Research in Criminology

Series Editors
Alfred Blumstein
David P. Farrington

Research in Criminology

continued after index

Klaus Sessar
Hans-Jürgen Kerner
Editors

Developments in Crime and Crime Control Research

German Studies on Victims,
Offenders, and the Public

Springer-Verlag
New York Berlin Heidelberg London
Paris Tokyo Hong Kong Barcelona

Klaus Sessar
Center for Youth Law and Youth Work, University of Hamburg, D-2000 Hamburg 13, Federal Republic of Germany

Hans-Jürgen Kerner
Institute of Criminology, University of Tübingen, D-7400 Tübingen, Federal Republic of Germany

Series Editors

Alfred Blumstein
School of Urban and Public Affairs, Carnegie-Mellon University, Pittsburgh, Pennsylvania 15213, USA

David P. Farrington
Institute of Criminology, University of Cambridge, Cambridge CB3 9DT, England

Library of Congress Cataloging-in-Publication Data
Developments in crime and crime control research: German studies on
    victims, offenders, and the public/Klaus Sessar, Hans-Jürgen
    Kerner, editors.
        p.   cm.—(Research in criminology)
    1. Criminology—Germany (West)   2. Criminology.   I. Sessar,
Klaus.   II. Kerner, Hans-Jürgen.   III. Series.
HV6022.G3D48   1990
364.993—dc20   89-26185

Printed on acid-free paper.

Typeset by Best-Set Typographers, Hong Kong.
Printed and bound by BookCrafters USA, Inc.
Printed in the United States of America.

9 8 7 6 5 4 3 2 1

ISBN 0-387-97081-9 Springer-Verlag New York Berlin Heidelberg
ISBN 3-540-97081-9 Springer-Verlag Berlin Heidelberg New York

Foreword

This collection is probably the most sophisticated, theoretically and empirically, that has appeared during the past quarter century in Germany. German criminology has been progressing for many years at the Max-Planck-Institute at Freiburg, and at the universities at Tübingen, Bielefeld, Hamburg, and Munster without appropriate knowledge and understanding by the English-speaking community of scholars. This gap, between what empirical criminology in Germany has produced and what English and American scholars know, has been unfortunate. German sociology and criminology have moved empirically far beyond Max Weber, but non-German scholars, in their provincialism, are generally unaware of the changes in scholarly research.

The scholars of this volume are abundantly aware of the importance of longitudinal studies, as represented by the studies of Karl F. Schumann and Reiner Kaulitzki, by Hans-Jürgen Kerner, and by Michael C. Baurmann in particular.

The National Commission on Law Enforcement and Administration, under President Lyndon B. Johnson's administration, was the first to launch a national survey on victimization. Germany has further developed victimization surveys, which is gratifying to those of us who helped to promote this kind of research. In the land that gave us Hans von Hentig and the earliest recognition of the importance of the victim, we now have excellent empirical studies of victimization and new models for research.

Studies of the fear of crime began in the United States, but the German studies in this book by Harald Arnold, Klaus Boers and Klaus Sessar, and Bernhard Villmow are marvelous examples of the use of the latest methodological strategies for exploring the topic, along with international comparisons.

Deterrence theory is also examined in this volume, even beyond the excellent provocative writings of Andenaes and Gibbs, by Susanne Karstedt-Henke. Prisoners on leave are a perennial problem in most countries, and Friedhelm Berckhauer and Burkhard Hasenpusch give us new and satisfying data to promote social policy. Hans-Jörg Albrecht has done the same with promoting day fines, and Bernhard Villmow has promoted victim compensation.

I am especially impressed with the remark by Boers and Sessar that ''Restitution contributes much more to conflict resolution than do fines or imprisonment;

it takes into account the victim's needs and interests; and it may even be a more effective form of rehabilitation for the offender.'' It is also very instructive to note that, as Albrecht informs us, only 3 to 5 percent of fined offenders end with a substitute imprisonment and that community service could probably alleviate those few from incarceration. Friedhelm Berckhauer and Bernhard Hasenpusch also enlighten us on the few offenses committed by prisoners on leave of absence.

The general thrust of the researches in the volume is that (1) German criminological research is up to date with the latest methodological and statistical techniques; (2) cross-national comparisons are more common coming from Germany than from the United States; (3) nonpunitive measures are acceptable and better employed in Germany than in the United States.

It is a pleasure for me to be a witness to these developments in German criminology. When I met my victimology mentor, Hans von Hentig, in Bad Tölz, FRG, shortly after World War II, criminology in Germany was in a relatively dormant stage of theoretical and empirical development. However, von Hentig told me that, like the economy of Germany, criminology would become modern and developed. His inspiration is present in this volume, and I hope that the rest of Europe and the United States will come to appreciate how firmly developed German criminology has become by reviewing this collection.

Marvin E. Wolfgang

Preface

Developments in Crime and Crime Control Research: German Studies on Victims, Offenders, and the Public contains nine chapters that represent essential aspects of modern German criminology, both in terms of the crime phenomenon and of crime control. The work is especially addressed to the English-speaking scientific community in the area of criminology, victimology, criminal policy, and criminal law.

For a long time, Anglo-American scholars knew hardly anything about German criminology, which was mainly a result of the language barriers. In recent years, however, several attempts have been made to overcome at least some of the communication problems by providing English readers with extensive overviews dealing with current research trends and research projects in Germany.[1] In addition, many German scholars are contributing to international meetings and English-speaking scholars are attending national and international criminological and victimological symposions and conventions in the Federal Republic of Germany. As a result, there has been a marked increase in the last decades in the scientific exchange of views, experiences, and research findings.

In spite of the different crime rates in various countries, crime is a basic social problem for all of them. However, regarding crime control, there are considerable differences that undoubtedly are connected not only with the different magnitude of the every day crime events but also with the different traditional and functional approaches to the crime problem. For example, highly elaborated North American diversion programs, mediation programs, and victim-offender-reconciliation programs have been adopted in Germany with great success. On

---

[1]These works are *Research in Criminal Justice* (1982), edited by the Criminological Research Unit of the Max-Planck-Insitute of Foreign and International Criminal Law, Freiburg im Breisgau, Freiburg: Max-Planck-Institute, *Deutsche Forschungen zur Kriminalitätsentstehung und Kriminalitätskontrolle/German Research on Crime and Crime Control* (1983), 3 Volumes, edited by Hans-Jürgen Kerner, Helmut Kury, and Klaus Sessar, Köln: Heymanns (the 65 articles are written in German but also include an English abstract; each volume has an English preface and subject index). *Criminological Research* in the 80's and Beyond. Reports from the Federal Republic of Germany, German Democratic Republic, Austria, Switzerland (1988), edited by Günther Käiser, Helmut Kury, and Hans-Jörg Albrecht, Freiburg: Max-Planck-Institute.

the other hand, the use of imprisonment as a sentence that is predominant in the United States and recently also in the United Kingdom, is gradually decreasing in Germany and is being replaced by the vast use of noncustodial sanctions such as probation and fines: these two sanctions make up 90 percent of all forms of convictions in adult cases. Similar results are found in cases of juveniles delinquency. In these cases, community service, admonition, and social training are the most common sentences. Deinstitutionalization has become one of the catchwords of modern criminal policy. Even nonintervention has been developed into an efficient pretrial educational measure and is now widely applied to a large scope of youth crimes resulting in a reduced recidivism.

Developments of this kind coincide with main trends in criminology. Some people even go as far as to say that criminology initiated or at least encouraged these developments. In fact, one of the central features of modern German criminology in revealing the "true nature of crime" follows the tradition of *enlightenment* as opposed to following the approach of the moral enterpreneurs and the criminal justice system. This perspective makes the whole concept of crime control the main target of empirical research. One focus of interest are the legitimizing concepts of criminal law such as deterrence or public needs for punishment. Many reseach findings question this legitimacy. Even where criminal behavior is investigated (e.g., the behavior of juveniles by using the experiences of American and English cohort studies), the endeavor is to reach a high degree of rationality in the reactions of the criminal justice system.

To grasp at least some of these aspects, the editors of this book could only select those topics that

- Fit explicitly or implicitly into a system perspective
- Pertain to policy matters of our present-day societies
- Are given priority in the literature and on criminological meetings in recent years.

Thus, although the contributions to this volume are not able to cover all aspects of the different criminological schools (for in-depth information see the literature in footnote 1), nevertheless, they do represent a large scope of perspectives in current German empirical criminology:

- Deterrence that can be explained by the juveniles' modes to see the world (Susanne Karstedt-Henke; Karl F. Schumann)
- The official picture of multiple offending and multiple offenders as drawn up by police statistics in opposition to empirical findings (Hans-Jürgen Kerner)
- The behavior of convicts during temporal release and work-furlough (Friedhelm Berckhauer and Burkhard Hasenpusch)
- Comparative victimology regarding the relationship between fear of crime and victimization in Germany and in the United States (Harald Arnold)
- The effects of victimization concerning sexual offenses (Michael C. Baurmann)
- The application and the efficiency of the German victim compensation scheme

and its comparison with similar schemes in other countries (Bernhard Villmow)
- The acceptance of restitution (*Wiedergutmachung*) as a sanction to replace punishment (Klaus Boers and Klaus Sessar)
- The policy of fining in Germany (Hans-Jörg Albrecht)

We hope that *Developments in Crime and Crime Control Research: German Studies on Victims, Offenders, and the Public* will contribute to a growing international criminology and will deepen the mutual interests in the social problems of other countries and throw light on ways of dealing with them.

Klaus Sessar
Hans-Jürgen Kerner

Contents

Contributors

Hans-Jörg Albrecht
Criminological Research Unit
Max-Planck-Institute for Foreign
and International Criminal Law
D-7800 Freiburg im Breisgau
Federal Republic of Germany

Born in 1950. Received his Dr. jur. from the University of Freiburg im Breisgau. Research Associate at the Criminological Research Unit of the Max-Planck-Institute for Foreign and International Criminal Law, Freiburg im Breisgau, FRG. Author of *Strafzumessung und Vollstreckung bei Geldstrafen*, 1980; *Legal bewährung bei zu Geldstrafe und Freiheitsstrafe Verurteilten*, 1982, and of numerous articles in German and English; coeditor of *Kriminologische Forschung in den 80er Jahren* (3 volumes), 1988.

Harald Arnold
Criminological Research Unit
Max-Planck-Institute for Foreign
and International Criminal Law
D-7800 Freiburg im Breisgau
Federal Republic of Germany

Born in 1951. Graduated with degree in psychology from the University of Freiburg im Breisgau. Currently Research Associate at the Criminological Research Unit of the Max-Planck-Institute for Foreign and International Criminal Law, Freiburg im Breisgau. Published several articles in the field of victimology, victim surveys, comparative criminology, and juvenile delinquency.

Michael C. Baurmann
Criminological Research Unit
Federal Criminal Police Office
(Bundeskriminalamt)
D-6200 Wiesbaden
Federal Republic of Germany

Born in 1946. Graduated with degree in psychology from the University of Mainz. Received his Dr.phil. from the University of Bremen. Former lecturer at the University of Mainz. Research associate at the Criminological Research Unit of the Bundeskriminalamt (Federal Criminal Police Office) in Wiesbaden, responsible for the field of victimology and currently leading a research project on violence. Author of *Sexualität, Gewalt und psychische Folgen*, 1983; *Gewalt. Aktuelle Diskussionen und Forschungsergebnisse*, 1985; *Perzeptionen und Erwartungen von Kriminalitätsopfern nach der Anzeige*, 1989.

Friedhelm Berckhauer
Ministry of Justice
Head of Criminological
Research Unit
Am Waterlooplatz 1
D-3000 Hannover 1
Federal Republic of Germany

Born in 1945. Received his Dr.jur. from the University of Freiburg im Breisgau. Head of the Criminological Research Unit, Department of Justice of Lower Saxony, Hannover. Published *Wirtschaftskriminalität und Staatsanwaltschaft*, 1977; *Die Strafverfolgung bei schweren Wirtschaftsdelikten*, 1981. Author of several articles in the field of criminology.

Klaus Boers
Senior Researcher
Institute of Criminology
University of Tübingen
D-7400 Tübingen
Federal Republic of Germany

Born in 1953. Lawyer and research associate at the Center for Youth Law and Youth Work, Faculty of Law I, University of Hamburg, currently at the Department of Criminology, University of Tübingen. He wrote a dissertation on fear of crime.

Burkhard Hasenpusch
Ministry of Justice
Criminological Research Unit
Am Waterlooplatz 1
D-3000 Hannover 1
Federal Republic of Germany

Born in 1949. Received his Ph.D. (Criminology) from the University of Montreal. Senior Researcher at the Criminological Research Unit, Department of Justice of Lower Saxony, Hannover. Author of *Future Trends in Crime and Crime Control in Canada*, 1982 and of several articles in the field of criminology.

Susanne Karstedt-Henke
Department of Sociology
University of Bielefeld
Universitätsstrasse
D-4800 Bielefeld 1
Federal Republic of Germany

Born in 1949. Received her Dr.phil. from the University of Bielefeld. Currently research associate at the Special Research Unit, Prevention and Intervention in Childhood and Adolescence, University of Bielefeld. Published *Alkohol am Steuer. Orientierungs- und Verhaltensmuster der Kraftfahrer*, 1986 (with E. Kretschmer-Bäumel), author of several articles focusing on deterrence and the knowledge and opinion of law.

Reiner Kaulitzki
Fachbereich Rechtswissenschaft
University of Bremen
D-2800 Bremen 33
Federal Republic of Germany

Born in 1954. Graduated from the Department of Social Sciences, University of Bremen. Coauthor of *Jugendkriminalität und die Grenzen der General prävention*, 1987. Currently Working at a diversion project in Bremen.

Hans-Jürgen Kerner
Professor of Criminology
Institute of Criminology
University of Tübingen
D-7400 Tübingen
Federal Republic of Germany

Born in 1943. Received his Dr.jur. from the University of Tübingen. Former professor at the Universities of Bielefeld, Hamburg, and Heidelberg. Currently professor of criminology at the Department of Criminology, University of Tübingen. Published *Professionelles und organisiertes Verbrechen*, 1973; *Verbrechenswirklichkeit und Strafverfolgung*, 1973; *Kriminalitätseinschätzung und innere Sicherheit*, 1980; *Strafvollzug. Ein Lehrbuch*, 1982 (with G. Kaiser and H. Schöch); coeditor of *German Research on Crime and Crime Control*, 1983 (with H. Kury and K. Sessar); author of numerous articles in the field on criminology, juvenile delinquency, corrections, and criminal law in German, French, and English.

Karl F. Schumann
Professor of Criminology
Fachbereich Rechtswissenschaft
University of Bremen
D-2800 Bremen 33
Federal Republic of Germany

Born in 1941. Received his Dr.phil. from the University of Tübingen. Currently professor at the University of Bremen. Published *Zeichen der Unfreiheit. Theorie und Messung sozialer Sanktionen*, 1968; *Der Handel mit der Gerechtigkeit*, 1977; coauthor of *Jugendkriminalität und die Grenzen der Generalprävention*, 1987. Many contributions in the field of criminology, sociology of law, and juvenile delinquency.

Klaus Sessar
Professor of Criminology
Center for Youth Law and
Youth Work
University of Hamburg
D-2000 Hamburg 13
Federal Republic of Germany

Born in 1937. Received his Dr.jur. from the University of Freiburg im Breisgau and his M.A. (sociology) from Boston University. Currently professor of criminology at the University of Hamburg. Published *Die Entwicklung der Freiheitsstrafe im Strafrecht Frankreichs*, 1973; *Rechtliche und soziale Prozesse einer Definition der Tötungskriminalität*, 1981; *Die Staatsanwaltschaft im Prozess strafrechtlicher Sozialkontrolle*, 1978 (with E. Blankenburg and W. Steffen); *Praktizierte Diversion*, 1989 (with E. Hering); coeditor of *Das Verbrechensopfer*, 1979 (with G.F. Kirchhoff); *German Research on Crime and Crime Control*, 1983 (with H.-J. Kerner and H. Kury); author of numerous articles in the area of criminology, victimology, and juvenile delinquency in German, French, and English.

Bernhard Villmow
Professor of Criminology
Fachbereich Rechts-
wissenschaft II
University of Hamburg
D-2000 Hamburg 13
Federal Republic of Germany

Born in 1945. Received his Dr.jur. from the University of Freiburg im Breisgau. Former research associate at the Criminological Research Unit of the Max-Planck-Institute for Foreign and International Criminal Law, Freiburg im Breisgau. Currently professor of criminology at the University of Hamburg. Published *Schwereeinschätzung von Delikten*, 1977; *Jugendkriminalität in einer Gemeinde*, 1983 (with E. Stephan); *Praxis der Opferentschädigung*, 1989 (with B. Plemper); author of numerous articles concerning criminology, victimology, victim compensation, and juvenile delinquency.

1
Limits of General Deterrence: The Case of Juvenile Delinquency

KARL F. SCHUMANN AND REINER KAULITZKI

Despite the abundance of research papers published in scientific journals on issues of deterrence during the last two decades, we hope there may be methodological as well as theoretical reasons to read about a deterrence study done in West Germany.

Although the scientific community agrees more (Grasmick, 1981) or less (Lundman, 1986) that the proper way to study deterrence on the level of individuals demands a panel design of some representative sample, very few studies comply with both standards. With the exception of Piliavin, Thornton, Garther, and Matsueda (1986), almost all panel studies were conducted with high-school or college students (Anderson, 1977; Bishop, 1982; Meier, Burkett, & Hickman, 1984; Minor & Harry, 1982; Rausch, 1982; Saltzman, Paternoster, Waldo, & Chiricos, 1982, Paternoster & Iovanni, 1986), leaving the issues of representativeness still unsettled. This gap may be filled by our study. The German panel consists of a representative sample of 740 juveniles (probability sample of all inhabitants of a metropolitan area who were born in 1964 or 1965). The design of our study has additional properties for theoretical reasons that will be discussed later.

On theoretical grounds it seems important to note the surprising lack of comparative thinking in deterrence research with individual data. In contrast, studies on aggregate levels depend completely on comparisons between states or countries (see Nagin, 1978). Also various studies have been completed in Scandinavian countries, England, and the United States comparing, for example, the deterrent effects of legal provisions against driving while intoxicated with reference to each other (see Ross, 1982, 1984). These studies imply that variations of features of the criminal justice system (CJS), such as different norms, sanctions, or types of law enforcement, may affect deterrence. If this assumption is valid, should not those differences be reflected too in the subjective knowledge of the law and the perception of certainty and severity of punishment? Would it be unreasonable to expect that states whose penal laws or styles of law enforcement are heavily influenced by the deterrence doctrine might produce among their citizens a stronger deterrence orientation? An example could be the Nazi regime in Germany, which in its final years heavily relied on deterrent sentencing practices (*Volksgerichtshöfe*) as well as on systems of informants to increase the certainty of punishment. Inasmuch as states use police forces and penal law to intimidate the people, this should have some impact on the findings of deterrence research in those countries. Deterrence research has so far ignored such a view. It aims at a general theory of deterrence. We doubt that such a view, which ignores the context of the state and political culture, is possible or, moreover, suitable.

Theoretical Frame of Reference

A first step toward such reflexivity can be seen in the insight by Williams and Hawkins (which they credit to an anonymous reviewer) that, whereas most research on deterrence on the individual level has been conducted with juveniles, the findings have been generalized also to adults irrespective of the fact that the juvenile justice system (unlike that of adults) is not designed to administer punishments for the purpose of deterrence (1986, p. 554). It was the intention of our research from the beginning (see Schumann, Berlitz, Guth, & Kaulitzki, 1984) that a comprehensive study of deterrence among juveniles who are controlled by an explicitly non-deterrent CJS should nullify the deterrence doctrine at least for that age group. We upheld this hypothesis in view of the possibility that juveniles gain their knowledge of punishments mostly from media coverage of adult cases because in Germany juvenile court cases against persons under 18 years are not open to the public. However, the flow of information on the traits and the functioning of the CJS and its contribution to the genesis of individual perceptions of severity or certainty of punishment has not been a main topic in our research.

Issues in Deterrence Theory

The relevance of both objective and subjective properties of the CJS has been stressed by Gibbs throughout his work, including his model of general

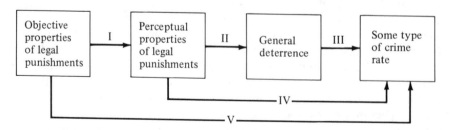

FIGURE 1.1. Gibbs's model of general deterrence.

deterrence (Williams & Gibbs, 1981, p. 594; see also Gibbs, 1979, p. 658) (see Figure 1.1): Gibbs's model covers the communication process (relation I), the generation of fear by knowledge about the CJS (relation II), and the effect of fear on decisions to act or suppress an act being possibly labeled as criminal (relation III). Gibbs stresses the fact that the effect of fear on action cannot be measured directly, at least not in survey research. Therefore deterrence can only be concluded from research on relation IV, or— using aggregate data—on relation V. Such conclusions could be valid only if all other variables with possible influence on the relationship between perceived punishments and (individual) crime rates are controlled for, as, for example, variables pointing to crime-generating factors and perceptual differences of the CJS.

Certainly the model of Gibbs offers a methodologically sound perspective for the evaluation and compilation of results of the mass of deterrence studies. Many of those studies on relation V, which rely on aggregate data (e.g., arrest rates, crime rates), suffer from various problems of design (see Greenberg, Kessler, & Logan, 1981). Among them are lack of consideration for perceptional differences and lack of control for intervening variables (Tittle, 1980b, p. 385). In fact, relation I has been studied only by few scholars. Parker and Grasmick established the relatively meager impact of mass media within this communication process (1979, p. 372). Erickson and Gibbs (1978, p. 259) did not find high correlations between the objective and perceived risks of being arrested for various crimes. More important, Williams and Gibbs (1981, p. 603) discovered that significant correlations between actual and perceived statutory maximum punishments disappeared (with one exception) when public disapproval of a crime was controlled. Apparently respondents perceive punishments in terms of what they think they ought to be, not what the penal code says they are. Personal moral positions are of greater importance for what persons perceive than legal threats. They seem to work like a filter in the perceptions of objective traits of the CJS. This is important because the moral acceptance of norms is of course strongly related to the individual's crime rate. It is well known that, among the many reasons for conformity, deterrence plays minor role beside such variables as lacking skills for deviance, belief in the legal order, approval of norms, habit, imitation of the behavior of reference persons (see Gibbs, 1975; Hofer & Tham, 1975, p. 262). If acceptance of norms influences both crime rate and perceptions of severity and certainty, this creates the danger of a spurious correlation if one studies relation IV in Gibbs's model. It would therefore be an important defect for any research on deterrence not to control for that variable (Erickson, Gibbs, & Jensen 1977). Beyleveld concluded his comprehensive review of deterrence research with the hypothesis that deterrence might have effects predominantly among persons who do not accept the respective norms (1980, p. 22). His suggestion relied on findings of Silberman (1976), Tittle (1977), and others. However, a most recent study by Piliavin et al. (1986), as well as the dissertation of Gartner (1985) falsify this hypothesis. Based on samples of serious and high-risk offenders (that is, persons like school dropouts, offenders, etc. who are enrolled in National Supported Work Programs), they found no effect of deterrence in a panel study. This leaves the relation between moral commitment to norms and deterrent effects of punishment again an open question to be researched.

Although we relied on the ideas of Gibbs, we do not consider his model as a theory. It provides a methodological frame of reference for the design of deterrence studies, especially through its message that any measurement of deterrence by way of survey research will necessarily be circumstantial, and its validity will rely on the comprehensiveness of controls for intervening factors. In the list of those factors have been included variables related to anomie theory, theories of subculture, and differential association theory (Tittle, 1977; Meier & Johnson, 1977). We followed this path in our study.

However, the consideration of crime-related factors to rule out alternative explanations is not in itself a step toward a theory of deterrence. This would only be the case if those factors were relevant for the cognitive as well as the motivational processes implied by the deterrence doctrine. Two variables may have such a status in addition to the acceptance of norms: the crime rate of peers and the risk of informal sanctions by friends or relatives.

Some authors argue that informal sanctions should be considered as part of the deterrence process itself (e.g. Tittle 1980a, p. 320). We doubt the theoretical soundness of that idea. Congruity between sanctions by the state and sanctions by peers cannot be imputed. Its degree is strictly an empirical matter. Furthermore, it makes a difference whether informal sanctions are caused by the formal punishment or by the behavior itself (irrespective of any formal sanction being applied). In the latter case informal sanctions may become a motivational factor in their own right (Williams & Hawkins, 1986, p. 563).

The crime rate of peers is not only a crime-generating factor as the theory of differential association claimed. In one rare three-wave panel study, Meier, Burkett, and Hickman (1984) demonstrated that persons select peers in view of their crime rate (e.g., marihuana smoking) rather than being affected by the behavior of the peers in the first place. Having established close contact with persons having a particular crime rate, that relationship may in turn influence their perceptions of sanction risks or stabilize their own deviant behavior (p. 76). It is important to note that the crime rate of peers may influence also the perception of certainty of punishment. Like norm approval, the crime rate of peers apparently influences both independent and dependent variables of the deterrence effect. Control for this intervening factor is necessary for this reason as well.

Issues of Criminological Theory

Before reporting on methods and findings of our research, a brief reflection on the consistency of deterrence research with criminological theory seems to be appropriate. It is especially useful to consider insights from the labeling perspective to get a clearer view of the problems involved. Actually the deterrence doctrine does not make much sense for labeling theory. So far, the contradictions between both approaches have been discussed in two respects. DiChiara and Galliher (1984) have pointed out that deterrence research boomed in the 1970s exactly because of its promise to undermine the message of labeling theorists. Its promise was to show that punishment reduces deviance instead of creating it. Other researchers treated both approaches as rival hypotheses to be tested against each other (Rausch, 1982; Thomas & Bishop, 1984). However, we want to stress a more epistemological issue.

According to labeling theory, an act becomes criminal only if it is so labeled (Becker, 1963). The labeling of an act, event, or actor takes place as an interaction with agents of social control who have the power to make a label stick. A prospective act, a vision of a possible chain of events, cannot be labeled. The actor may himself judge his fantasies or ideas according to his understanding of penal law. Thus, a vision of an act may be self-labeled by a person as a criminal act where a judge or policeman would not see any, and vice versa. The mechanism of deterrence depends completely on such self-labeling processes of projected actions (or first steps toward actions). Deterrence theory expects persons to judge their behavior correctly and subsume it under the appropiate penal-code provisions to figure out the threatening sanctions. In reality persons are simply not able to do that. Although they are certainly able to judge prospective behavior on moral grounds, they do not know case law well enough to find out the punishment. Also, it is unclear whether there is sufficient congruency between their moral positions and the penal code. Incomplete knowledge on local conviction routines, legal ignorance, lack of precision of the law, effective techniques of neutralization, innovative or idiosyncratic inter-pretations of the law are among the mechanisms to distort and prevent a judgment sufficiently congruent with probable judges' subsumption.

Deterrence studies on the individual level produce results based on subjectively distorted understandings of norms. Respondents relate the abstract norms to their daily practice and subsume their own behavior under their individual understanding of the norm. According to that personal version of the norm, they report perceptions of punishment as well as their personal crime rate. How distorted the individual version of the norm exactly is remains hidden from the researcher. Actually this does not matter at all for deterrence research. If both perceived punishments and crime rate are related to the same distortion of the norm this will not influence the strength of the deterrence relation. More important, however distorted the understanding of norms by a person is, it remains the one and only cognitive basis to be used in the cost-benefit calculus implied by deterrence doctrine. Deterrence is a matter of the minds. This includes the however distorted process of subsumption of situations under legal norms.

Deterrence studies thus may produce quite valid data on the respondent's self-disciplinary mechanisms but cannot reveal in just how distorted a manner those mechanisms function compared to penal law. Those discrepancies would only be observable if respondents were tested according to their ability to subsume given situations of possibly deviant behavior correctly under the respective norms, as we did in our study.

First, we included a test on ability to subsume cases of behavior under the penal law that was being studied. Limited space unfortunately does not allow us to discuss the findings at length: Whereas for many laws the data show a sufficient overlap of individual subsumption with legal doctrines, for some (e.g., assault, drug taking) they do not (see Schumann, 1988, for more details). Second, we measured crimes committed after the first interview by self-report as well as by official registrations. We requested information about registered crime for the whole sample at the Bundeszentralregister, the Germany central agency for registering any criminal case decided in the country. Thus, we were able to test the deterrence doctrine against a subjective as well as an official crime rate of individuals (however distorted by selective law enforcement that may be). It should be noted that legislators do not have self-report data (the dark figure) in mind when they are talking about possibilities of deterrence. They look at registered crimes. Only if an officially defined crime rate is used, is it possible to avoid a researcher finding correlations highly consistent with the deterrence doctrine without knowing whether the behavior contemplated by the respondents was indeed forbidden by the law, and, conversely, whether the illegal behavior was indeed what the respondents had in mind.

Research Design and Methods

The longitudinal study is based on a sample of young people born in 1964 and 1965. The sample was randomly selected from a list of all citizens of a metropolitan area born in those years by permission of the residents registration office (*Einwohnermeldeamt*). The 740 boys and girls of the panel were questioned in 1981 about their perceptions of certainty and severity of punishments for specific deviant acts. In addition, data on other variables related to theories of juvenile delinquency were collected, for example, differential association, family background, social bonds, moral assessment of deviant acts. In 1982 we asked the same juveniles for the delinquent acts they committed last year using a list of 14 criminal offenses

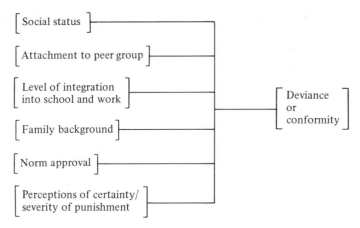

FIGURE 1.2. Overview of sets of variables.

that make up the bulk of juvenile crime. In 1984 the official penal records of the sample were gathered from the Federal Central Registration Office in Berlin (*Bundeszentralregister*). Thus a measure for registered criminal activities can be used as dependent variable as well as self-reported delinquency.

Figure 1.2 offers a scheme of the sets of independent, intervening, and dependent variables included in the research. The questionnaire (first wave) included 144 items. The interviews of both waves were conducted predominantly at the homes of the juveniles. The self-reported crimes were written down on a separate sheet of paper by the juveniles themselves, sealed in an envelope, and mailed by the juvenile via a lawyer to the research team. This procedure to grant anonymity (the lawyer used a link-file-list known only to him) was necessary because researchers do not have in Germany the privilege of refusing testimony in court. The use of a lawyer for anonymity was of course employed for the questionnaires too, to be able to link all data to the dependent variable.

Most of the items were considered in the regression analysis to cover as comprehensively as possible the relevant factors contributing to the occurrence of deviance. However, only a limited number of variables contributed significantly to one or more of the models resulting from regression analysis.

Results

Self-reported Delinquency

Table 1.1 shows the self-reported delinquency between the first and second interview. The minimum time span between both interviews was 12 months.

TABLE 1.1. Self-reported delinquency for the period between the two interviews.[a]

Offenses	Offenders %	Nonoffenders N	Nonoffenders %	Number of acts (offenders) Mean
Theft	15.4	606	84.6	4.7
Shoplifting	20.5	569	79.5	5.8
Car theft	3.1	694	96.9	2.6
Burglary	3.9	688	96.1	3.1
Theft of any type	30.0	501	70.0	6.9
No ticket (concerts)	42.7	410	57.3	4.6
No ticket (transportation)	58.4	298	41.6	10.4
Any services without ticket	68.3	227	31.7	11.8
Assault	5.2	679	94.8	2.1
Assault with a weapon	0.6	712	99.4	3.6
Assault of any type	5.3	678	94.7	2.5
Joy-riding	18.3	585	81.7	4.1
Vandalism	17.3	592	82.7	4.7
Drug use	18.2	585	81.8	40.7
Fraud	5.3	678	94.7	1.7
Robbery	2.9	695	97.1	3.4
Driving without license	38.8	438	61.2	12.4

[a] $N = 716$.

Less than 10% of the sample reported robbery, fraud, burglary, car theft, and two types of assault. The frequency of offending was quite high for other offenses. More than half of the sample reported using public transportation services without paying the fare, every fifth person reported one or more shoplifting cases. Driving without a license was committed by almost four out of ten. Next to drug use it has the highest frequency per person (mean, see column 3). Seventy-eight percent of the sample reported a violation of at least one of the norms of the penal code (in 1981, 83% had been offenders).

We will now report the results of correlation analysis between perceived severity and certainty of punishment in 1981 and self-reported delinquency in 1982.

Deterrent Effects of Perceived Severity of Punishment

Does severity of punishment produce any drift to conformity? A hypothesis according to deterrence doctrine would predict that subjects who expect lower punishments will deviate more often than persons who are expecting severe punishments. Table 1.2 examines the relationship between perceived severity of punishment and self-reported delinquency (Pearson's R, 5% level of significance).

TABLE 1.2. Zero-order correlations between perceived severity of punishment and self-reported delinquency.[a]

Offenses	Severity of expected punishment		
	Lowest	Most probable	Highest
Shoplifting			
Theft			
Burglary			
Car theft			
No ticket (concerts)	−0.06		−0.09
No ticket (transportation)			
Joy riding	+0.07		
Fraud			
Assault with a weapon			
Assault		−0.10	−0.10
Vandalism			
Robbery			−0.09
Drug use	−0.11	−0.09	
Driving without license		−0.11	−0.10

[a] Pearson's R; significant coefficients only (5% level).

Most correlations are insignificant, one is significant but positive. Some are significant negative, but generally the correlations are quite low. The level of punishment (minimum, maximum) does not make any difference. Perceived severity of punishment has little or no effect on deviance. Thus a common finding in deterrence research is repeated in our study, which was to be expected given the fact that the juvenile justice system is not designed for deterrence.

Deterrent Effects of Perceived Certainty of Punishment

According to prior research, the risk of getting caught seems to be a stronger inhibitor of offenses against the penal code than the perceived severity of punishment. For each of the 14 offenses we asked the juveniles how often they might commit this offense until the police would catch them. The mean estimated arrest ratios per 100 offenses are presented in Table 1.3.

The second column of Table 1.3 presents zero-order correlations between the perceived risk of being caught and frequencies of deviant acts. Given the rather strong skewness of the distributions, the raw data were transformed to logarithms before correlation analysis.

Table 1.3 shows that all coefficients have the expected direction. The juveniles who think in 1981 they can violate a penal norm more frequently before getting caught by the police report more offenses in 1982 than juveniles who do not. The strongest bivariate correlations involve shoplifting, theft of any type, driving without a license, obtaining services of any type without paying, and drug use. These offenses are in part minor

TABLE 1.3. Perceived arrest rate (per 100 offenses) and self-reported delinquency.[a]

Offense	Perceived risk of getting caught (per 100 deviant acts) %	Correlations Perceived certainty 1981: self-reported delinquency 1982		
		R	R^2%	s[b]
Theft	38.2	0.10	1.0%	**
Shoplifting	42.0	0.22	5.0%	**
Car theft	64.6	0.05	0.3%	
Burglary	55.1	0.08	0.7%	*
Theft of any type	—	0.21	4.5%	**
No tickets (concerts)	35.3	0.21	4.4%	**
No tickets (transportation)	21.9	0.19	3.5%	**
Any service without ticket	—	0.22	4.6%	**
Assault	81.3	0.16	2.6%	**
Assault with a weapon	85.1	0.05	0.3%	
Assault of any type	—	0.13	1.8%	**
Vandalism	45.4	0.14	1.9%	**
Joy riding	50.9	0.03	0.1%	
Drug use	41.9	0.20	4.2%	**
Fraud	54.6	0.06	0.4%	
Robbery	67.8	0.07	0.4%	*
Driving without license	37.8	0.23	5.1%	**

[a] R = Pearson's R; R^2 = determination coefficient in %.
[b] Level of significance: * = 5%, ** = 1%.

ones. The correlations are not very high. Explanations of variance are 5% or less, leaving 95% unexplained.

According to the zero-order-correlations there is some evidence for deterrence. This raises the question whether correlations between perceived certainty and subsequent delinquency still exist if other crime-generating factors are controlled for or will turn out to be spurious.

The Effects of Control of Extralegal Factors

The social world seems to be more complex than the deterrence model suggests; theories of juvenile delinquency name a lot of rational motives for deviance. The influence of legal factors may fade away if extralegal factors are controlled for (see Rausch, 1982; Saltzmann, et al., 1982).

We used multiple-regression models to assess the influences of legal and extralegal factors on subsequent behavior. The total explanatory power of a model that includes legal and extralegal factors may be compared with variance explained by perceived risk of punishment alone; both coefficients are given in Table 1.4. The coefficients are the results of 17 different regression models for single offenses or groups of offenses.

Column 1 of Table 1.4 presents the total-explanation power of regression models including all significant legal and extralegal factors (multivariate R^2). Percentages of explanation of subsequent deviant behavior vary from 3.8% (assault with a weapon, an offense that was seldom carried out) to 27.5% (drug use). Column 2 presents the contribution of perceived certainty to the explanation of behavior. A comparison of the results of bivariate analysis and multivariate analysis shows to what extent the bivariate analysis leads to overestimations of the power of risk assessment.

Only in six regression models is there some influence of perceived certainty of punishment on subsequent behavior left, if extralegal factors are controlled for. Those offenses or groups of offenses are shoplifting, and—under the category of shoplifting—all types of theft, obtaining entrance without paying, traveling without ticket, assault, and driving without licence. For the remaining 11 offenses, or groups of offenses, the perceived risk of getting caught does not contribute toward explaining the frequency of deviant behavior. For theft, burglary, robbery, and drug use, former significant correlations are not reproduced within multivariate

TABLE 1.4. Legal and extralegal factors for juvenile delinquency.[a]

	Total behavior explanation[b]		For comparison[c]
Offenses	Multivariate R^2(%)	Certainty multivariate β^2 (%)	Certainty bivariate R^2 (%)
Theft	9.9		1.0
Shoplifting	10.5	2.7	5.0
Car theft	9.3		
Burglary	10.0		0.7
Theft of any type	15.2	1.3	4.5
No tickets (concerts)	16.4	1.4	4.4
No tickets (transportation)	12.9	1.0	3.5
Any service without ticket	15.6	0.6	4.6
Assault	12.2	1.4	2.6
Assault with a weapon	3.8		
Assault of any type	12.7	0.8	1.8
Vandalism	15.9	0.6	1.9
Joy riding	8.4		
Fraud	4.6		
Drug use	27.5		4.2
Robbery	4.1		0.4
Driving without license	20.5	1.1	5.1

[a] Determination coefficients R^2 and standardized regression measures β^2; only significant coefficients (5% level).
[b] Regression sets (R^2) for every offense. The amount of variance of the dependent variable, which is explained by perceived certainty of arrest *only*, is given by the multivariate β^2 coefficient.
[c] See Table 1.3.

regression models. In the case of car theft, assault with a weapon, joy-riding, and fraud, no bivariate correlation existed in the first place.

These modifications reflect the fact that conformity is not necessarily evidence of deterrence, but may be attributed to extralegal factors. As Gibbs argues (1975; p. 12), there is only evidence of deterrence if an individual contemplates a deviant act and refrains only or mainly from committing it for fear of legal consequences.

Relevance of Extralegal Social Factors

Gender, activities in leisure time, association with delinquent peers, and moral commitment to penal laws are among the social factors that explain most of the variance of deviant behavior.

These social factors may determine the number of situations in which opportunities to deviate exist. Not each situation in which deviance occurs is a situation in which threats of punishment are contemplated. Attachment to friends, for example, may prevent a rational calculus of advantages and disadvantages of deviance.

One may safely say that:

Gender is a complex indicator for normative patterns that determine interest in crime.

Attachment to specific social worlds, especially in *leisure time*, creates opportunities to deviate.

Given these opportunities the juveniles will, before committing deviant acts, calculate risks based on their participation in the lifestyle of peers, and by learning from those who are skilled at offending. Those influences are helpful also to neutralize and devalue the costs of deviant activities.

Finally there are thresholds of individual *moral commitments*, which may prevent deviant acts despite an interest in delinquency and opportunities. Conversely, they may prevent the individual from considering any deterrence arguments.

Table 1.5 shows the most important β-coefficients for 5 of the 22 regressors included in the regression analysis.

Gender, conventional leisure activities, association with delinquent peers, and acceptance of norms contribute substantially to the explanation of juvenile delinquency though the magnitude of relationships differs. Except for shoplifting, where perceived certainty of punishment remains the strongest predictor for deviance or conformity, social factors predict behavior better than perceived risk of getting caught.

Living conditions that are based in the social structure of society (different education according to gender) and that frame the social world of juveniles (evaluating the norms and values of society in the context of peers), individual belief systems that result from external and internal

TABLE 1.5. Social and legal factors as predictors of juvenile delinquency.[a]

β	Gender	Conventional leisure activities	Unconventional leisure places	Association to delinquent peers	Moral commitment	Perceived certainty
Theft	-0.13	-0.13		0.13	-0.13	
Shoplifting		-0.12		0.11	-0.13	0.16
Car theft		-0.14		0.17		
Burglary	-0.09			0.23		
Theft of any type	-0.11	-0.14		0.16		0.11
No ticket (concert)	-0.15	-0.11		0.20	-0.12	0.12
No ticket (transportation)		-0.12		0.09	-0.21	0.10
Any service without ticket			0.11	0.14	-0.18	0.08
Assault	-0.08	-0.15			-0.11	0.12
Assault with a weapon			0.11	0.10		
Assault of any type	-0.09	-0.15			-0.15	0.09
Vandalism	-0.17	-0.21		0.08	-0.12	0.08
Joy riding	-0.10			0.12	-0.08	
Fraud				0.08	-0.09	
Drug use		-0.09	0.12	0.21	-0.33	
Robbery	-0.11				-0.10	
Driving without license	-0.21	-0.10		0.13	-0.13	0.11

[a] Multiple regression: standardized regression coefficients beta; only significant coefficients (5% level)

moral sources seem a stronger influence on the number of deviant acts than subjective perceptions of certainty of punishment.

It may even be that both deviance and perceived certainty of punishment are results of extralegal social factors; this would suggest that bivariate deterrence correlations are mainly spurious.

Varying subjective perceptions of certainty of punishment seem not to be related to objective risks of being arrested. Rather they seem to be a result of individual moral beliefs, group values, or deliquency experiences than of a realistic perception of the activities of the criminal justice system.

Perceived Certainty and Official Penal Records

According to labeling theory, acts are not deviant or criminal by themselves, but only when they are defined so by relevant others. Such labels are imposed by policemen or judges. Those officials have the power to define what is criminal. Laymen, and especially juveniles, may underestimate or overestimate the relevance of the penal code for everyday actions. What they report as crimes may not be valid subsumptions under the penal code. Therefore we checked the deterrence model using official data on crime.

Only 6% of the panel had been registered for one of the 14 types of crime committed between the two interviews. To retain enough cases for regression analysis we had to restrict it to theft and traffic offenses. Compared to the self-reports the official crime figures are small. 30% of the sample reported theft in the questionnaire but only 2% of the sample were officially prosecuted for theft in the same time period. A similar 2% was found for traffic offenses whereas 39% of the sample reported they committed traffic offenses.

If self-reports of theft and traffic offenses are substituted by official penal records, regression analysis shows even less evidence of the deterrence doctrine. Zero-order correlations between perceived certainty of punishment and official crime rates explain only 0.8% of the variance of theft and 1.1% of the variance of traffic offenses. In regression analysis perceived certainty of punishment does *not* contribute at all to the explanation of crime in the models, whereas social variables (e.g., acceptance of norms) still do.

If only official crime rates were considered in studies on the deterrence model, evidence for its assumptions would be even smaller compared to crime measurement by self-reports. Certainly deterrence is a product of subjective decisions: If deterrence is to work, the individual has first of all to view the act as contrary to the law. On the other side it is necessary to establish that the behavior deterred would be considered criminal when judged by official criteria. Unfortunately this can be checked only for nondeterred acts. According to them, however, no relation to perceived features of punishment could be found.

Discussion

Severity of Punishment

As expected, a juvenile justice system which is constructed according to principles of rehabilitation and education apparently has no deterrent impact. Its perceived severity is not linked to deviance. It is important to note that juveniles rank punishments differently compared to the ranking of punishments built into the system. Fines for example seem to frighten juveniles more than short-term incarceration. However, if this subjective evaluation of punishments is used as a measure of severity, no substantial deterrent effects can be found. The predictive power of severity can also not be improved if it is weighted by certainty, that is, if an integrated measure of both aspects is being used.

The argument that the lack of explanatory power of severity is due to nondeterrent features of the juvenile justice system may be doubted on the ground that we did not compare systems that differed in their degrees of deterrence as, for example, Ruhland, Gold, and Heckman (1982) tried to do. We accept this criticism but want to point out that the lower zero-order correlation between severity and deviance seems to give additional evidence for our view. Although the punishments of the German juvenile justice system (JGG) are in fact more lenient, the arrest rate for juveniles is higher compared to the adult population. Police apparently controls juveniles much more closely. Thus, contrary to Williams and Hawkins's view that perceptions of certainty should have less of an effect on crime rates of juveniles than adults (1986, p. 554), the relationship should be more close.

Certainty of Formal and Informal Sanctions

The moderate zero-order correlation between certainty and deviance disappears for most crimes if one controls for theoretically relevant variables. This result provides further evidence to the thesis that juveniles might be less deterrable than adults (Green, 1985, p. 639; Meier, 1978, p. 236). If the relationship of certainty of being caught and the individual crime rate disappears after controlling—among other factors—for the crime rate of peers (a measure for differential association), which is next to norm approval the most important intervening variable, this may stress the impact of informal reactions to deviance. Crime rates of the peers may be considered as a proxy for informal sanctions of peers. We unfortunately asked only regarding three (assault, shoplifting, fraud) out of 14 crimes for the reaction a respondent expected to be offered by his peers to his deviant behavior. There were high correlations between the crime rate of the peers and their expected reaction patterns. Thus the understanding of crime rate as a proxy for informal reaction by peers seems warranted. A direct measure would have been preferable.

It seems to be important to distinguish between informal and formal reactions by using separate questions for certainty that a crime may become known at all and that it become known by police. Although we did not use such a distinction ourselves, we now are convinced also by Williams and Hawkins (1986, p. 563) that both are distinct instruments of social control. A deviant act may be informally punished even if it is not known to the police. Furthermore, if informal stigmatizations follow an arrest, this does not necessarily mean just a multiplication of the official sanction. Rather they may be sanctions in their own right that might have been applied anyway if the behavior had been ascertained in a way other than by arrest.

A final reason to insist on a distinction between formal and informal sanctions—as Meier et al. (1984, p. 68) want us to do—should be the insight that informal sanctions are beyond the influence of penal law. Thus for a politician who wants to frighten persons away from certain types of behavior, the scope of informal sanctions is unavailable, or useless.

Deterrence of Petty Crimes

According to our results lesser crimes have a higher chance to be reduced by an increase of perceived certainty of being caught. This finding is consistent with results of Chambliss (1967) and Watson (1986). Both authors found that petty violations of law (parking violations, not using mandated seatbelts) may be influenced by variations of law enforcement. Such types of law breaking that can be done almost any time with little effort (in our study: shoplifting, traffic violations, travel without ticket) seem to be partially influenced by the perceived certainty of detection. Those types of deviance seem to offer only marginal gains. Compliance with the respective norms is neither difficult nor does it imply much self-restraint to any given person. The behavior involved in petty crimes is mostly instrumental.

Those findings stress the importance of paying attention to differences between various types of norm-breaking behavior. How do deviant acts vary in terms of the rationality involved? A good example may be consumer fraud. As a rational, business-type practice, the possibility of deterrence has been demonstrated by variations of the risk of detection (Jesilow, 1982).

It should be safe to expect that most forms of conscious deviant behavior (those not committed under the influence of alcohol or narcotics and not conducted under emotional stress) will imply a short reflection on the risks of detection. If the risk is considered substantial (a criterion defined individually at different levels) the activity may be restructured (to minimize the risk) or even postponed for a less risky situation. If the behavior is carried out it is because the risks involved are, after all, considered to be not substantial in the given situation. To measure certainty of punishment as a general feature of a type of crime seems to be somewhat misleading. It might be more feasable to find out levels of risk that preclude for respondents certain types of deviant acts in appropriate situations. Certainty of punishment should be considered as a feature of a crime-prone situation rather than a general attribute of norms.

Summary

In the case of petty or everyday offenses, delaying such behavior by increased control is possible. Such a delay may in effect imply a reduction for a given time span. In the case of more serious crimes a delay of the act may lead only to the search for a more suitable situation because after all the reasons for that act (e.g., poverty) might continue to be pressing.

Sources of Error in Panel Research

Some features of our study allow a rebuttal of criticism offered against panel studies on deterrence. Lundman stresses the problem of mortality,[1] which, in his opinion, undermines the external validity of that kind of research (1986, p. 79). Although the problem of mortality may be a serious one, it must not necessarily imply distortion of the results. In our research we drew a probability sample of 1,538 juveniles: 842 participated in the first wave, 740 in both waves of the panel study. The loss of more than 50% did not distort the representativeness of the panel with respect to social-status variables (gender, level of education, etc.) but, more important, it was unrelated to deviance. We were able to check this at the *Bundeszentralregister*. The percentage of persons registered officially for any criminal case in the panel was 15.1%. Among the persons who could not be interviewed or dropped out of the panel ($n = 798$), 15.2% were registered for a criminal case. Thus our findings may claim generalizability, especially for issues of deterrence related to officially known crimes.

We were able to test the deterrence doctrine for self-reported as well as registered official crimes with the result that the deterrence doctrine was rejected more strongly if official data were used. However, there remains an unsolved problem in methodology: Some authors have doubted the validity of judgments on certainty of punishment for the whole time span between the two waves of a panel (see Williams & Hawkins [1986] and Lundman [1986] for elaboration). Notwithstanding the critique we ourselves would like to offer against that variable (see discussion on deter-

---

[1] Panel mortality: respondents of the first wave of interviews do not agree with or are not available for a second interview.

rence theory), we think that the problem is not so much one of lacking stable perceptions of certainty, but of measuring the interaction between perceptions at time 1 with the experiences of the respondent himself or his peers with subsequent undetected and detected deviance. Every deviant act may virtually change the judgment on certainty. The lack of significant correlations between perceived certainty and the individual crime rates may partly be caused by erronous measurement of the independent variable at time 1 without any chance to adapt those data to interactions with interim criminality. Further research on causes of perceived certainty seems to be necessary for any control of this interaction process.

Morality and Penal Law

Finally the important role of the approval of legal norms as an intervening variable in deterrence research needs to be discussed. There is a tendency to see moral commitment to the legal norms as an indirect effect of deterrence. In this view, certainty and severity of punishments are signals for individuals on how important those norms are in society. Thus the deterrent features are supposed to influence the degree of approval (see Gibbs, 1975; Williams & Hawkins, 1986, p. 559). This consideration of both deterrence and normative validation as two related aspects of general deterrence has actually been always promoted by Andenaes (1974). His position was influenced by the thinking of a German philosopher of penal law, Mayer (1936), who claimed for penal law a creative role in regard to morality. It is important to insist on the principle that, contrary to Mayer and Andenaes, the morality validating effect of penal law must be treated as an open empirical question rather than a component of the doctrine of general prevention. To mix normative validation with the deterrence doctrine will create the danger of immunizing general prevention against any attempt of falsification forever. There is simply no society existent that does not have social norms which partly overlap with penal law. Thus the impact of social norms is in danger everywhere of being credited to the impact of penal norms.

This at least happened in Germany. Although deterrence is a rather suspect principle for German legal philosophers given the bad experiences during the Nazi regime with the massive use of sentencing and even executions as deterrents, the notion of "positive" general prevention is very acceptable and has in recent years gained a reputation as a leading principle to legitimize penal law. German research on deterrence, which, consistent with American research, established the importance of norm approval as an intervening variable in the deterrence context (Albrecht, 1980, Schöch, 1985) tended to give credit for this influence also to the penal law (evidence for positive general prevention). Such interpretations are beyond the proof available from social research so far. But although research in this area is still just beginning, there is evidence that penal norms may be even counterproductive for morality. Walker and Argyle (1964) found a boomerang effect: The criminalization of an act led to a reduction of disapproval of that behavior. We found the same result in our panel study. Between the two waves of our panel the German drug laws were changed: The range of prohibited behavior was enlarged and punishments were increased, effective January 1, 1982. The moral disapproval of drug taking decreased from the first to second wave (Schumann, 1988) and the crime rate increased. The tightening up of the law neither deterred nor caused a higher approval of the drug laws. It seems necessary to start a complete new range of empirical studies on the relationship between penal law and norm acceptance to prevent the danger of producing handy legitimations for penal law provisions simply because they happen to overlap partly with the autonomous or socially based morality of the people.

References

Albrecht, H.J. (1980). Die generalpräventive Effizienz von strafrechtlichen Sanktionen. In Kaiser, G. (Ed.), *Empirische Kriminologie* (pp. 305–327). Freiburg: Max-Planck-Institut.

Andenaes, J. (1974). *Punishment and deterrence*. Ann Arbor; MI: University of Michigan Press.

Anderson, L.S. (1977). *Longitudinal study of the deterrence model*. Ann Arbor; MI: University Microfilms International.

Becker, H.S. (1963). *Outsiders. Studies in the sociology of deviance*. New York: Free Press.

Beyleveld, D. (1980). *A Bibliography on general deterrence research*. Westmead: Saxon House.

Bishop, D.M. (1982). *Deterrence and social control: A longitudinal study of the effects of sanctioning and social bonding on the prevention of delinquency*. Doctoral dissertation, SUNY-Albany. Ann Arbor, MI: University Microfilms International.

Chambliss, W.J. (1967). Types of deviance and the effectiveness of legal sanctions. *Wisconsin Law Review*, 703–719.

DiChiara, A., & Galliher, J.F. (1984). Thirty years of deterrence research: Characteristics, causes and consequences. *Contemporary Crises, 8*, 243–263.

Erickson, M.L., Gibbs, J.P., & Jensen, G.F. (1977). The deterrence doctrine and the perceived certainty of legal punishment. *American Sociological Review, 44*, 305–317.

Erickson, M.L., & Gibbs, J.P. (1978). Objective and perceptual properties of legal punishment and the deterrence doctrine. *Social Problems, 25*, 253–264.

Gartner, R.I. (1985). *The perceived risks and returns of crime: An individual-level panel study of deterrence*. Ann Arbor, MI: Microfilms.

Gibbs, J.P. (1975). *Crime, punishment and deterrence*. New York: Elsevier.

Gibbs, J.P. (1979). Assessing the deterrence doctrine. *American Behavioral Scientist, 23*, 653–677.

Grasmick H.G. (1981). The strategy of deterrence research: A reply to Greenberg. *Journal of Criminal Law and Criminology, 72*, 1102–1108.

Green, G.S. (1985). General deterrence and television cable crime: A field experiment in social control. *Criminology, 23,* 629–645.

Greenberg, D.F., Kessler, R.C., Logan, C.H. (1979). Aggregation bias in deterrence research: An empirical analysis. *Journal of Research in Cime and Delinquency, 18,* 128–137.

Hofer, H., Tham, H. (1975). Beware of general prevention! In National Swedish Council for Crime Prevention (Ed.), *General deterrence* (pp. 257–270). Stockholm: NSCCP.

Jesilow, P.D. (1982). *Deterring automobile repair fraud: A field experiment.* Ann Arbor: Microfilms.

Lundman, R.J. (1986). One-wave perceptual deterrence research: some grounds for the renewed examination of cross-sectional methods. *Journal of Research in Crime and Delinquency, 23,* 370–388.

Mayer, H. (1936). *Das Strafrecht des Deutschen Volkes.* Stuttgart: Enke.

Meier, R.F. (1978). The deterrence doctrine and public policy: A response to utilitarians. In Cramer, J.A. (Ed.), *Preventing crime* (pp. 233–246). Beverly Hills: Sage.

Meier, R.F., Burkett, S.R., & Hickman, S.A. (1984). Sanctions, peers, and deviance: Preliminary models of a social control process. *The Sociological Quarterly, 25,* 67–82.

Meier, R.F., & Johnson, W.T. (1977). Deterrence as social control: The legal and extralegal production of conformity. *American Sociological Review, 42,* 292–304.

Minor, H.W., & Harry, J. (1982). Deterrent and experiental effects in perceptual deterrence research: A replication and extension. *Journal of Research in Crime and Delinquency, 19,* 190–203.

Nagin, D. (1978). General deterrence: A review of the empirical evidence. In Blumstein, A., Cohen, A., & Nagin, D. (Eds.), *Deterrence and incapacitation: Estimating the effects of criminal sanctions on crime rates.* (pp. 95–139). Washington, D.C. Government Printing Office.

Parker, J., Grasmick, H.G. (1979). Linking actual and perceived certainty of punishment. *Criminology, 17,* 366–379.

Paternoster, R., & Iovanni, L. (1986). The deterrent effects of perceived severity: A reexamination. *Social Forces, 64,* 751–777.

Piliavin, I., Thornton, C., Gartner, R., & Matsueda, R.L. (1986). Crime, deterrence and rational choice. *American Sociological Review, 51,* 101–119.

Rausch, S.P. (1982). *Perceptions of sanctions, informal controls, and deterrence: A longitudinal Analysis.* Ann Arbor; MI: Microfilms.

Ross, L.H. (1982). *Deterring the drinking driver.* Lexington; MA: Ballinger.

Ross, L.H. (1984). Social control through deterrence: drinking-and-driving laws. *Annual Review of Sociology, 10,* 21–35.

Ruhland, D.J., Gold, M., & Heckman, R.J. (1982). Deterring juvenile crime. *Youth and Society, 13,* 353–376.

Saltzman, L.E., Paternoster, R., Waldo, G.P., & Chiricos, T.G. (1982). Deterrent and experiental effects: The problem of causal order in perceptual deterrence research. *Journal of Research in Crime and Delinquency, 19,* 172–189.

Schöch, H. (1985). Empirische Grundlagen der Generalprävention. In Vogler, T. (Ed.), *Festschrift für Hans Heinrich Jescheck* (pp. 1081–1105). Berlin: Duncker & Humblot.

Schumann, K.F., Berlitz, C., Guth, H.W., & Kaulitzki, R. (1984). Lassen sich generalpräventive Wirkungen des Jugendstrafrechts nachweisen? In DVJJ (Ed.), *Jugendgerichtsverfahren und Kriminalprävention* (pp. 281–286). München: DVJJ.

Schumann, K.F., Berlitz, C., Guth, H.W., & Kaulitzki, R. (1987). *Jugendkriminalität und die Grenzen der General-prävention.* Neuwied: Luchterhand.

Schumann, K.F. (1989). *Positive Generalprävention. Ergebnisse und Chancen der Forschung.* Heidelberg: Müller.

Silberman, M. (1976). Toward a theory of criminal deterrence. *American Sociological Review, 42,* 442–461.

Tittle, C.R. (1977). Sanction fear and the maintenance of social order. *Social Forces, 55,* 579–596.

Tittle, C.R. (1980a). *Sanctions and social deviance.* New York: Praeger.

Tittle, C.R. (1980b). Evaluating the deterrent effects of criminal sanctions. In Klein, M.W., & Teilman, K.S. (Eds.), *Handbook of Criminal Justice Evaluation* (pp. 381–402). London: Routledge.

Thomas, C.W., & Bishop, D.M. (1984). The effect of formal and informal sanctions on delinquency: A longitudinal comparison of labeling and deterrence theories. *The Journal of Criminal Law and Criminology, 75,* 1222–1245.

Walker, N., & Argyle, M. (1964). Does the law affect moral judgements? *British Journal of Criminology, 24,* 570–581.

Watson, R.E.L. (1986). The effectiveness of increased police enforcement as a general deterrent. *Law and Society Review, 20,* 292–299.

Williams, K.R., & Gibbs, J.P. (1981). Deterrence and knowledge of statutory penalities. *The Scoiological Quarterly, 22,* 591–606.

Williams, K.R., & Hawkins, R. (1986). Perceptual research on general deterrence: A critical review. *Law and Society Review, 20,* 544–572.

2

Attribution Theory and Deterrence Research: A New Approach to Old Problems

SUSANNE KARSTEDT-HENKE

Introduction

About 1980 criminologists in the Federal Republic of Germany (FRG) took a new approach to deterrence theory and research. Although the topic of "general prevention" had been discussed within the community of the practitioners of penal law, it had been dormant within the scientific community.[1]

At this time, theoretical discussion (Andenaes, 1974; Gibbs, 1975; Zimring & Hawkins, 1973), empirical research, and the discussion of methodological issues was fairly advanced elsewhere. The developing field of research on "general prevention" or "general deterrence"[2] derived great benefit from this situation. Meanwhile, a few studies have been completed,[3] but none has yielded evidence of strong and consistent linkages between formal sanctions and deviance. In sum, it can be stated that deterrence variables are not operating in a "social vacuum" (Minor, 1977, p. 119) and that their effects, compared to those of other "control-inhibitory variables" (Paternoster, Saltzmann, Waldo, & Chiricos, 1983) such as moral commitment (Kretschmer-Bäumel & Karstedt-Henke, 1986; Schumann, Berlitz, Guth, & Kaulitzki, 1985) or disapproval by others (Schumann et al., 1985; Karstedt-Henke, 1988), are small or negligible. In fact, these results do not differ from the results yielded by the considerable amount of research in the United States.[4] The problems that accompany

---

[1] An exception is the work of Kaiser (1970) on traffic laws and traffic behavior.

[2] See Andenaes for the "European" connotation of these terms (1974, p. 173).

[3] These are mainly: a two-wave survey study of a cohort of 16-year-old adolescents by Schumann, Berlitz, Guth, and Kaulitzki (1985), a cross-sectional study of offenders and young soldiers by Dölling (1985), a study of drinking-and-driving habits by Kretschmer-Bäumel and Karstedt-Henke (1986), a cross-sectional study by Karstedt-Henke (1985b, 1987), and a study of seat-belt-laws on the aggregate level in Switzerland by Killias (1985).

[4] See the report and criticism by Lundman (1986).

empirical research on general deterrence since its early days and that have been clearly stated by Gibbs (1975) are still to be solved. Summing up what the results have in common and developing and testing new approaches to deterrence doctrine and research seem to be promising.

First, it seems to be appropriate to conceptualize the deterrence variables being "organized around a set of rules" (Paternoster et al., 1983, p. 282), which includes the perception not only of a single regulation but also of a whole set of norms and laws defined by the penal code (Grasmick & Green, 1980; Silberman, 1976).

Second, the resulting set of perceptions is not established independently from the whole set of cognitions and beliefs about the law, the penal code, and the system of criminal justice on the one hand, and about morale, deviance, and outsiders on the other hand. Consequently, deterrence research deals only with one component of the "belief system" (Converse, 1964) concerning law and morality among the public at large. Thus, identification of the position of the deterrence factors within this cognitive structure, analysis of the process of formation of the belief system,[5] and determination of the role of "experience" versus other channels of information[6] require the integration of other theories of deviance,[7] of theories of mass communication, theories of knowledge and opinion of the law, as well as theories of moral development (Banfield, 1968; Kohlberg & Turiel, 1978).

Third, belief systems seem to be relatively stable, once they have been established (Converse, 1964), especially the belief system concerning the penal code and the system of penal justice (see, e.g., Stinchcombe et al., 1980). Comparing several two-wave studies, Lundman (1986, p. 374) concludes that "evidence of considerable perceptual instability is at worst mixed."[8] Effects of deterrence variables, which are traceable for naive offenders (Bridges & Stone, 1986) or in samples of adolescents (high-school and college students, see, e.g., Paternoster et al., 1983), might vanish as soon as the belief system is established. Further, the belief systems as to the law and the penal system do not radically differ among the sexes, ages, and status groups,[9] although there seems to be evidence implying that within deviant subcultures the belief system differs from the one of the law-abiding majority.[10] Still, the question remains: Why are the

---

[5] See Bridges and Stone (1986) for the susceptibility of "naive offenders" to sanctions.
[6] See Parker and Grasmick (1979) for the importance of personal experience and interpersonal communication.
[7] See, for example Minor (1977), Silberman (1976), Geerken and Gove (1975).
[8] See Paternoster, et al. (1983) for evidence of instability.
[9] See Tittle (1980).
[10] See cultural deviance theories, Miller's theory of lower-class culture, the theory of neutralization by Sykes and Matza (1957).

radical differences between the crime rates of males and females, young and older people, lower and higher classes—according to official crime reports as well as to self-reports—not accompanied by respective differences between the perceptions of the control-inhibitory factors?[11]

The task of studying an organized set of perceptions or a cognitive pattern requires establishment of the principles governing the formation of this pattern.[12] In this chapter I will analyze these principles within the framework of attribution theory. "Attribution refers to the process through which individuals seek the causes and meanings of their behavior and the behavior of others" (Howard & Levinson, 1985, p. 192), how observers make inferences about people and the surrounding environment, and how they conclude with a causal judgement about behavior.

The basic principles of justice, as they are defined in the penal law, mainly in the code of criminal procedure, govern the "just" and "justified" attribution of an offense to an offender: "One must be reasonably certain that the actor is the cause of his behavior" (Howard & Levinson, 1985, p. 193), not the circumstances; it must be proven that the behavior is the result of his willing intent (or of gross negligence); otherwise he will be more or less excused.[13]

The obvious parallels between the attribution process and the principles of justice suggest an analysis of the belief system surrounding penal law and the system of criminal justice according to the principles of internal versus external attribution of offenses and the related information profiles.

After reviewing the field of attribution theory I will present several hypotheses about the attribution process and the relationship between moral and legal inhibitory factors and crime rates. I will focus in particular on the relation between "the social (extralegal) evaluation of particular crimes" (Erickson, Gibbs, & Jensen, 1977) and the perceived risk of arrests and I will report on the results of a survey study.

Attribution Theory and Deterrence Theory

Attribution Theory and the Social Evaluation of Crimes

It was only recently that criminologists have recognized attribution theory and its potential. Stryker and Gottlieb (1981) and Crittenden (1983) criticize the wasteful duplication of effort that follows from mutual

---

[11] The results of our study on drinking and driving showed that females are much more law abiding than males in special situations as well as in their general habits—but that they almost do not differ with respect to their cognitive patterns supporting conformity or deviance (Kretschmer-Bäumel & Karstedt-Henke, 1986).

[12] See Converse (1964) for the formal principles of belief systems.

[13] See Hart (1968) for the principles of responsibility in the penal law.

interdisciplinary ignorance. Criminology offers a rich field for the application of attribution theory: the process of the offenders being labeled by the institutions of social control as well as by the general public, the evaluation of the seriousness of crimes and criminality, decisions of judges concerning recidivism and arrests, and the principles of criminal law itself.[14]

In the original formulation of attribution theory by Heider (1958), the factors that contribute to a causal judgement about behavior were conceptualized as internal to the actor (ability, effort, intention) or external to the actor (task- and situation-related factors, luck). Kelley (1967, 1973) specified the kinds of information we use in making attributions and the rules by which this information is combined: the behavior of an actor in response to a particular stimulus in his environment, his behavior toward other stimuli, and finally the behavior of others toward the same stimulus (Howard & Levinson, 1985, p. 193). From this information, patterns are arranged pointing to an attribution to the actor himself or to internal causes on the one hand and to the environmental stimulus or to circumstances—external causes—on the other hand. Three of these patterns or "forms of covariation" are especially apt to discriminate between an attribution to the actor (internal attribution) and an attribution to the environment (external attribution): (a) the *consensus* between the actor's behavior and the behavior of others; (b) the *consistency* of the actor's behavior toward this stimulus at various times and in various modalities; and (c) the *distinctiveness* of his behavior toward this stimulus compared to other stimuli[15] (Howard & Levinson, 1985, p. 193). The information profile supportive of an internal attribution is the "high-consistency, low-consensus, low-distinctiveness" profile (Howard & Levinson, 1985, p. 193): If the offender is assumed to react mainly in this way toward the stimulus (high consistency), if his behavior strongly differs from the "normal" behavior or the behavior of almost everyone (low consensus), and if he is assumed to react in the same way in any other circumstances (low distinctiveness), he will be found guilty, his behavior will be morally condemned, and his character will be judged negatively.

Conversely, more positive judgments of his character and a less severe condemnation of his offense are associated with the "high-consistency, high-consensus and high-distinctiveness" pattern that supports external attribution or attribution to the environment (Howard & Levinson, 1985, p. 193). A modification of the information profile that supports an external attribution seems to be appropriate, for low consistency of the behavior

---

[14] See, for example, Abele and Volbert (1979) for an application of attribution theory to the labeling of female offenders; Albrecht and Karstedt-Henke (1987) for an analysis of the labeling by the institutions of social control and its perception by young offenders.

[15] For a review of the literature see Harvey, Ickes, and Kidd (1976, 1978, 1981).

marks the offender as a person who could not withstand an opportunity, who was induced by others, or who just once committed an offense.

The principles of justice and the principles of labeling and moral condemnation as well rely on these informational patterns for the purpose of the correct internal or external attribution of an offense to an offender, that is, of the identification of the willing and destructive intent of the offender on the one hand, or of the circumstances on the other hand causing his behavior. These principles of appreciation apply to the causal judgment made by offenders and law-abiding persons about their own behavior and the behavior of others as well as about offenses: The rating of offenses according to their seriousness and to their moral condemnation will be based on a similar attribution process.[16]

The more offenses are attributed to the internal factors—that is, to the willing intent of the offender—the higher will be the public recognition of their seriousness and their subsequent moral condemnation; the more they are attributed to environmental stimuli or circumstances, the less will be their perceived seriousness and moral condemnation. Accordingly, the social evaluation of crimes will result in a rank order of offenses the first places of which will be occupied by offenses mostly attributed to internal factors. On the other hand, if offenders do not differ much from everyone else or if most people commit the offense (high consensus), if offenders are usually law abiding (high distinctiveness), and if opportunities are overwhelming (high consistency), in short, if the offense is a "folk-crime" (Ross, 1960), moral condemnation of the offense will be low.

Attribution Theory and the Legal Inhibitory Factors

The legal and social factors inhibiting crime—the risk of arrest and the severity of sanctions, formal as well as informal—are part of the "opportunity structure" or situational setting of the offense.[17] They are environmental stimuli inhibiting a prospective offender by surpassing his (normally bad) intentions and the prospective benefits the offender derives from committing the offense. Accordingly, external attribution implies the ascription of the commitment of the offense to the impact of the deterrent factors to a marked degree. Conversely, moral commitment as an inhibiting factor is assumed to operate more or less independently from the environmental stimuli: In various situations (high consistency) and for different offenses (low distinctiveness) a person will not change his moral commitment, even when facing the best opportunities. Thus, moral

---

[16] See Sellin and Wolfgang (1964) for the importance of intentions with regard to the evaluation of the seriousness of crimes.

[17] For the relevance of situational settings see Clarke (1980), Karstedt-Henke (1981), Kretschmer-Bäumel and Karstedt-Henke (1986), especially the process of "crime spillover" (Hakim & Rengert, 1981).

commitment and "bad intentions" as its counterpart are related to the internal attribution of offenses, implying that the deterrent factors are of small or no importance. Reconsidering the rank order of the social evaluation of crimes according to their internal or external attribution, we find that the legal inhibitory factors will have a stronger impact on the lower ranks, which include less serious crimes, whereas the more serious and socially condemned crimes are, to a marked degree, less susceptible to their influence.[18]

Thus, we find within the realm of deterrence theory several typologies of crimes and offenders coinciding with the results of the application of attribution theory: The discrimination between "mala in se" and "mala prohibita" (Zimring & Hawkins, 1973), between "expressive" and "instrumental" crimes, and between offenders with high and low commitment to a criminal or deviant life style (Chambliss, 1966), characterizes offenses and offenders according to their susceptibility to the process of rational decision making with regard to the deterrent factors, that is the tenet of deterrence doctrine.[19] Thus, the findings of empirical studies vary according to their dependent variables; in other words, they vary according to the type(s) of offenses chosen for the study. (Lundman, 1986, pp. 379–380; Paternoster, Saltzman, Waldo, & Chiricos, 1985, p. 430). A closer look at the information patterns supporting internal versus external attribution will help us "to identify the process involved in the formation of individual perceptions of sanctions ..." (Tittle, 1980, p. 240) and especially to analyze these perceptions as they are related to the various components of the belief system (Erickson et al., 1977; Parker & Grasmick, 1979).

The high-consensus, high-distinctiveness and high- or low-consistency information profile supporting external attribution is associated with low perceived or objective certainty of arrests. In the case of high consensus, the offender does not differ from the majority or from people who commit the same offense, but reacts similarly to the specific environmental stimuli; consequently it will be difficult to detect the offender and to arrest him. The same holds for high distinctiveness and low consistency, for offenders who react to specific opportunities in their environment are equally hard to detect. On the other hand, the high-consistency, low-consensus, and low-distinctiveness information profile supporting internal attribution is valid for those offenders who differ from the behavior of others (low consensus), who react mainly in this special deviant way (high consistency) in any circumstances, and in response to any opportunities (low distinctiveness):

[18] See the results of Erickson et al. (1977, p. 316), which led them to conclude that "the combination of a low crime rate ... and high objective or perceived certainty of legal punishment would reflect the social (extralegal) evaluations of particular types of crimes, not deterrence."
[19] See Andenaes' criticism of Chambliss typology (1974, p. 84).

Their difference from other persons makes them more easy to detect. Thus, the combination of a high crime rate (official as well as unofficial), low perceived and objective rates of detected offenses (people usually know which are the crimes they mostly get away with), and a low degree of moral condemnation is the result of the underlying informational pattern that supports external attribution. The reverse combination of low crime rates, high perceived and objective rates of detected offenses, and a high degree of moral condemnation is linked to internal attribution of offenses.

Similarly, the perception of the severity of sanctions fits into the scheme of internal versus external attribution of offenses. The threat of penalties for an offense must surpass the intentions of the typical prospective offender; therefore, the more a crime is attributed internally to the actors, the more severe the perceived and actual sanctions will be. The informational profile—high consistency, low consensus, low distinctiveness—points to crimes that are seldom committed and socially condemned to a marked degree (Erickson et al., 1977, p. 316).

The impact of the legal factors depends on the processes of informal social control. Informal as well as legal control require information to identify the offense and the offender precisely. This task will be more easy in the case of information profiles supporting internal attribution and more difficult in the case of the high-consensus, high-distinctiveness, high/low-consistency pattern supporting external attribution. The intensity of informal control varies with respect to the external versus internal attribution of offenses to an offender.

This short outline of the attribution processes resulting in the formation of a belief system about the legal and moral inhibitory factors focuses on the formation of perceptions by the mass public, the more or less law-abiding majority. Table 2.1 presents the proposed impact of the information profiles on the various components of the belief system among the public at large based upon information about the frequency of offenses.

Information about offenses and offenders is gathered from many sources, the experience of offenders being only one; others are experiences of victimization (Parker & Grasmick, 1979, p. 372; Stinchcombe et al., 1980), experiences by others, or sources like the mass media (Parker & Grasmick, 1979, p. 372). There is no reason to assume that commission of offenses has a stronger and longer-lasting impact than other sources, as is often done. On the contrary, it is reasonable to assume cumulative effects of being an offender and a victim.[20] Besides the different information gathered by offenders in contrast to the law-abiding majority, the differences between perceptions of offenders and nonoffenders may result

---

[20] See Lasley (1986) whose study reveals that both victims and offenders share common lifestyle determinants. The results of my own study show a high correlation between the commission of offenses and victimization on the individual level as well as on the aggregate level for categorical rates.

TABLE 2.1. Legal, moral, and social inhibitory factors and their relationship to information profiles supporting external vs. internal attribution.

	Frequency of offenses	Perceived risk of arrest	Perceived severity of sanctions	Perceived impact of the legal inhibitory factors	Moral condemnation	Intensity of social control
High	High consensus High distinctiveness High/low consistency	Low consensus Low distinctiveness High consistency	Low consensus Low distinctiveness High consistency	High consensus High distinctiveness High/low consistency	Low consensus Low distinctiveness High consistency	Low consensus Low distinctiveness High consistency
Low	Low consensus Low distinctiveness High consistency	High consensus High distinctiveness High/low consistency	High consensus High distinctiveness High/low consistency	Low consensus Low distinctiveness High consistency	High consensus High distinctiveness High/low consistency	High consensus High distinctiveness High/low consistency

☐ External attribution;
┆ ┆ Internal attribution.

from a tendency of offenders to attribute their behavior externally, for example, by techniques of neutralization (Sykes & Matza, 1957). Thus, the information profile of marijuana users will support an external attribution to the extent that they are members of a subculture (Becker, 1963), whereas that of nonusers will suggest an internal attribution.

The research presented below examines:

1. Whether the process of attribution applies to various components of the belief system,
2. How according to the process of attribution the perception of the certainty of arrests is related to other parts of the belief system
3. Whether self-reported crime rates and victimization rates are sources of information related to the legal and moral inhibitory factors as well as to the other parts of the belief system according to the presuppositions of attribution theory.

Methods

Sampling

A questionnaire was mailed to a sample of 1,500 inhabitants of the FRG, who belonged to the electorate.[21] The codable response rate was 33% (510 completed questionnaires). A comparison with official data showed that the sample rather well approximated the composition of the population in the FRG, regarding sex, age, education, and marital status, as well as the rural and urban population.

Variables

The central variables were estimates of the risk of arrest for a generalized other, the perceived impact of the legal inhibitory factors (certainty of arrests and severity of sanctions) on the crime rate, the disposition to take active part in informal control (the tendency to report offenders to the police), the moral condemnation of crimes, the estimate of the growth of crime rates, and the perceived consent to the penal law. Each questionnaire included a self-report criminal-involvement inventory and a self-report of victimization for the past 3 years. Each question was answered for a list of offenses, including drunk driving, robbery (unarmed), grand fraud (white-collar crimes), burglary, sexual offenses, shoplifting, willful destruction

---

[21] They were 18 years and older and had German citizenship. It was a two-stage sample; the first stage was a sample from the inventory of communities according to their size. Three big cities (Hamburg, Berlin, Munich) were added. On the next stage subjects were randomly selected from the registers of inhabitants.

(vandalism), assault-battery, cheating (small-scale), possession and use of drugs, murder and homicide, and free riding on trains and buses.[22]

The measure of the perceived risk of arrests asked the respondents to estimate the percentage of offenders (generalized other) who are caught by the police on a scale from 0% (no one) to 100% (all), steps of 10% taken at a time. The measure of the perceived impact of the risk of arrests asked the respondents whether the crime rate would grow, remain unchanged, or would decline should the police substantially reduce their efforts to arrest offenders; the same measure was applied to the severity of sanctions, asking the respondents what would happen to the crime rates were all sentences to be reduced by half. The measure of informal control asked the respondents what they would do if they observed a person committing a crime; five ordinally ranked response options from "doing nothing" to "arresting and reporting the person to the police" were given. Moral condemnation was measured by the necessity to hold the offender responsible; the scale included 5 points from "absolutely not necessary" to "absolutely necessary." The growth of the crime rate for the last 3 years was estimated by the respondents for every offense, whether it happened now "more often," "equally often," or "less often." Moral consensus within the population was measured by estimating whether the majority would "fully consent," "fully dissent," or whether consent and dissent were balanced for the several laws.

The analysis of individual data[23] showed that the belief system concerning the law and the institutions of criminal justice is based on general political-legal orientations according to the cleavages between liberalism and conservativism (Karstedt-Henke, 1985a, 1985b, 1987). The comparison of types of offenses was based on aggregation according to offenses.[24] Two measures of central tendency, the mean and the median, were used to describe the responses to each question. In the case of the self-reports on offending and victimization, the "categorial rate" (Gibbs, 1975) was computed; this is the proportion of subjects who reported at least one offense or one victimization. To identify the rank order of offenses resulting from attribution, rank-order correlations (Kendall's τ) were computed for 8 offenses.[25]

---

[22] From the self-report inventory for victimization, crimes without "personal victims" (shoplifting, free riding, possession and use of drugs) were excluded; none of the self-report inventories included murder and homicide.

[23] A regression approach for categorial data was used (Forthofer & Lehnen, 1981) to establish theoretical and empirical models.

[24] See Erickson et al. (1977) and Inglehart (1985) for the aggregate analysis of individual data on belief systems.

[25] These coefficients seemed to be more appropriate to the small sample and the nonlinear relations reported by Erickson et al. (1977, p. 311). It should be kept in mind that the cases (offenses) are not randomly selected and there might be a

Findings

Comparison between Estimates and Official Reports

Official crime reports are severely biased.[26] Despite their flaws, they represent a rank order of offenses according to their frequency, their arrest rates, and their growth rates that shapes the respective impressions and information patterns of the general public. Comparing the rank orders of official clearance rates and their estimates by the respondents, a significant positive correlation was found ($\tau = .42; p = .00$).[27] The rank order of the growth rates was less well matched ($\tau = .33; p = .17$), although the positive relation indicates a general synchronization between estimates and official sources. Compared to the official rates, offenses and offenders showed little agreement, whereas reported victimization matches the official records well ($\tau = .55; p = .02$). The results show that—with respect to rank orders of offenses—the public belief about crimes is rather accurate (Warr, 1980); the experience of victimization especially is supported by official sources.

Rank Order of Offenses

The rank order of the perceived risk of arrests for various offenses clearly follows the attribution process outlined above: for murder and homicide (1), assault-battery (2), and robbery (3) the estimated arrest rate is highest, whereas on the last ranks we find willful destruction (vandalism) (11), small-scale cheating (10), white-collar crime (9), and drunk driving (8), which are mostly externally attributed according to the high-consensus, high-distinctiveness and high/low-consistency pattern. Mainly at its extreme points, this rank order is matched by the moral condemnation of offenses. The findings concerning the perceived impact of the deterrent factors on the crime rate are inconsistent: On the one hand drunk driving, shoplifting, and white-collar crime are offenses for which subjects estimate the highest impact of sanctions; on the other hand, the lowest impact is assumed for assault-battery, willful destruction, and murder and homicide, a result that fits into the scheme of external versus internal attribution with the exception of willful destruction. The results of the rank order according to the impact of arrests show the same offenses in the lowest ranks, whereas offenses with a high impact of arrests are possession and use of drugs,

---

correlation between cases. In order to compare the results with those obtained by Erickson et al., Pearson's rho was computed. The results did not differ markedly from the rank-order coefficients, but in parts they showed better results.

[26] See Kerner (1973).

[27] Shoplifting, drug use, and small-scale cheating were excluded from the computation because of serious biases in the official reports.

drunk driving, and shoplifting. The "false" ranking of willful destruction may result from a more internal attribution according to its ranking among the "aggressive" offenses.

The rank order of offenses according to the intensity of informal control shows some inconsistencies: small-scale cheating, drunk driving, and shoplifting will not be reported to the police by most of the respondents, whereas nearly all will report burglary, damaging a car, and assault-battery. The inconsistent ranking of damaging a car can be attributed to the "special relationship" the Germans have to their cars.

Relations between the Components of the Belief System

The results of the correlation analysis for the several components of the belief system are not consistent overall with the hypotheses derived from attribution theory. Although the signs of the coefficients point to the predicted direction, coefficients are in part low and not significant. Strong and significant correlations ($\tau = .60$; $p = .04$) are found between the perceived risk of arrests and moral condemnation as had been predicted. The relationship between the perceived risk of arrests and the perceived impact of arrests and sanctions on the crime rates is negative, according to attribution theory, but small and not significant ($\tau = -.12$; $p = .29$). Although the negative coefficient indicates that respondents believe in a higher impact of the legal inhibitory factors on offenses with a low rate of arrests, moral condemnation could not be identified as an essential factor of these relations; there are no correlations with the measures of the impact of legal factors to be found.[28]

The results concerning the intensity of informal control are consistent with the internal versus external attribution of offenses and the related information profiles. Offenses for which respondents estimate a high risk of arrest will evoke a higher degree of informal social control ($\tau = .33$; $p = .09$), and accordingly, moral condemnation is related to its intensity ($\tau = .47$; $p = .09$). Further, a negative correlation ($\tau = -.47$; $p = .03$) between the estimated impact of sanctions and the intensity of informal control is consistent with external versus internal attribution and indicates a compensatory function of the legal factors, especially of the impact of the severity of sanctions: If informal social control will not be activated to a marked degree, severe sanctions and a high risk of arrest ($\tau = -.20$; $p = .3$) are assumed to decrease the crime rate instead. The result shows that in the case of folk crimes their prosecution is left to the system of criminal justice.

---

[28] A partial rank-order coefficient was not computed, although Kendall's τ offers this opportunity; a test of significance is not yet available because the distribution of the partial rank-order coefficient is not known (Siegel, 1976, p. 217).

Impact of Information about Offenses

The information profiles governing the process of attribution are collected from various sources, the most important information being crime rates. The correlation analysis focuses on the relation between the information variables—self-reported offenses and victimizations—and the legal and moral inhibitory factors. Additionally, the relationship between information variables and the perceived growth rate of crimes as well as consent to the respective law is examined.

For both sources of information and experience two measures were constructed: the mean and the median indicate the frequency of personal experience; the categorial rate indicates the frequency of sources of information in the general public or in smaller social networks. Both sources are related, obviously the categorial rates ($\tau = .60$; $p = .04$), although the correlation coefficient for the measures of individual experience is small and not significant[29] ($\tau = .33$; $p = .17$).

Table 2.2 reports the data concerning the relationship between the frequency of offenses and the legal and moral inhibitory factors. The findings support the predicted inverse relations between the frequency of offenses, the estimated risk of arrests, and the moral condemnation of crimes. This is consistent with the high-consensus, high-distinctiveness and high/low-consistency information profile resulting from a high frequency of deviant acts. Furthermore, the findings of Erickson et al. (1977) could be repeated and were confirmed (see columns 1 and 2). Both measures—frequency of personal experience and frequency of sources of information— yield similar results.

Similarly, the impact of the legal factors on the crime rate is rated according to external versus internal attribution of offenses: Frequent and less serious offenses that are externally attributed are assumed to increase to a marked degree if the sanctions and the certainty of arrest were reduced, thereby changing the inhibiting stimuli in the environment. The relationship between the frequency of offenses and the impact of sanctions is slightly stronger, thereby indicating that the certainty of arrest is assumed to have a more constant effect on all crimes. This conforms with scientific deterrence theory, supposing that the certainty of arrest is the main deterrent factor.

Furthermore, the intensity of informal control is related to the high-consensus, high-distinctiveness, and high/low-consistency information profile characterizing mass offenses, as is supported by the negative coefficients; their small scale suggests that the disposition to exert informal control seems to be only loosely linked to the belief system and will be

---

[29] See note 20.

TABLE 2.2. Correlation (Kendalls' τ) between values pertaining to the frequency of self-reported offenses and victimization and the components of the belief system concerning penal law.[a]

Measures of frequency of self-reported offenses	1 Perceived risk of arrests[b]	2 Moral condemnation	3 Perceived impact of the risk of arrests	4 Perceived impact of the severity of sanctions	5 Intensity of informal social control	6 Estimate of increase of offenses	7 Perceived consent to the Legal norm
Mean	-.47***c	-.60**	.50**	.61**	-.21	-.33	.52**
Median	-.50	-.73**	.32	.59***	-.33	-.58**	.71***
Categorical	-.64	-.73**	.47**	.59**	-.33	-.58**	.71***
Measures of frequency of self-reported victimization[d]	1	2	3	4	5	6	7
Mean	-.80***	-.73**	-.14	-.09	-.14	.33	-.38
Median	-.71**	-.88***	-.23	-.14	-.04	.33	-.30
Categorical	-.71**	-.73**	-.14	-.04	-.04	.33	-.33

[a] Data from a sample of the population of the FRG, 1981. $n = 8$ for each coefficient.
[b] For columns 1–7, median values were entered into the computations.
[c] $*p \leq .1i **p \leq .05i ***p \leq .01$.
[d] $n = 8$ for each coefficient; offenses without personal victims were excluded from the computations.

better explained within the framework of general personal dispositions and traits.

The perception of the increase of crimes is inversely related to the frequency of self-reported crimes: While stability is assumed for mass offenses, a higher growth rate is estimated for the rare ones, a possible consequence of the general overestimation of rare crimes. Mass deviance from legal norms seems to be perceived as a matter of daily life, not as an alarming situation. Accordingly, folk crimes are perceived as being fully consented to by the majority; the laws are violated by the majority, but they are neither doubted nor dissented to.[30] Frequent violation of the legal norm has little or no impact on the stability and "validity" (Gibbs, 1975) of the respective norm.

In the next section, Table 2.2 reports the data on the impact of information about and through victimization on the belief system. In the computation only offenses involving victims personally were included.[31] In contrast to the first section of Table 2.2, most of the correlation coefficients are negligible while partially showing a direction opposite to the prediction. There are two interpretations of this result: On the one hand, information on victimization seems to have a small or negligible impact on the belief system, partially independent of information resulting from the commission of offenses. On the other hand, the results of the first part of table 2.2 might be mainly attributed to victimless crimes like drunk driving and drug use.

Columns 1 and 2 show that information about and through victimization is inversely related to the perceived risk of arrests and to moral condemnation. This is in accordance with the information profile resulting in external attribution of the most frequent offenses. Combined with the corresponding inverse relation to moral condemnation, both results confirm that a constant information profile produces substantial attributions, and they explain why victims normally do not alter the moral condemnation of the offense or their punitiveness (Langworthy & Whitehead, 1986; Stinchcombe et al., 1980). Especially with regard to folk crimes, for victims as well as for offenders these events are more or less matters of daily life and consequently victims would consent to having the offender go unpunished, if the damage done is compensated (Sessar, 1986).

In contrast to offense information, victimization information is inversely related to the estimated impact of the arrest rate on the crime rate. This refers to a spurious, but reasonable effect of information through and about victimization: Offenses with high rates of victimization seem to be

---

[30] The lowest consent is estimated for murder and homicide, sexual offenses, white-collar crimes and drug use. Dissent seems not to be induced by dissent on the norm itself but by dissent on appropriate—more severe or lenient—sanctions.
[31] See note 22.

less susceptive to the impact of the risk of arrests, an indication that a change toward internal attribution might take place as a consequence of high victimization rates.[32] Reasonably, growth rates are estimated to be higher when victimization is frequent, and consent decreases. Insofar as the estimated consent seems to be mainly linked to the consent on sanctions, a decreasing consent might hint to a tendency of the general public to be increasingly divided on the question of appropriate sanctions. These interpretations of the data are based on the constant direction of the coefficients, while their small scale, compared to the strong and significant relationship to the certainty of arrest and moral condemnation, indicates that information on victimization is mostly unrelated to, and not integrated into, the belief system by processes of internal vs. external attribution.

Conclusion

The results show support, though mixed, for conceptualizing the deterrent factors as part of a belief system, which is organized according to external versus internal attribution of offenses. Several problems of deterrence research, especially of survey research, seem to be induced by the nature and structure of the belief system: different effects of the deterrent factors on various crimes, the stability respectively instability of the perceptions of the deterrent factors, and the impact of various experiential effects on perceptions of the deterrent factors.

Furthermore the results show again the necessity to integrate theories of deviance and suggest "that the statement of the deterrence doctrine as a sophisticated theory may be far more difficult than any version of the doctrine suggests" (Erickson et al., 1977, p. 315). The findings provide evidence for starting renewed examinations of cross-sectional perceptual deterrence research. Deterrence research is still a field good for new explorations.

References

Abele, A. & Volbert, R. (1979). Are female defendants judged differently than male defendants? Quantitative vs. qualitative parameters of social judgement. Unpublished paper, Department of Psychology, Universität Bielefeld, Bielefeld.

Albrecht, G., & Karstedt-Henke, S. (1987). Alternative methods of conflict-settling and sanctioning: Their impact on young offenders. In Hurrelmann, K., Kaufmann, F.-X., & Lösel, F. (Eds.), *Social intervention: Potential and constraints* (pp. 315–332). New York: de Gruyter.

---

[32] Thus, the inconsistent ranking of willful destruction with regard to the impact of the legal inhibitory factors pointing to internal attribution might be caused by the high rate of victimization.

Andenaes, J. (1974). Punishment and deterrence. Ann Arbor, MI: University of Michigan Press.

Banfield, E. (1968). The unheavenly city. Boston: Little Brown.

Becker, H.S. (1963). Outsiders. Studies in the sociology of deviance. New York: Free Press.

Bridges, G.S., & Stone, J.A. (1986). Effects of criminal punishment on perceived threat of punishment: Toward an understanding of specific deterrence. Journal of Research in Crime and Delinquency, 23 (3), 207–239.

Chambliss, W.J. (1966). The deterrent influence of punishment. Crime and Delinquency, 11, 70–75.

Clarke, R.V. (1980). "Situational" crime prevention: Theory and practice. British Journal of Criminology, 20, 136–147.

Converse, Ph.E. (1964). The nature of belief systems in mass publics. In Apter, D.E. (Ed.), Ideology and discontent (pp. 206–261). New York: Free Press.

Crittenden, K.S. (1983). Sociological aspects of attribution. Annual Review of Sociology, 9, 425–446.

Dölling, D. (1985). Rechtsgefühl und Perzeption des Stafrechts bei delinquenten und nicht delinquenten Jugendlichen und Heranwachsenden. In Lampe, E. & Rehbinder, M. (Eds.), Das sognenannte Rechtsgefühl. Jahrbuch für Rechtssoziologie und Rechtstheorie (Vol. 10, pp. 240–256). Opladen: Westdeutscher Verlag.

Erickson, M.L., Gibbs, J.P., & Jensen, G.F. (1977). The deterrence doctrine and the perceived certainty of legal punishments. American Sociological Review, 42, 305–317.

Forthofer, R.N., & Lehnen, R.G. (1981). Public program analysis. A new categorical data approach. Belmont, CA: Lifetime Learning Publications.

Geerken, M., & Gove, W. (1975). Deterrence: Some theoretical considerations. Law and Society Review, 9, 497–514.

Gibbs, J.P. (1975). Crime, punishment and deterrence. New York: Praeger.

Grasmick, H.G., & Green, B. (1980). Legal punishment, social disapproval and internalization as inhibitors of illegal behavior. Journal of Criminal Law & Criminology, 71, 325–335.

Hakim, S., & Rengert, G.F. (Eds.) (1981). Crime Spillover, Beverly Hills, CA: Sage Publications.

Hart, H.L.A. (1968). Punishment and responsibility. Oxford: Oxford University Press.

Harvey, J.H., Ickes, W., & Kidd, R.F. (Eds.) (1976, 1978, 1981). New directions in attribution research (Vol. 1, 1976; Vol. 2, 1978; Vol. 3, 1981). Hillsdale, NJ: Erlbaum.

Heider, F. (1958). The psychology of interpersonal relations. New York: Wiley.

Howard, J.A., & Levinson, R. (1985). The overdue courtship of attribution and labeling. Social Psychology Quarterly, 48 (3), 191–202.

Inglehart, R. (1985). Aggregate stability and individual-level flux in mass belief systems: The level of analysis paradox. The American Political Science Review, 79, 97–116.

Kaiser, G. (1970). Verkehrsdelinquenz und Generalprävention. Tübingen: Mohr.

Karstedt-Henke, S. (1981). Das Trunkenheitsdelikt im Strassenverkehr—Studie zur Theorie der Wirksamkeit von Strafgesetzen. Unpublished dissertation, Universität Bielefeld, Bielefeld.

Karstedt-Henke, S. (1985a). Die Stützung von strafrechtlichen Normen und Sanktionen durch das Rechtsgefühl. Ein kognitions-zentrierter ansatz. In Lampe, E. & Rehbinder, M. (Eds.), *Das sogenannte Rechtsgefühl. Jahrbuch für Rechtssoziologie und Rechtstheorie* (Vol. 10, pp. 210–239). Opladen: Westdeutscher Verlag.

Karstedt-Henke, S. (1985b). Die Einschätzung von Strafen und ihren Wirkungen— Ein Beitrag zur Sanktionsforschung. *Zeitschrift für Rechtssoziologie, 6,* 70–89.

Karstedt-Henke, S. (1987). Die Einschätzung der generalpräventiven Faktoren und ihrer Wirksamkeit durch die Bevölkerung—Ergebnisse einer empirischen Untersuchung. *Kriminologisches Journal, 19,* 66–78.

Karstedt-Henke, S. (1988). Alternative Konfliktlösungs- und Sanktionspraktiken: Auswirkungen auf strafrechtlich Auffällige. *Bericht aus dem Teilprojekt,* C 3. SFB 227, INFO 4, 8–15.

Kelley, H.H. (1967). Attribution theory in social psychology. In D. Levine (Ed.), *Nebraska Symposium on Motivation.* Lincoln, NE: University of Nebraska Press.

Kelley, H.H. (1973). The processes of causal attribution. *American Psychologist, 28,* 107–128.

Kerner, H.-J. (1973). *Verbrechenswirklichkeit und Strafverfolgung—Erwägungen zum Aussagewert der Kriminalstatistik.* München: Goldmann.

Killias, M. (1985). Zur Bedeutung von Rechtsgefühl und Sanktionen für die Konformität des Verhaltens gegenüber neuen Normen. Das Beispiel der Gurtanlegepflicht. In Lampe. E., & Rehbinder, M. (Eds.), *Das sogenannte Rechtsgefühl. Jahrbuch für Rechtssoziologie und Rechtstheorie* (Vol. 10, pp. 257–272). Opladen: Westdeutscher Verlag.

Kohlberg, L. & Turiel, E. (1978). Moralische Entwicklung und Moralerziehung. In Portele, G. (Ed.), *Sozialisation und Moral* (pp. 13–80). Weinheim: Beltz.

Kretschmer-Bäumel, E. & Karstedt-Henke, S. (1986). *Orientierungs- und Verhaltensmuster der Kraftfahrer. Ergebnisse einer Befragung. Untersuchungen zu Alkohol und Fahren (Research on Drinking and Driving),* (vol. 13). Köln: Bundesanstalt für Straßenwesen (Federal Agency of Traffic Affairs).

Langworthy, R.H., & Whitehead, J.T. (1986). Liberalism and fear as explanations of punitiveness. *Criminology, 24,* 575–591.

Lasley, J.R. (1986). *A causal analysis of victimization and offending.* Ann Arbor, MI: UMI Dissertation Information Service.

Lundman, R.J. (1986). One-wave perceptual deterrence research: Some grounds for the renewed examination of cross-sectional methods. *Journal of Research in Crime and Delinquency, 23,* 370–89.

Minor, W.W. (1977). A deterrence-control theory of crime. In Meier, R.F. (Ed.), *Theory in criminology. Contemporary Views* (pp 117–137). Beverly Hills, CA.: Sage publications.

Parker, J., & Grasmick, H.G. (1979). Linking actual and perceived certainty of punishment: an untested proposition in deterrence theory. *Criminology, 17,* 366–379.

Paternoster, R.L., Saltzmann, L.E., Waldo, G.P., & Chiricos, T.G. (1983). Estimating perceptual stability and deterrent effects: The role of perceived legal punishment in the inhibition of criminal involvement. *Journal of Criminal Law and Criminology, 74,* 270–297.

Paternoster, R.L., Saltzmann, L.E., Waldo, G.P., & Chiricos, T.G. (1985). Assessment of risk and behavioral experience. *Criminology, 23,* 417–436.

Ross, H.L. (1960). Traffic law violation: A folk crime. *Social Problems, 8,* 231–241.

Schumann, K.F., Berlitz, K., Guth, H.-W., & Kaulitzki, R. (1985). *Jugendkriminalität und die Grenzen der Generalprävention.* Bremen: University of Bremen.

Sellin, Th., & Wolfgang, M.E. (1964). *The measurement of delinquency,* New York: Wiley.

Sessar, K. (1986). Neue Wege der Kriminologie aus dem Strafrecht. In Hirsch, H.J., Kaiser, G., et al. (Eds.), Gedächtnisschrift für Hilde Kaufmann (pp. 373–391). Berlin: de Gruyter.

Silberman, M. (1976). Toward a theory of criminal deterrence. *American Sociological Review, 41,* 442–456.

Siegel, S. (1976). *Nichtparametrische Statistische Methoden.* Frankfurt am Main: Fachbuchhandlung für Psychologie.

Stinchcombe, A.L., Adams, R., Heiner, A.C., Scheppele, K.L., Smith, T.W., & Taylor, D.J. (1980). *Crime and punishment. Changing attitudes in America.* San Francisco: Jossey-Bass.

Stryker, S. & Gottlieb, A. (1981). Attribution theory and symbolic interactionism: A comparison. In Harvey, J.H., Ickes, W., & Kidd, R.F. (Eds.), *New Directions in Attribution Research* (Vol. 3). Hillsdale, NJ: Erlbaum.

Sykes, G., & Matza, D. (1957). Techniques of neutralization: A theory of delinquency. *American Sociological Review, 22,* 664–670.

Tittle, Ch. R. (1980). *Sanctions and social deviance. The question of deterrence.* New York: Praeger.

Warr, M. (1980). The accuracy of public belief about crime. *Social Forces, 59,* 456–470.

Zimring, F., & Hawkins, G. (1973). *Deterrence: The legal threat in crime control.* Chicago: University of Chicago Press.

3

Offenses by Prisoners on Leave of Absence: A Representative Study from Lower Saxony

FRIEDHELM BERCKHAUER AND BURKHARD HASENPUSCH

Introduction: The Prison System in the Federal Republic of Germany

The prison system in the Federal Republic of Germany is regulated by a federal law: the Act on the Execution of Prison Sentences and on Measures for Correction and Protection Involving Deprivation of Liberty (Corrections Act) of March 16, 1976 (*Strafvollzugsgesetz*). The law is administered by the eleven *Länder* (states) of the Federal Republic.

In July 1989, there were 173 prisons in the Federal Republic of Germany (among them 22 minimum-security institutions) with a capacity of 59,668 beds. Table 3.1 shows how many prisoners were housed in the various types of prisons on July 31, 1989 (Bundesminister der Justiz, 1989). According to their presumed dangerousness, prisoners are assigned to the institutions. The security standards of the prisons differ (maximum vs. minimum security) according to the criminal career of their inmates (first prison sentence vs. two or more prison sentences). According to the law, minimum-security institutions ought to be the rule, but actually they are not: Only 15% of the prisoners serve their sentence in minimum-security prisons. If possible, the prisoner is prepared for his release by a transfer to an open institution some time before the expiry of his prison term.

Despite the general rejection of short-term prison sentences (up to 6 months) in principle because of their desocializing and destabilizing effects, the proportion of such sentences is still relatively high (some 20% of all prison sentences served have an expected duration of up to six months).

According to figures published by the Council of Europe (Tournier, 1986), Germany used to have until recently a relatively high rate of prisoners per 100,000 population (cf. Table 3.2). In 1987, Germany's detention rate of 87 ranked seventh among 19 European nations, however, and was surpassed by the detention rates in Austria, Turkey, Luxembourg, Great Britain, and France. When evaluating such figures, however, one has to consider the differences in the administration of criminal justice in

TABLE 3.1. Prisoners in different types of institutions in the Federal Republic of Germany as of July 31, 1989.

Type of prisoner or detention	Maximum security		Minimum security		Total
	N	%	N	%	N
Remand prisoners (male)	11,338	100	2	0	11,340
Remand prisoners (female)	666	100	0	0	666
Adult prisoners (male)[a]	23,941	78	6,620	22	30,561
Adult prisoners (female)	1,042	84	195	16	1,237
Nonpayment of fine (male)	1,410	73	510	27	1,920
Nonpayment of fine (female)	101	90	11	10	112
Sociotherapy (male)	488	88	64	12	552
Sociotherapy (female)	17	81	4	19	21
Young offenders (male)	3,558	86	561	14	4,119
Young offenders (female)	110	100	0	0	110
Other prisoners (male)	1,090	100	2	0	1,092
Other prisoners (female)	61	100	0	0	61
Total prisoners (male)	41,825	84	7,759	16	49,584
Total prisoners (female)	1,997	90	210	10	2,207

[a] Including preventive detention.

these countries. In the Netherlands, for example, incarceration is on the average only one third of the time served in Germany, but the rate of persons incarcerated annually is considerably higher because, owing to the shorter period of incarceration, the number of persons passing through the prisons must be three times higher to attain a given incarceration rate on a given day.

Leave of Absence

Leave of absence is meant to help in the prisoner's reintegration into society. The Corrections Act specifies the following forms of leave:

Work outside the institution with or without supervision by correctional staff (extramural occupation and work-furlough, respectively, section 11 subsection 1 figure 1)

Temporary absence from the institution for several hours with or without supervision by correctional staff (taking-out and day-out, respectively, section 11 subsection 1 figure 2)

Leave for up to 21 days within one calendar year (section 13)

Taking-out, day-out, or leave of up to 7 days for important reasons (section 35)

Since the Corrections Act came into force in 1977, the various forms of leave have been granted more and more extensively. It is hardly possible, however, to determine their relative frequency because they cannot reasonably be related to the available figures on the prison population:

TABLE 3.2. Rates of prisoners per 100,000 population in selected European countries (as of February 1st).

Country	Year	Prisoners (total)	Prisoners per 100,000 population[a]	Percent remand prisoners
Austria	1984	8,516	114.0	23.8
	1985	8,493	111.5	23.2
	1986	8,286	109.0	22.9
	1987	7,297	96.0	22.7
Great Britain	1984	45,950	83.9	18.4
	1985	50,717	90.0	21.8
	1986	53,127	94.2	20.3
	1987	55,729	98.2	22.2
France	1984	41,545	74.2	51.9
	1985	44,969	79.7	50.9
	1986	45,754	80.7	49.4
	1987	52,494	92.0	41.3
Federal	1984	64,091	104.4	25.4
Republic of	1985	60,911	99.7	23.8
Germany	1986	56,285	92.2	23.8
	1987	53,039	86.7	22.6
Denmark	1984	3,430	70.0	25.7
	1985	3,478	68.0	23.4
	1986	3,513	69.0	24.0
	1987	3,515	69.0	26.9
Spain	1984	14,691	38.2	40.9
	1985	19,541	50.7	50.4
	1986	23,550	61.2	47.6
	1987	27,793	69.2	42.9
Italy	1984	43,348	76.3	73.9
	1985	44,174	77.5	64.1
	1986	43,855	76.7	57.5
	1987	35,589	62.0	54.6
Sweden	1984	4,742	57.0	17.0
	1985	4,807	58.0	17.6
	1986	4,649	56.0	16.3
	1987	5,150	61.0	20.4
Netherlands	1984	4,500	31.0	42.2
	1985	4,933	34.0	35.9
	1986	5,133	35.0	38.3
	1987	5,291	36.0	38.5

Source: Tournier (1984, 1985, 1986, 1987, 1988).
[a] Includes unconvicted prisoners.

44   F. Berckhauer and B. Hasenpusch

neither the number of prisoners on a given day nor the average number of prisoners per year is a valid denominator for such a rate. The recorded number of leaves of absence would have to be related to the number of persons passing through the prison system each year, and this figure is not known reliably. There are nevertheless appreciable differences between the eleven Länder regarding the granting of leave of absence, but there is no relationship between these differences in administrative practice on the one hand and the rate of failures on the other hand. Any cross-sectional analysis of this issue is hampered, however, by the limited comparability of the respective statistics. A longitudinal comparison of data on Lower Saxony nevertheless shows that an increasing number of leaves granted does not result in an—albeit plausible—increase in the proportion of failures (cf. Table 3.3).

The survey of corrections in the Federal Republic of Germany by Dünkel and Rosner (1982) documents the development of prison leave. Even before the Corrections Act came into force in 1977, day-out, leave and work-furlough were on the rise, which continued under the new legislation. For the period 1977 to 1980, the authors report rates of increase of 66% for leave, 76% for day-out, and 51% for work-furlough.

The official statistics also show how often prisoners fail to return on time or to return on their own (technical failures). The rate of such failures per 1,000 leaves of absence is relatively low. However, this figure does not indicate the abuse of leave for new offenses or other forms of deviance, such as intoxication. Table 4.3 shows the number of times the various forms of leave were granted in Lower Saxony as well as the respective percentages of technical failures (Niedersächsischer Minister der Justiz, 1987). There seems to be a negative correlation between the frequency of leave and the rate of technical failures—provided these statistics can be trusted at all.

TABLE 3.3. Leave of absence and failure rates in Lower Saxony 1977 to 1986.

Year	Day-out Granted (N)	Day-out Failures (%)	Leave Granted (N)	Leave Failures (%)	Work-furlough Granted (N)	Work-furlough Failures (%)
1977	17,701	2.1	9,040	5.9	651	10.9
1978	25,812	2.0	11,808	4.0	825	10.5
1979	31,273	1.8	15,151	3.1	1,222	4.7
1980	35,737	1.7	16,244	3.2	1,925	2.3
1981	43,161	1.5	17,270	2.9	1,926	4.1
1982	51,002	1.2	17,388	2.9	2,524	0.8
1983	63,125	1.0	18,142	2.8	2,233	0.9
1984	69,727	0.8	20,453	2.3	2,494	1.6
1985	81,776	0.6	21,066	2.2	2,148	2.0
1986	73,347	0.6	22,625	2.1	1,905	2.2

The present administration of leave of absence did not remain undisputed, however. Particularly the police have expressed their discontent, but the mass media are also fueling public discussion by sometimes sensational coverage of individual, spectacular offenses committed by prisoners on leave. The shooting of two plainclothes detectives by prisoners on leave in Lower Saxony in the fall of 1987, for example, has resulted in considerable political pressure on the prison administration to tighten up the granting of leave. Subsequently, the minister of justice decided to continue the current practice in principle, but to raise the procedural standards in general and for certain violent offenders in particular.

Public opinion on offenses by prisoners on leave is so far not based on reliable empirical evidence, apart from the anecdotal support by individual cases. This limits the scope for objective analysis, and the present study is intended to provide sound data for the numerous political and correctional decision-making processes regarding leave of absence.

In any comprehensive cost-benefit analysis, leave of absence from prison must be considered not simply with the goal of reducing the abuse of leave by prisoners, but rather in relation to the following four more general issues:

Which are the disadvantages for corrections arising from abuses of leave of absence, particularly from nonreturn or involuntary return (so-called technical failures)?

Which are the disadvantages for society at large arising from new offenses by prisoners on leave of absence?

Which are the advantages for rehabilitation arising from leave of absence?

Which are the effects of leave of absence on the conduct of prisoners within the institution?

Understandably, for the prisons it is most important in how far their work and organizational procedures are disturbed by technical failures by prisoners on leave. This is documented by the prison statistics, which only show late or involuntary returns, but do not record how many prisoners commit offenses while on leave and how the recidivism rates are for prisoners with or without leave.

Particularly the latter question, which ought to be of special concern, can so far not be answered conclusively: Too many methodological problems are in the way of a reliable response. But even the issue of new offenses by prisoners on leave of absence is of vital importance to corrections. This issue, however, cannot be resolved on the basis of routinely collected information, so that special studies were necessary.

Several institutions have analyzed data on offenses by prisoners on leave (cf. Table 3.4), but these studies are either out of date, too narrow in scope, or cannot be generalized for other reasons. In view of the continued discussion of this problem, a representative study of offenses by prisoners on leave of absence was conducted in Lower Saxony in 1983. Lower

TABLE 3.4. Overview of studies on offenses by prisoners on leave of absence: Federal Republic of Germany, 1970–1984.

Author	Year	N	Sample, Results	Failure rate (%)
Landeskriminalamt Hamburg (quoted in Gehrkens, 1980)	1980	349	Adult prisoners: 189 offenses by 111 suspects	32
Department of Justice Hamburg (Jürgensen & Rehn, 1980)	1980	43	Adult prisoners, technical failures only: 23 suspects	53
		20	Young prisoners, technical failures only: 3 suspects	15
Landeskriminalamt Bremen (1984, personal communication to the authors)	1983	117	Prisoners not returning from day-out only: 21 offenses by 16 suspects	14
		95	Prisoners not returning from leave only: 5 offenses by 5 suspects	5
		43	Escaped prisoners only: 13 offenses by 43 suspects	12
Nesselrodt (1979)	1970 to 1974	469	Prisoners from maximum-security institutions: 59 suspects	13
		374	Prisoners from medium- and minimum-security institutions: 22 suspects	6
Department of Justice Northrhine-Westphalia (1981)	1977	13,736	Prisoners on leave of absence and escaped prisoners: 107 offenses within 4 months	1
Academy for Public Administration Bremen (Berger et al., 1985)	1982	960	Prisoners from minimum-security institutions: 65 offenses within 3 months	7
Criminological Research Institute of Lower Saxony (Beckers & Beckers, 1983, personal communication to the authors)	1979 to 1982	166	Prisoners from 3 maximum-security institutions: 10 suspects	6
Department of Justice Hamburg (Süss, 1984)	1982	1,641	All prisoners who were granted leave of absence in 1982: 207 offenses by 188 suspects	12
Dolde & Rössner (1987)	1983 to 1984	314	Adult short-term prisoners on work-furlough only: 11 suspects	4

Saxony is one of the Länder of the Federal Republic of Germany with about 7 million inhabitants; its capital is Hannover.

Representative Study in the Lower Saxony Prison System on Offenses by Prisoners on Leave of Absence

Sampling

Three samples were formed of prisoners who had been granted leave, work-furlough, or day-out in 1983. In order to generalize the findings and to avoid multiple reference to identical prisoners, it was necessary for the statistical analysis to replace the events "leave," "work-furlough," and "day-out" by the individual prisoner as unit of analysis. This is possible by referring for the sampling procedure to the prisoner's first leave in the year 1983. This only affects the access to the cases in the sample, but not the access to leaves granted: All instances of leave of absence, work-furlough, and day-out of the selected prisoners were examined for new offenses.

For the year 1983, the institutions were requested to report every 20th prisoner who had been granted leave of absence or day-out for the first time in that year and every 10th prisoner who had been granted work-furlough. This procedure results—particularly in institutions with relatively small numbers of prisoners granted leave—in a reduction of the sample size, compared to the sampling design.

The sample actually consists of:

153 inmates with leave of absence = 4.1% of all such inmates
175 inmates with work-furlough   = 8.5% of all such inmates
248 inmates with day-out   = 4.8% of all such inmates.

Sampling—compared to the unfeasible analysis of all cases—inevitably has the side effect that serious, but very rare offenses by prisoners on leave of absence are not likely to be included in the analysis. The study, then, is representative in the statistical sense, but not comprehensive. It was necessary to examine the occurrence of serious offenses in other ways (reports by the institutions to their superior authorities). For medium- and less-serious criminality, however, the sample results should be more accurate than the results according to these reports.

Evaluation Criterion

Particularly in view of the objections by the police against the granting of leave for prisoners, it seems appropriate to evaluate the prisoners' conduct during leave with reference to as comprehensive a criterion as possible. Therefore, all new offenses registered by the police and committed during leave granted in 1983 were included in the analysis. Technically, this was made possible by a search of files belonging to the Lower Saxony *Landeskriminalamt*. Thus, the names of all prisoners in the sample were checked against the names of suspects known to the police.

This procedure results in the following limitations of the study's generalizability:

Offenses not known to the police are not included in the analysis.

Offenses registered by police agencies outside Lower Saxony are not included in the analysis.

Traffic offenses are not included in the analysis because they are not registered in the police file on criminal offenses.

On the other hand, this approach allows consideration of the complete criminal proceedings by the prosecution and the courts and does not take place at the end of an already completed process of judicial decision making.

Extent of Registration by the Police

The initial formal check of the police records against the times spent outside the institution by the sample of prisoners on leave of absence, day-out, or work-furlough yields the following results:

11 suspects with 16 offenses out of 153 prisoners on leave of absence
 6 suspects with 21 offenses out of 175 prisoners on work-furlough
21 suspects with 33 offenses out of 248 prisoners on day-out

These global rates, however, require further scrutiny because offenses during leave, work-furlough, and day-out should only be counted in the subsample of prisoners on leave, work-furlough, and day-out, respectively. The time of each offense therefore must be examined for the type of leave during which it was committed because there is considerable overlap, particularly among work-furlough and day-out, which may be granted consecutively on the same day. Furthermore, the police records also include offenses committed within the institution.

Following this refinement, the failure rates are:

 7 suspects with 12 offenses among 153 prisoners on leave of absence— failure rate 4.6% (2 assaults, 7 thefts, 1 further property offense, 2 other offenses)
 2 suspects with 15 offenses among 175 prisoners on work-furlough— failure rate 1.1% (15 thefts)
10 suspects with 14 offenses among 248 prisoners on day-out—failure rate 4.0% (2 assaults, 9 thefts, 1 drug offense, 2 other offenses)

Because of the small number of cases, an evaluation of the types of offenses does not seem appropriate.

Comparison of Types of Leave Regarding the Frequency of New Offenses

The failure rates quoted above are prisoner related, they thus describe the conduct of prisoners on leave, work-furlough, and day-out. These rates provide little information, however, for the evaluation of their conduct with regard to the time spent outside the institution. In this respect, there ought to be a difference in the opportunities for abuses ranging from work-furlough over leave of absence to day-out. It may be, however, that the institutions do consider this circumstance in advance when selecting prisoners for leave.

In order to assess the impact of time spent outside the institution, the prisons were requested to list in detail each leave granted in 1983. It was found that prisoners on work-furlough performed best: The 175 prisoners were outside prison walls on a total of 1,793 days and committed 15 offenses during this time, that is, 0.84 per 100 man/days. This may be due to a positive selection process and to the small amount of unsupervised spare time during work-furlough. Day-out occupies an intermediate position with 1.59 offenses per 100 man/days outside the institution (248 prisoners, 14 offenses, 879 man/days outside prison). Leave of absence, finally, has a relatively poor record with 1.76 offenses per 100 man/days (153 prisoners, 12 offenses, 682 man/days outside prison). This rate—twice as high as the one of prisoners on work-furlough—may be attributed to the almost total lack of supervision during leave of absence, apart from the one provided by persons (normally the family) to whom the prisoner is released.

Offenses by Prisoners on Leave in Relation to Overall Criminality

The estimated total impact of offenses by prisoners on leave on the overall crime-rate is shown in Tables 3.5 and 3.6. For a conservative estimate, the maximum value quoted is relevant: The probability for the actual value to be lower than that is 90%.

According to these estimates, some 151 to 430 offenses may have been committed by 89 to 253 inmates out of 3,725 who had been granted leave of absence in Lower Saxony in 1983. Of the 2,062 inmates on work-furlough, between 2 and 43 may be suspected of having committed between 15 and 323 offenses. The respective figures for the 5,175 prisoners on day-out amount to some 129 to 285 registered suspects with 181 to 399 offenses. Taken together, some 220 to 581 prisoners should have been registered with 347 to 1,152 offenses committed in Lower Saxony in 1983. Quantitatively, these offenses have no practical importance for the overall crime rate: they amount at most to 0.53% of all cleared offenses; the propor-

TABLE 3.5. Estimated number of suspects among prisoners on leave.

Type of leave	Standard error of proportion	Suspects in the sample (%)	Suspects among all prisoners on leave		
			Minimum	Mean	Maximum
			(80% Confidence Interval)		
Leave of absence Sample: 153 Total : 3,725	1.7	4.6	89	171	253
Work-furlough Sample: 175 Total : 2,062	0.8	1.1	2	23	43
Day-out Sample: 248 Total : 5,175	1.2	4.0	129	207	285
Total			220	401	581

TABLE 3.6. Estimated number of offenses committed by prisoners on leave.

Type of leave	Number of offenses per suspected prisoner	Number of offenses by prisoners on leave		
		Minimum	Mean	Maximum
		(80% Confidence Interval)		
Leave of absence	1.7	151	291	430
Work-furlough	7.5	15	173	323
Day-out	1.4	181	290	399
Total	—	347	754	1,152

tion of prisoners on leave among the registered suspects amounts at most to 0.41%.

Extent of Serious Criminality

Because of the methodological approach it was unlikely that serious, but infrequent offenses were included in the sample. In order to avoid even the semblance of "dying in fast colors," serious offenses were assessed separately. The prison administration records serious offenses committed by prisoners on leave for administrative purposes, so that a complete review of such cases is possible. In 1983, the following offenses were reported to the Lower Saxony Department of Justice: one arson, one grievous assault, one rape, five serious robberies (including extortions), two attempted manslaughters, one attempted murder, and one murder. These are the isolated, spectacular cases drawn on by the press and thus influencing public opinion. These 12 offenses not included in the sample have no appreciable quantitative impact on overall criminality, but are important because of their quality.

Summary and Conclusions

The police stereotype of the prisoner on leave is based essentially on a distorted perception. The policeman recalls primarily those suspects with particularly numerous or serious offenses. This group usually includes a large number of prisoners, despite their representing a relatively small proportion of all offenders. Offenses by prisoners on leave subjectively gain more weight than they objectively have because their repeated occurrence reinforces certain "common sense" assumptions, which in addition are endorsed by the media. The distortion results from disregarding and forgetting the large number of offenders who do not appear again and again. Actually, the majority of new offenses by prisoners is committed after release from prison and thus may at best testify to the (in)effectiveness of incarceration.

The results of the present study indicate that, in 1983, some 200 to 600 prisoners were charged by the police in Lower Saxony with some 350 to 1,150 offenses committed while on leave. Compared to the grand total, these offenses amount to about 0.5%.

The crime rate of prisoners on leave should not be regarded as overly serious because prison inmates are a particularly crime-prone group of persons, compared to other groups of offenders, and in view of traditional prognostic criteria, one would actually expect a higher level of offenses committed on leave. Apparently, the prison staff succeed in reducing the risk of new offenses substantially by careful selection, preparation for the time of leave, and the threat to refuse leave in the future in case of new offenses.

Leave of absence from prison is meant to prepare and facilitate the prisoner's reintegration into society. Leave and day-out also further the cohesion of the prisoner's family. The decision to grant leave must balance these goals against the risk of new offenses, and because new offenses can never be ruled out with certainty, this decision is bound to result in occasional failure. This risk, however, has been seen and accepted by the legislators.

Leave of absence, however, has also become a significant feature of life in the institutions. On the one hand, the granting (and refusing) of leave causes a considerable workload for the staff, not to mention the administration of disciplinary measures after failure to return on time or criminal proceedings after new offenses. On the other hand, leave has made life in prison more humane, and the granting or refusing of leave has become an important tool for governing the prisoners' conduct: Because every prisoner wants to have his leave, he will do his best not to lose it. A general tightening of the rules for granting leave in order to reduce problems with prisoners outside the institutions may thus also create new problems with prisoners inside the institutions.

References

Beckers, C., & Beckers, D. (1985) Urlaubsvergabepraxis in drei Justizvollzugsanstalten des geschlossenen beginnenden Vollzugs in Niedersachsen. In Kury, H. (Ed.) *Kriminologische forschung in der Diskussion: Berichte, Standpunkte, Analysen* (pp. 605–616). Köln: Carl Heymanns Verlag.

Berger, B., Dähn, P., Diete, P., et al. (1985). *Hat sich der offene Strafvollzug bewährt? Kriminologische Projektarbeit der Hochschule für öffentliche Verwaltung (Projektleiter: Dr. Karl Thomas)*. Bremen: Hochschule für öffentliche Verwaltung.

Bundesminister der Justiz (1987). *Bundeseinheitliche Strafvollzugsstatistik für den Monat August 1987*. Bonn: Bundesminister der Justiz.

Department of Justice Northrhine-Westphalia (1981). Information des Presse- und Informationsamtes der Landesregierung Nordrhein-Westfalen vom 17. 07. 1979. *Zeitschrift für Strafvollzug, 30*, 44.

Dolde, G. & Rössner, D. (1987). Auf dem Wege zu einer neuen Sanktion: Vollzug der Freiheitsstrafe als Freizeitstrafe. Ein Programm zum Vollzug kurzer Freiheitsstrafen und seine empirische Bestätigung. *Zeitschrift für die gesamte Strafrechtswissenschaft, 99*, 425–451.

Dünkel, F. & Rosner, A. (1982). *Die Entwicklung des Strafvollzugs in der Bundesrepublik Deutschland seit 1970. Materialien und Analysen* (2nd ed). Freiburg i.Br.: Max-Planck-Institut für ausländisches und internationales Strafrecht.

Gehrkens, E. (1980). Bedenkliche Behandlung Schwerkrimineller. *Der Kriminalist, 12* (3), 102–108.

Jürgensen, P., & Rehn, G. (1980). Urlaub aus der Haft. *Monatsschrift für Kriminologie und Strafrechtsreform, 63* (4), 231–241.

Nesselrodt, J. (1979). *Der Strafurlaub im Progressionssystem des Freiheitsentzuges. Funktion und Wirkung der Beurlaubung Gefangener hessischer Vollzugsanstalten.* Dissertation, University of Marburg.

Niedersächsischer Minister der Justiz (1987). Strafvollzug in Niedersachsen 1977–1986. Ein Auszug aus den Statistiken. Hannover: Niedersächsischer Minister der Justiz.

Süss, W. (1984). *Abschlussbericht: Urlaubsuntersuchung.* Unpublished manuscript. Hamburg: Justizbehörde.

Tournier, P. (1984). Statistics concerning prison populations in the member states of the Council of Europe. *Prison Information Bulletin, 3*, 17–30.

Tournier, P. (1985). Statistics concerning prison populations in the member states of the Council of Europe. *Prison Information Bulletin, 5*, 16–27.

Tournier, P. (1986). Statistics concerning prison populations in Council of Europe member states. *Prison Information Bulletin, 7,* 23–31.

Tournier, P. (1987). Statistics on prison populations in the member states of the Council of Europe. *Prison Information Bulletin, 9,* 16–26.

Tournier, P. (1988). Statistics on prison populations in the member states of the Council of Europe. *Prison Information Bulletin No. 11,* 18–20.

4

Sexuality, Violence, and Emotional Aftereffects: A Longitudinal Study of Victims of Forcible Rape and Sexual Deviance in Cases Reported to the Police[1]

MICHAEL C. BAURMANN

Introduction

Whenever people in our society talk about sexuality, and especially when they discuss deviant sexual behavior or sex offenses, the discussion tends to be filled with emotional upset. Prejudice is widespread in the field of indecent assault and leads to warnings addressed to children and young women with the intention of preventing sexual criminality:

"Watch out for strange men!"
"Never take shortcuts through alleys, dark streets, or wooded areas, and don't play in abandoned buildings or new constructions sites!"
"Never accompany a stranger. Don't accept candy or other treats from strangers!"
"Be careful of the exhibitionist! He might turn out to be a brutal child molester, rapist, or even murderer."
"Be careful of the homosexual! He might harm you for the rest of your life."

---

[1] This article is a summary of a larger final report of a research project conducted at the Criminological Research Unit of the *Bundeskriminalamt* (Federal Office of Criminal Police) of the Federal Republic of Germany. A summary was given at the Fourth International Symposium on Victimology in Japan (see Baurmann, M.C. (1986). Longitudinal study of cases of sexual assault: Typology and emotional aftereffects. In K. Miyazawa & M. Ohya (Eds.), *Victimology in Comparative Perspective* (pp. 211–217). Tokyo: Seibundo). The complete study was published in 1983 under the title "Sexualität, Gewalt und psychische Folgen. Eine Längsschnittuntersuchung bei Opfern sexueller Gewalt und sexueller Normverletzungen anhand von angezeigten "Sexualkontakten" (for translation, see chapter title) BKA-Forschungsreihe (Vol. 15). Wiesbaden, FRG. This final report contains all methodological and statistical details, as well as a comprehensive bibliography.

"Don't answer when people stop you for directions!"
"You can only trust your relatives and acquaintances."

One of our assumptions at the beginning of the research project was that the rate of sexual offenses cannot be reduced by this kind of information. We supposed that the reality contradicts the ideas expressed in those bits of advice. We feared that the attitudes underlying those statements even might injure the victims (secondary victimization).

What the victim's situation actually looks like, and where the real dangers for the sexual victim lie, were the subject of an empirical, comprehensive longitudinal study in the state of Lower Saxony (Federal Republic of Germany).

Main Questions of the Study, Methodology, and Crime Numbers

The Criminological Research Unit of the Bundeskriminalamt (Federal Office of Criminal Police) of West Germany undertook a longitudinal study dealing with the situation of the victims of indecent assault. During a period of four years (1969–1972) all cases reported to the police in Lower Saxony, which had not necessarily been tried in court, were analyzed from a victimological point of view ($N = 8,058$).

In a panel study 6 to 10 years later (1980/1981), 112 victims representing the total sample were explored extensively by psychologists and subjected to a battery of psychological tests. Depending on the age of the subject, four psychodiagnostic inventories were used:

A biographical inventory (MBI or BIV, depending on the age of the subject) to measure outstanding behavior patterns

Freiburg Personality Inventory (FPI), which is a German version of the combination of MMPI, MPI, EPI, and 16PF

A scale measuring anxiety (AFS–MA), which is based on the American CMAS and TASC

A special inventory measuring neuroticism and extraversion (EPI or, depending on age, HANES).

The interviews normally lasted from 2 to 4 hours and were face-to-face talks in the home of the victim, in most cases only between the victim and a male or female (50:50) psychologist.

In a third part of the project, 131 files of cases of indecent assault that had been tried in court were studied for comparison. All of these files contained a psychological expert report on the credibility of the victim's testimony.

As the distribution of the reported indecent assaults in Lower Saxony do not differ significantly from the corresponding distribution in the Federal

Republic of Germany, the results of this longitudinal study characterize the situation in West Germany.

The main groups of sexual offenses registered are (1988):

Exhibitionism (§183 German Penal Code)	27.3%
Sexual assault on children (§176 German Penal Code)	30.6%
Forcible rape (§177 German Penal Code) and sexual assault under duress (§178 German Penal Code)	24.2%
Others	17.9%

A relatively small number of incestuous contacts was also included in this project although the German Penal Code regards them not as "sexual offenses" but as "offenses against the institution family". The German Penal Code—in contrast to some other codes—considers forcible rape as a sexual offense and not as violent crime primarily.

The main questions posed in this study were:

1. What kind of sexual offenses are actually reported to the police? What role does the use of force or of violence play?
2. Is there a single type of sexual offense or are there different typical constellations?
3. How does the victim view the reported sexual contact years after the charge was made?
4. What was the situation like for the victim? How did others in the social environment react? How did representatives of the authorities act?
5. How many of the victims feel violated or injured? In which cases does emotional injury occur?
6. In the opinion of the victim, what causes psychological injury, if it occurs? Is it so-called primary injury triggered by the criminal act itself, or so-called secondary injury, which occurs later, as a result of the negative influences of the social environment on the victim?
7. Is it possible to determine a typology of victims or of perpetrators or is there rather a typology of interactions between the two persons?

Results of the Study

In 80% to 90% of the cases reported to the police in Germany, sexual victims are girls and women. The age group varies according to the nature of the offense. Nearly two thirds of children who are sexually assaulted are between 7 and 13 years of age. In the area of forcible rape, primarily young women between the ages of 14 and 20 are endangered. The age range of women who encounter an exhibitionist is more widespread, but the incidence is higher in the younger age groups.

Of the suspects and perpetrators, 99.8% were men, primarily between the ages of 16 and 35. The wide-spread opinion that the majority of indecent assailants are older or aged men is incorrect. The age difference between victim and accused is, on the average, 25 years; in cases of violent sexual assault, however, only 7 years. Sexual victims are therefore mainly young women and girls threatened by men who are "in the best years of their lives".

The exhibitionists were men unknown to the women and children in almost all cases (93.0%). In the other reported sexual contacts, however, most of the sexual perpetrators were either known previously or related to the victim (53.6% of *these* cases). In all cases *brought to trial*, 93.8% of the offenders were acquaintances or relatives of the victim. Warnings against unknown sexual assailants therefore is preventively ineffective and, as far as sexual education and upbringing is concerned, highly dubious, as they convey feelings of threat by strange men, whereas, for example, forcible rape is usually inflicted by an acquaintance in the close social environment. With increasing acquaintance between victim and perpetrator, there is an increase in the intensity of the sexual contact ($r = 0.58$) and often in the psychological injury to the sexual victim.

If the incident was reported to the police (the estimated dark figure is 1:3 to 1:10), then it was the cases of violent sexual assault and exhibitionism that were more quickly reported by the victim or relatives. Among the victims of forcible rape, this declaration is usually an expression of indignation, fear, anger, and affliction on the part of the victim. With exhibitionism, in contrast, it is more the indignation of the relatives of the victim about the deviant sexual behavior of a strange man. As the accused is a stranger, there is less scruple about reporting him.

The situation is quite different in cases of child molesting (§176 of the German Penal Code). In many of the more superficial cases the sexual contacts are not given much importance by the children, and sometimes they do not even tell anyone so that the deed becomes known accidentally. Even in serious incidents, parents are often reluctant to report it as the accused is often an acquaintance. In both cases it is possible that—for different reasons—secondary injury to the victim may easily occur, as when the child incurs additional injury from the behavior of persons in the environment, or injury even first results from this behavior (secondary victimization).

Homosexual contacts played no significant statistical or criminological role in this study. On the one hand, they composed only 10% to 15% of the cases, and on the other, the sexual contacts were described by the victims themselves as "harmless", almost exclusively without the use of violence by the suspect. None of the male victims questioned felt themselves to have been injured. No injury could be determined in these cases with the help of test procedures.

In studying the literature, it was very interesting to note that only few attempts have been made to set up a definition for the term *injury* that could be operationalized for diagnostic purposes. Therefore injuries caused by sexual offenses were defined for this study as follows:

Injury as a result of a sexual contact is a reactive, sexual, social, emotional, and/or physical disturbance, which the injured person is subjected to by a guilty party. This disturbance can either be subjectively recognized by the injured person him- or herself, or it can be diagnosed by specific scientific methods. The disturbance can be caused directly by the event itself, or indirectly.

The measurement of injury was operationalized in an *index of injury* (Schadensindex = SI) ranging from zero (no injury) to 100 (maximum injury). Half of this index was determined by symptoms reported actively by the victim when questioned whether he or she had noticed, at any time afterwards, any physical, social, emotional, or sexual problems that were caused by the sexual offence. Twenty five percent of the index contained the answer to a checklist of possible injuries, drawn from the literature, and another 25% the extreme results (SN < 4 or > 6) in the psychological tests listed above.

This method of operationalizing the measurement of injury emphazises the subjective judgment of the victim, as we think that the victim knows best whether she was hurt or not. This method is in contradiction to that of many scientist who have reported on injuries without having asked the victims themselves about the symptoms and their causes.

About half of the victims of indecent assault (48.2%) showed no injury at all, 17.9% a lower index and 33.9% a higher or very high index of injury. On an average the index of injury was 8.7. In cases of forcible rape it went up to SI = 22.3. The highest index explored in this survey was SI = 50.0. *Injured* victims suffered from the sexual attack for an average of 4 years and 8 months.

If injured, the victims were asked what they thought is or was the *main reason* for their suffering. Of the reported sexual contacts with injuries, half of the sexual victims claimed the sexual act itself as being the main cause of their injury, one third some other behavior of the suspect, and one tenth each the behavior of relatives, friends, or the police. This indicates that the police are less often responsible for psychological injuries of sexual victims than some have assumed up to now, but even these few cases should encourage reflection and improvement of police work.

From the point of view of protecting the victim of crime and of improving the quota of cleared cases of serious sexual offenses, it is intolerable that some victims suffer injury primarily from the criminal prosecution system itself or at all.

It can be assumed that the distribution of primary and secondary victimization would be different if tried cases had been studied exclusively. In tried cases it can be expected that relatively more victims are secondarily injured by the behavior of family members or representatives of the authorities.

Further evaluation of the composed index of injury revealed that *self-reported* injuries had the highest degree of validity. In contrast, common psychological tests usually used for other purposes did not provide sufficient information. This means that for the future victimologists have to develop special methods, that is, to construct special inventories to measure objectively the grade of injury from which the victims suffer. For the years to come we then might be able to compare the victim assessment of injury in different groups of criminality with each other.

In addition to the main causality for the injury, the victims were also asked to judge all conversations they had about their experience with other people. Talks with friends, her boyfriend, siblings, teachers, psychologists, her lawyer, specialists, and the interviewers of this study were generally experienced as pleasant and helpful.

Talks with school acquaintances and parents on the other hand, were generally rated as neutral. Closer analyses showed that some parents had behaved injuriously, others in a helpful manner.

In such situations, the parents assume an important role, as they are particularly close to the sexual victim emotionally. Therefore, the impact of their contribution on the ability of the child or young woman to work through the incident without long-term injury was a powerful one. Conversations with medical doctors and officials of the Department of Juvenile Welfare, the police, and the courts, as well as with the attorney of the accused were experienced as mildly to very injurious.

In a large proportion of the *declared* sexual contacts, there was no court proceeding. The situation of the victim in court and the effects of the proceedings on the victim require an additional analysis.

Specialists in the field of police work are becoming increasingly aware of this problem. This can be attributed to groups specializing in victim assistance who publicize injurious circumstances. In Germany, some of these organizations are the Rape Crisis Centres, self-help groups for molested girls ("Wildwasser"), hotlines for children in trouble, and houses for battered women. Special private victim assistance associations exist for victims in general, like the so-called "Weißer Ring" and Arbeitskreis der Opferhilfe" (Association for Victims' Aid) and finally one government-supported victim assistance program in Hanau in the state of Hessia ("Hanauer Hilfe").

The characteristics of injured versus noninjured victims were determined. The following variables correlated significantly to the degree of injury:

The injured victims were all female.
The injured victims were significantly older than the noninjured ($p < 0.01$; $r = 0.34$).
Because the injured victims on the average were older, they tended to have had more sexual information ($p = 0.045$) and more sexual experience before the offense ($p < 0.05$).
The injured victims had not started dating at an earlier age than the noninjured.
Injured victims had often been brought up with relatively strict regulations

concerning going out in the evening ($p = 0.035$).
Injury was associated with violent or threatening behavior of the assailants ($p = 0.0003$; $r = 0.47$) and defensive behavior or attitude of the victims ($p = 0.0016$).
Most of the sexual contacts that resulted in injury to the victims were of an intensive nature, such as sexual intercourse ($p = 0.001$; $r = 0.43$).
Most of the injured victims went directly to the police to declare their victimization ($p = 0.028$). They often reported the offense themselves and had more conversations about the attack ($p = 0.004$) than noninjured persons.

As expressed before, only half of the declared victims (51.8%) of indecent assault suffered from injuries or even severe trauma. The other half (48.2%) reported no primary or secondary injury in connection with the experience. In most of these cases, the sexual offense was relatively superficial and harmless and/or the so-declared victim consented to the offense.

Many experts in the field have assumed that sexual victims without primary injuries are rare. It certainly appears that this must be reevaluated. Adults who hold the opinion that any sexual behavior is traumatic for children and young people have to face the fact that in many cases the young person becomes a victim only because grown-ups expect him or her to become a victim. On the basis of this expectation they may act in such a way that the child really becomes victimized. This behavior then has a labeling function (*labeling as a victim*).

This kind of secondary victimization can easily occur after exhibitionism and other nonviolent sexual contacts when the child comes from a family with particularly strict sexual attitudes, a family that creates fear about "immoral assaulters", or a family that, out of helplessness and fear, dramatizes the victimization. Members of prosecuting authorities such as policemen and -women, can unfortunately not be excluded as sources of secondary victimization.

In this study it was not possible to determine a typology of victims of indecent assault, nor was it possible to determine a typology of the sexual offender in general. In the field of indecent assault it seems to be necessary to differentiate on the offender's side between violent assailants and nonviolent offenders. In all probability, violent sex assailants have more in common with other groups of violent perpetrators. In addition, it could not be proved that the criminal career of a perpetrator begins with exposing the genitals and leads to forcible rape.

This finding should have much influence on preventive interventions. Up to now, many parents and educators in general fear that an exhibitionist or fondler is a potential violent rapist or even murderer. The contrary is true. In situations of exhibitionism and superficial fondling, similar to doctor games, the perpetrator almost never becomes violent.

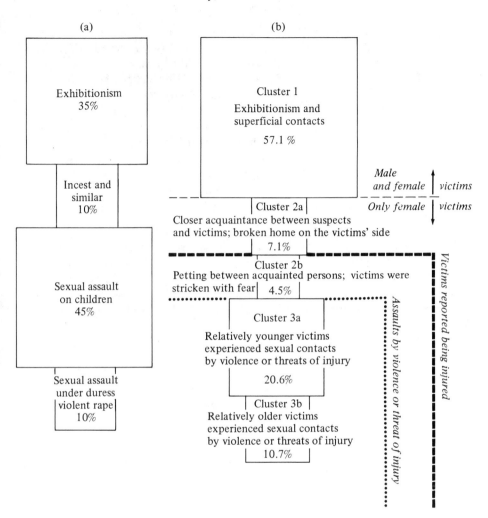

(a)   (b)

Exhibitionism
35%

Cluster 1

Exhibitionism and
superficial contacts

57.1 %

*Male
and female* | *victims*

Incest and
similar
10%

Cluster 2a

Only female | *victims*

Closer acquaintance between suspects
and victims; broken home on the victims' side

7.1%

Cluster 2b

Petting between acquainted persons; victims were
stricken with fear   4.5%

Sexual assault
on children
45%

Cluster 3a

Relatively younger victims
experienced sexual contacts
by violence or threats of injury

20.6%

Assaults by violence or threat of injury

Victims reported being injured

Cluster 3b

Relatively older victims
experienced sexual contacts
by violence or threats of injury

10.7%

Sexual assault
under duress
violent rape
10%

FIGURE 4.1.

Because most of the offenses of indecent assault—violent or non-violent—are first of all interactions between two or more persons, the situation should be analyzed as a unit. We expected to find a typology of victimizing interactions or situations rather than a typology focused on the isolated participants. To find an answer to this question we calculated a cluster analysis with 38 variables for each case. Reported indecent assaults could be divided into three groups (Figure 4.1).

Group 1 (57.1%)—cluster 1. The numerically largest group includes
   exhibitionism and comparatively harmless erotic sexual contacts with
   younger victims. All the male victims are found here. Injury was very
   rare in this group.

Group 2 (11.6%)—cluster 2a and 2b. This group includes sexual contacts of a more intensive nature. The suspects were mostly known or related to the victim; the victim's family situation could be considered as disturbed. One part of the (only female) victims of this cluster showed no injury at all, another part had an injury index that fell within the average range of the entire investigation.

Group 3 (31.3%)—cluster 3a and 3b. In this group are sexual assaults under duress, forcible rape, and sexual contacts with highly emotional defensive behavior or attitude of the victim. The (exclusively) female victims were older, the suspects younger than the average and the assaults were reported immediately to the police. Victims of this cluster had the highest indices of injury.

The typology of interactions and cases discovered differs very much from the typology suggested by the penal code. It also contradicts the commonly held ideas about indecent assault, especially as the two large groupings of cases (the first and the third) have nearly nothing to do with each other.

Any preventive, legislative, prosecuting, or victim-supporting activities should be influenced by these findings. All of the opinions and bits of advice to which we referred at the beginning of the chapter are misleading and can injure victims secondarily or even make victims out of persons who would not have become one by dramatizing situations that are not really dangerous.

Conversely, mixing nonviolent and violent situations without any differentiation may result in playing down the really dangerous cases of brutal sexual attacks. In our society there is a widespread general attitude of tolerance toward violent sexual behavior. Brutal sexual victimization however mostly happens in the neighborhood, within the circle of friends, or even in the family.

Consequences

For the future it is urgent to pay more attention to the situation of the exclusively female victims from group 3 and some of those in group 2. Political, preventive, and social measures to improve their situation are absolutely necessary.

With respect to prejudicial attitudes toward the assailant, his deed, and the sexual victim, there is no homogenous type of indecent assault in general. Rather there are three clearly different constellations of deviant sexual interactions. Until recently, conventional opinion has confused infringements of sexual norms and violent assaults in the sexual sphere. Other studies have revealed, however, that attitudes regarding sexual violence are very ambivalent: Although there is a formal ban on sexual violence it is, at the same time, tacitly tolerated. Sexual violence, like other types of violent behavior, is very common and belongs, criminologically, more to the group of violent crimes than to the group of sexual assaults.

The ambivalent attitudes of the general population toward sexual violence may pose problems when measures are undertaken. It is difficult to outlaw sexual violence effectively if at the same time violent behavior is tolerated in the society at large. These problems fall basically into the fields of sociology and politics and can only be effectively solved if tackled as a whole. The results of this survey suggest that the situation of the victims of violent and indecent assaults should be improved by applying suitable short- and medium-term measures.

Differentiation

To change public attitudes, the three main phenomena of deviant sexual behavior should be clearly differentiated from one another:

a. Exposure of the genitals
b. Relatively superficial, nonviolent erotic and sexual practices
c. Sexual violence and duress

Dedramatization and Elucidation

Objective and unbiased information about the phenomenology of indecent assaults and their after-effects would reduce dramatization in case groups a and b and elucidate the violent character of the other assaults in group c. To protect potential victims it is necessary to differentiate between disagreeable or undesirable sexual molestation or menacing and brutal sexual attacks. We should clarify that hardly any criminal career starts with exposure of the genitals and leads up to forcible rape and murder. The present survey reveals that—contrary to the German Penal Code—the situation of forcible rape has much in common with other violent offenses and that recidivism of any violent assailant can rather be expected in offenses like forcible rape and sexual duress than in exhibitionism and fondling. If nonviolent molesters and exhibitionists relapse, the probability is high that they will resort to their previous form of deviant behavior. It is improbable that a relapsed exhibitionist will display violent sexual behavior.

These results should have a strong influence on prevention programs, prosecuting strategies, and victim-assistance programs. The police can work more effectively and cooperatively with the victim if these results are taken into consideration in day-to-day work.

Informing Target Groups

The objective description of the phenomenology of punishable sexual contacts, their causes and consequences should influence the following areas:

1. The in-service training of officials responsible for victims should be improved.
2. When asked, specially qualified police officials should inform groups of teachers and educators.
3. Parents and professional educators should be fully informed and provided the opportunity for further training in sexual education. The problems of sexual deviation should be integrated into modern sexual education.
4. The results of the present survey should be widely publicized so as to influence public opinion.
5. Corresponding laws in the Penal Code should be subjected to unbiased evaluation.

Coordination

The different institutions that professionally deal with the problems of sexual victims should cooperate more effectively. In the Federal Republic of Germany many officials responsible for victims still do not know that there are organizations in most German cities that partially or fully deal with crisis intervention. There are, for instance, capable institutions for psychotherapy; there is a nationwide organization, called Pro Familia, which gives advice in cases of sexual problems (especially birth control), there are rape crisis centers in larger cities with their telephone hotlines (*Notrufe für vergewaltigte Frauen*) and houses for battered women (*Frauenhäuser*); there are hotlines for children and youth (*Sorgentelefon*), and some children's shelters. In nearly every town there is a day and night hotline for any acute problems (*Telefonseelsorge*). During the last few years private organizations like *Weißer Ring* and the Arbeitskreis Opferhilfe (Association for Victim's Aid) have developed and specialized in granting financial and personal professional support to victims of crime. Furthermore, the Department of Justice of the State of Hessia has installed a Victim's Aid Program in the city of Hanau (*Hanauer Hilfe*) with my support. In addition there is a special federal law that guarantees financial aid to victims of violent offenses (*Opferentschädigungsgesetz*; see Chapter 5 by Villmow) and a new law to protect victims in the criminal process (*Opferschutzgesetz*).

Until now, the victim in need and the experts in the field have usually not been aware of the existence of appropriate institutions owing to lack of cooperation and exchange of information. We still have a lot to learn from the American victim-assistance programs.

If victim-assistance programs are initiated, care should be taken not to treat the victim as a sick person. Labeling the victim as mentally ill is another form of structural victimization. The aim of victim-assistance programs should be the reintegration of the victim into her social environment, which is just as necessary as the social reintegration of the offender.

This reintegration should lead to regaining or strengthening the victim's self-confidence. To be more effective, victim-assistance programs must be linked with an information service aimed at informing the public about how structural victimization may cause individual victimization.

The situation of victims of sexual offences in the Federal Republic of Germany requires that we develop and organize training programs for professionals and volunteers as well as strengthening the organization of assistance programs for victims. Current problems in the Federal Republic are as follows:

1. The phenomenon of sexual violence should be subjected to further empirical analysis. We would welcome a psychological analysis of structural victimization and a victimological analysis of the situation surrounding sexual violence, that is, what the situation is like between offender and victim shortly before the offense occurs (analysis of the interaction process).
2. The public must be informed about the problems and background of sexual violence.
3. Police officials who deal with sexual victims must establish contact with women working in victim-assistance programs in order to obtain feedback on their work and promote an exchange of ideas.
4. In-service training programs for police officials should be developed similar to those training programs in the states of Hessia, Baden-Württemberg, Bavaria, Lower Saxony, and—since 1988—in Northrhine-Westfalia.
5. Cooperation between the different responsible institutions and advisory boards should be improved in the interest of the victims.
6. Victims who are in the crisis situation should be provided with solid information about several institutions they can trust.
7. The present survey should be extended to study the effects of court procedures upon the victims.
8. While discussing the laws dealing with sexual offenses, objective and scientific arguments should be clearly seperated from emotional and/or moral opinions.

5

Victim Compensation in Some Western Countries

BERNHARD VILLMOW

Introduction

State compensation for crime victims nowadays is widespread and has found a certain acceptance. The earliest programs were established in New Zealand (1963) and in Great Britain (1964). During the last two decades many other countries followed with similar regulations: more than 30 states in the United States, all of the states in Australia, and a number of European countries, for example, Austria, Denmark, Finland, France, Germany, Ireland, the Netherlands, Norway, and Sweden. Plans are in preparation in other countries (see, e.g., Council of Europe, 1978; Joutsen, 1987).

Numerous articles have discussed the development, structure, and justifications of these programs. The main purpose of this chapter, however, is to provide an overview of their functioning and the possible effects the regulations have on the victims of crime. As Carrow states, "the evaluation of victim compensation programs can facilitate the effective administration of programs, help to improve program services to crime victims, enhance the formulation of appropriate policies and procedures ... and promote the development of more effective and efficient programs in the future" (1980, p. 173).

Statistics from various countries, for example, showed that only a minority of victims have benefitted from these schemes. Evaluation studies tried to discover the reasons for this unsatisfactory situation. Up to now, there are only a few concrete and comprehensive empirical studies of actual programs. So this report can only summarize the results of research from Great Britain, Canada, and the United States. However, they give an interesting picture of the different schemes and the present situation of victim compensation.

Some findings of a recently finished German study will be added. But because this research only has the character of a pilot study, the results concerning German victim compensation may be preliminary and restricted.

Because the terms *restitution* and *compensation* are often used interchangeably, a necessary distinction has to be made here: Restitution is generally defined as a formal sanction or requirement imposed by a justice-system official that obligates an offender to repay the victim in the form of either money or personal services, whereas compensation is usually paid from state funds through programs that are relatively independent of the criminal-justice system. Consequently, compensation programs are able to provide payment to victims, whether or not an offender is apprehended (Harland, 1981, p. 2; see also Burns, 1983, p. 102; Galaway 1981, p. 278).

Program Objectives

The aims of the different programs are not always clear. Often there is a mixture of expectations, rationales, and legislative philosophies. Sometimes it has been noted that they are even contradictory or too vague to be of any real value for use in program evaluations (Carrow, 1980, p. 174).

Generally, many different underlying philosophies or justifications are discussed, for example, the strict liability theory, the government negligence theory, the equal protection theory, the humanitarian theory, the social obligation theory, and the social welfare theory (see Elias, 1983a; Burns, 1983; Kirchhoff, 1983/84). In summary, the programs presented in this chapter have been justified in the following ways:

In Great Britain two elements were emphasized: The compensation scheme should show "social solidarity and the desire to express public sympathy for the victim of crime" (Shapland, Willmore, & Duff, 1985, p. 119; Weintraud, 1980, p. 181). For Canada, particularly the Quebec program and its evaluation will be considered. Most Canadian schemes are based on the moral duty of the state to aid innocent victims because the justice system is unable to guarantee the prevention of crime (humanitarian model). The Manitoba and Quebec programs, however, are administered through the provincial workers' compensation board, following an insurance approach based on the concept of social justice or collective responsibility (see Baril, Laflamme-Cusson, & Beauchemin, 1984; Canadian Federal Provincial Task Force 1983, p. 97; Hastings, 1983, p. 32).

The American evaluation research done by Elias (1983a) measured the effectiveness of compensation programs in New York and New Jersey. In both states the regulations are based on egalitarian and humanitarian motives, but political and crime-prevention aspects can be found as well. The main difference lies in New York's awarding compensation as welfare whereas New Jersey grants payments by right (social welfare theory versus social obligation approach) (Elias, 1983a, p. 146).

The German victim-compensation act is primarily based on the consideration that the community has a special responsibility for those who have suffered through an intentional criminal act. It is the state's duty to protect citizens from violent offenders. If it does not fulfill this duty, it is obliged to provide for the compensation of the victims (Bundesregierung, 1974, p. 7; for other aspects, see Kirchhoff 1983/84, pp. 20–22).

Most of the schemes are clearly directed at the so-called innocent victims. There is a special image of the victim as an innocent party, sometimes brutally subjected to a deliberate, sudden and unprovoked assault by the offender (Joutsen, 1987, p. 267). The problems combined with this stereotype will be presented in the following sections of the chapter describing the special regulations of the programs and their application.

The Scope of the Schemes

Despite their common concerns and partly similar backgrounds, the programs represent a process that varies somewhat from country to country. The scheme in Great Britain was established on a nonstatutory basis to provide ex gratia compensation to the victims of crimes of violence and to those hurt as a result of attempts to arrest offenders and to prevent offenses. Compensation includes payment for medical expenses, for the pain and suffering caused by the injury, and for loss of earnings or earning capacity as well as for out-of-pocket expenses. In cases of death, funeral expenses can also be claimed. To restrict the number of petty claims, a minimum award limit of £400 was set (for details, see Joutsen, 1987, pp. 258–260; Weintraud, 1980). The amount of compensation can be reduced or the application rejected if (before or after the incident) the conduct of the victim, his character, or way of life make it inappropriate for him to be granted a full award. For instance, the scheme draws special attention to provocation in sexual offenses or offenses arising out of a sexual relationship (for other excluding aspects see Joutsen, 1987, p. 264; Miers, 1983, p. 207). The incident must be reported to the police without undue delay.

The Quebec violent-crime-victims program provides financial compensation for temporary or permanent loss of ability resulting from a crime. If the victim is killed, the scheme pays an annuity to the dependants as well as funeral expenses and a special allowance. In addition, the victim is reimbursed for all medical expenses and—if he played a part in preventing crime or assisted in an arrest—material damage up to a certain amount is covered, too (Baril et al., 1984, p. 4; for details, see Hastings, 1983, pp. 37–44). Compensation can be denied when the victim, by gross fault, contributed to his own injury or death and when the claimant was a party to the offense that caused the victim's death. Concerning cooperation with law-enforcement agencies, the victim must have reported the act to the police (Baril et al, 1984, p. 4; Hastings, 1983, pp. 39–44; McKie, 1987, pp. 8–10).

The programs of New Jersey and New York provide compensations only for losses due to violent crimes. Those losses include medical expenses, rehabilitation costs, funeral costs, lost income, but not pain and suffering.

In New York the claimants must report the victimization to the police within 48 hours, and in New Jersey within 30 days, and they are required to cooperate with the law-enforcement officials. Furthermore, the victims have to make a claim within 90 days in New York and within one year in New Jersey. Excluded claimant groups are those having a past or present relationship with the offender and those found to have been an accomplice or conspirator in the crime committed. Another reason for disqualification can be provocation of a crime against oneself. Maximum and minimum award limits are set in both regulations to reduce the costs and to filter out small claims. Additionally, in New York a claimant has to demonstrate "serious financial hardship" (Elias, 1983, pp. 153–154).

Pursuant to the German Victim Compensation Act, benefits are awarded to a person who has suffered bodily harm due to an intentional, unlawful attack directed against himself or another person or to a person who defended himself lawfully against such an attack with the result that he has to endure lasting physical or economic damage. If the person attacked dies of his injuries, surviving dependants can claim certain benefits. The act provides for benefits pursuant to the Federal War Victims Maintenance Act (BVG). Thus pensions, or regular monthly benefits, are granted, but only to victims whose earning capacity has been permanently reduced by at least 25% and for a period of more than 6 months. In that case, however, the payments are independent of other income. In addition, the act provides for benefits for medical treatment as well as financial help for vocational rehabilitation. Damages for pain and suffering are not provided for, nor can damages to property be compensated. Pursuant to the act, benefits must be denied if the injured party has culpably caused the injury or when it would be unfair to grant compensation for other reasons—particularly in connection with the behavior of the claimant himself. Moreover, benefits may be refused if the injured party omitted to do everything reasonably feasible to assist in the investigation of the case, in particular if he did not report the incident without delay to the police.

This summarizing overview shows that compensable offenses are limited almost entirely to violent crimes and that compensable losses are almost exclusively limited to medical costs, loss of earnings due to physical injury, and funeral costs. Property losses are virtually never compensable. Compensation for pain and suffering is provided only in some countries. The use of minimum-loss criteria has been criticized by many contributors, who point out that the threshold limitation poses problems to the poor victim to whom the statutory minimum may be a significant sum. In addition, estimations showed that the program costs would not be substantially increased by elimination of minimum-loss criteria (Carrow, 1980, p. 19).

Attempting to reduce "unjust" attainment of benefits, some programs have excluded victims related to the offender and victims who contributed to their own injury. Many critics have stated that the first condition often denies compensation to deserving and needy individuals (female spouses and children) and in Great Britain, for example, such victims have been included in the scheme since 1979 (Burns, 1983, p. 107; Miers, 1983, p. 207). The second restriction too has been discussed widely in the victimological field. The difficulty of ascertaining the existence of victim responsibility and assessing its extent has been noted and some contributors also argue that the questionable stereotype of the "innocent victim" quite obviously plays an important role (Burns, 1983, p. 106).

In sum, one can state that virtually all schemes contain a series of restrictive eligibility requirements. As a result of these and other limitations on benefits, most crime victims are not covered by the programs.

Add to this that some statutory descriptions of grounds for denying benefits are to be regarded as overly vague, for example, when the British scheme draws attention to the conduct of the victim, including conduct before and after the event, and his or her character and way of life. Another example is the Federal Republic rule that denies compensation entirely if, in the light of the victim's own conduct, it would appear inequitable to grant the award. It is unclear which attitudes and moral principles held by the officials in the compensation process influence their decisions. Obviously, certain victims or specific forms of behavior of victims are not accepted and various programs differentiate in this context between "innocent" and "guilty" victims. Developing special stereotypes, for example, may lead to broad interpretations given to statutory grounds for denying applications. So the scope of the schemes may be considerably limited in a second way, namely, by exercise of discretion by members of the boards. It would therefore appear that Joutsen is right when he states: "The schemes are clearly to the benefit of the ideal, innocent victim, but they will not benefit those victims who, in the opinion of the decision-making tribunal, were to an appreciable degree responsible for their victimization. In some countries, moreover, the restrictions operate to the disadvantage of those whose lifestyle is regarded with severe disfavour" (1987, pp. 267–268).

Evaluation of the Compensation Programs

The importance of systematic planning studies and program evaluations has been increasingly recognized as essential to the success, continuation, and improvement of projects in this field. Up to now there have been relatively few attempts to evaluate state victim-compensation programs (Carrow, 1980, p. 173; Baril et al., 1984, p. 1). In his overview Elias comes to the conclusion that "the existing studies purporting to evaluate compensation programs are inadequate because they are either too small or incomplete, or fail to question victims or simply fail to live up to what their titles promise" (1983b, p. 217).

The Studies

Elias attempted to fill that gap by contrasting the New York and New Jersey compensation schemes, and by comparing a control group of victims having no contact with their state's compensation scheme to an experimental group that had applied. He asked to what extent crime victims were being compensated, and if compensation produced the supposed improvement in attitudes and willingness to cooperate with criminal justice and government generally. Telephone interviews were completed for 98 nonclaimants and 85 claimants in Brooklyn, and for 80 nonclaimants and 79 claimants in Newark. A further data source included interviews with board members and investigators from each compensation board. They were questioned about their board's purposes, goals, procedures, eligibility requirements, and about decision-making influences (Elias, 1983a, pp. 53–61). With the responses given, the study tried to examine the following hypotheses: "Victim compensation programs are not adequately compensating victims. . . . A 'rights' approach would be more successful than a 'welfare' approach. . . . Adequately compensated victims do have better attitudes toward criminal justice and government. . . . A victim's denial of any or adequate compensation will produce negative attitudes toward criminal justice and government. . . . Financial reward will make a victim more likely to participate in the criminal-justice process" (Elias 1983a, p. 51).

Similar comprehensive research was done in Britain by Shapland et al. (1985) between 1979 and 1982. They studied the experiences, attitudes, and difficulties of 276 victims of violent crime (physical assault, sexual assault, and robbery) as their cases passed through the criminal-justice system, including applications for compensation to the various compensation agencies. In a longitudinal study the victims were interviewed several times over a period of up to three years. Additionally, police officers, prosecution solicitors, justices' clerks, other court staff and compensation-agency personnel were questioned; police files, compensation-agency files, and newspaper reports were also examined (Shapland et al., 1985, pp. 4–9). Concerning compensation, the task was to explore the reasons for the low application rate. Shapland et al. wanted to know whether victims wanted compensation, whether they knew of any source of compensation, why they decided to apply or not to apply, and whether there were any other personal factors that appeared to differentiate between those who applied and those who did not (Shapland et al., 1985, p. 121). In addition, they tried to find out the levels of satisfaction with the compensation process, the amounts of awards, and the principles on which the compensation board operated (Shapland et al., 1985, pp. 151–152).

In Canada Baril et al. studied the effectiveness of the Quebec crime-victims compensation scheme in 1981/82. The main objective was to give a description of the claimants, the program, and the operation of the scheme, and to assess the program's impact on beneficiaries (Baril et al., 1984, p. 1). They analyzed 1,251 files (applications in 1979/80) concerning characteristics of victims, circumstances of crime, legal proceedings, personal consequences of victimization, and applicant–program relationship. In a second step, 43 victims were interviewed to obtain more information on victimization as an experience, on the needs of victims, and their level of satisfaction with the compensation program (Baril et al., 1984, pp. 6–10).

Simultaneously, but without any knowledge of the other studies, we began our research concerning the application of the German victim-compensation act in Hamburg. We had similar research questions concerning the situation of the victims, their decision to apply for compensation, their experiences with the administration, and the outcome of the compensation case, and we tried to find out which criteria influenced the decision-making process. In our opinion there is no comprehensive theoretical framework that covers all questions to be studied, so we proceeded from a relatively rough filter/selection approach, which includes very different aspects.

Analysis on the level of the legal program, reveals that injuries below a certain degree of seriousness are not covered by the system, which primarily provides for rehabilitation and for securing the victim's livelihood (see also Kirchhoff, 1983/84, p. 23).

On the administrative level, you may find various factors that exclude certain groups of victims. Many agencies lack interest in passing on information about the act. Arguments range from strategies for avoiding higher work loads (Weintraud, 1980, p. 92) to problems for the responsible administration in cases of high financial demands (Vaughn and Hofrichter 1980, p. 38), to the notion that the victim compensation scheme is only "symbolic legislation," which would mean that application of the act is of secondary importance (Elias, 1983b, p. 214; Miers, 1983, p. 211). In addition, administrators may harbor some notion of the "ideal type" of victim worthy of compensation, who therefore will be granted benefits. In contrast claimants who are injured in similar situations, but who do not meet the stereotype of "innocent victim," are denied benefits either due to lack of sufficient evidence or due to "unworthiness." In analyzing the exercise of discretion, we tried to include concepts of the so-called labeling approach in our search for an explanation (Miers, 1980, p. 3). We had to investigate which groups of the nonstereotypical compensable victims were often said to have contributed to their injuries, were regarded as tardy in making an application, and offered no explanation or who appeared reluctant to cooperate with the police. Miers has noted that "those who fall within this class are characterized by their advertised willing participation in risk situations, their similarity in socioeconomic terms to offenders and their participation in activities which are perceived by the schemes' administrators as constituting unacceptable departures from conventional standards of behaviour, that is, those standards subscribed to by innocent victims" (1980, p. 14).

On the third level, finally, that of the victims, it is imaginable that they intentionally refrain from claiming compensation because they feel stigmatized by societal reaction and wish to avoid "official recognition" as victims. Many victims suffer disadvantages in the course of "secondary victimization" caused by the reaction of persons in their social environment as well as by interactions with the criminal justice system (Kirchhoff & Kirchhoff, 1979, p. 279). It may also be relevant that victims of violent crime often belong to social classes and groups that generally find it difficult to deal with administrative agencies (see Mayntz, 1985, pp. 241–245; Hoffmann-Riem, 1980).

Furthermore, financial benefits alone might not satisfy the primary needs of this group of victims. In a study on problems faced by victims, Knudten and Knudten found that 57% complained of psychological and emotional difficulties, 25% of family problems, and 12% of difficulties with friends (1979, p. 461; see also Shapland, 1984, p. 142). Thus it becomes clear why more and more organisations offering support to victims have been founded over the past few years, trying to tackle the most immediate problems directly with the victim, that is, emotional help, counseling, and information (Weigend, 1981; see Williams, 1983, for a discussion of Britain).

Obviously, the three levels and their various aspects and factors are not independent of each other. Therefore the study combined analysis of 403 compensation-agency files with interviews of 96 victims who decided to apply for compensation and 51 victims who did not apply. In addition, the compensation administration personnel of Hamburg and Bremen were questioned to contrast their attitudes toward and experiences of the act with those of the victims.

Findings of the Studies

In the following section, only an overview can be given of some main results of the studies primarily concerning the situation of the victims and the compensation process. Some investigations, for example, those of Elias and Shapland et al., have covered in detail more topics that are not discussed here.

Registered Number of Violent Crimes and Number of Applications

American research already has shown that only a small proportion of all victims of violent crimes, mostly less than 10%, apply for compensation (Vaughn & Hofrichter, 1980, p. 30). The application ratios cited by Carrow (1980, p. 102) for some other American states are even lower (2%–7%) and in the New York/New Jersey study less than 1% of all

violent crime victims filed a claim (Elias, 1984, p. 110). The numbers found
by Baril et al. for Montreal are similar (1984, p. 16). Of course, the ratio
depends on the definition of "violent crime," and in Germany, for
example, there is considerable dispute about the range of the term (see
Villmow & Plemper, 1984, pp. 73–74). However, numerous other factors
affect the outcome of the figures. Structure of crimes of violence, structure
of the population, public information, and awareness of the act, are only
some of those aspects. Further, many applicable criminal provisions are
constructed in such a way that violent offenses in the true sense can be
recognized as having been committed where a threat with a specific act of
violence occurred. Many violent acts registered in the police statistics may
have been carried out without any bodily injury being suffered and respective consequences (see Baril et al., 1984, p. 16). If you consider, therefore, only serious violent crimes such as homicide and aggravated assaults,
you will get higher application ratios. In the Netherlands, calculations
indicate that approximately 20% of all potentially eligible crime victims do
file a claim (van Dijk, 1984, p. 4), in Germany the percentages vary
between 8% and 20% in the individual states (Villmow & Plemper 1989).

Characteristics of Applicants, Kinds of Crimes, and Effects of the Offenses

Numerous studies showed that social factors influence the risk of being
victimized (Elias, 1986, pp. 59–65), and there has been developed a model
of personal criminal victimization, the lifestyle/exposure model (Hindelang,
1982, pp. 156–163). Of course, there may be differences between the
group of victims of violent crimes and the special group of applicants
because of certain selection processes.

Examination of the applicants' social background, however, serves an
additional function because it can be assumed that those factors play an
important role when the boards have to decide about worthiness or
unworthiness of the claimants.

In Elias's study, most victims were between ages 15 and 45 (74%), two-
thirds were male, and 46% were married. The results indicated that
socioeconomic status was not high: 42% of the victims were unemployed
and nearly the same percentage received welfare payments (1983a, pp.
69–71). The results of the Canadian study of Baril et al. correspond to the
American ones. About 60% of the applicants were between the ages of 14
and 45, nearly two-thirds were men, but only 36% married. Two out of five
victims had no gainful employment at the time of the crime that resulted in
their applying for compensation (1984, pp. 25–29).

In the British study the victims in assault and robbery cases were
primarily men (75%). The age group 18 to 22 years contained one-third
of all victims. Most of the sample were single, and no more unemployed
than the rest of the population in Coventry and Northampton. So Shapland et al. came to the conclusion: "According to victimization studies,

the picture of the typical victim in our study is the correct one" (1985, p. 12).

The research done in Hamburg again showed that 75% of the claimants were male and approximately two-thirds stated that they were unmarried, divorced, or separated. Nearly 80% belonged to the age group 14 to 49. For one-third of the sample there was no information about characteristics influencing socioeconomic status. Taking profession as a criterion of economic well-being, for the other part of the sample the following picture emerges: 40% were of low social status, 54% belonged to the middle class, and 6% to the upper class. However, it is difficult to compare these data with the results found in the other studies because in Hamburg foreign workers were excluded, whereas in the American study 57% of the victims were minorities (Elias, 1983, p. 70), and the British study, too, covered nonwhite victims.

An interesting result in the American study and the German research was that no significant difference could be found in the social background of claimants and nonclaimants. It seems that those factors are not a major determinant when deciding a compensation claim (Elias, 1983a, p. 79; Villmow & Plemper, 1989).

The greatest number of applications in Quebec stemmed from assault causing bodily harm and robbery (together approximately 55%), followed by murder, homicide, and sexual offenses (Baril et al., 1984, pp. 30–31). In contrast, in the American study homicide and rape were eliminated from consideration; therefore, two-thirds of the interviewed claimants were victims of assault and one-third victims of robbery (Elias, 1983a, pp. 67, 268). The German data show that the most common offense giving rise to a compensation claim was assault, which appeared in more than 80% of the cases. The other applications were made for incidents defined as homicide, rape, and robbery.

Examination of the victim–offender relationship is of special interest because some regulations eliminate claimants having a past or present relationship with the offender (see Carrow, 1980, pp. 42–43; Joutsen, 1987, pp. 263–264). The results of the studies correspond very well. In the British research, 61% of the victims were assaulted by offenders unknown to them. The known perpetrators were primarily relatives or friends, followed by business associates and neighbours (Shapland et al., 1985, pp. 10–11). The Quebec study also showed that 61.5% of assailants were strangers to the victims; the other offenders were friends or acquaintances or were related to the victims (Baril et al., 1984, p. 43). Elias found that a little over one half of the perpetrators were strangers, one-third were acquaintances, and one in five cases could be defined as close relationships (1983a, p. 87). The remarkable point, however, was the difference in the pattern of relationships between claimants and nonclaimants. Intimate relationships, which can be the basis of refusing an award, were reported by 29% of the nonclaimant group whereas the claimants showed 5%. Elias assumed that potential claimants disqualified themselves by not applying after having noticed the restriction in the official program brochures (1983a, pp. 88–89). For the German study, which found the same tendencies concerning the relationship differences between claimants and nonclaimants, this explanation cannot be used directly. Neither do the regulations explicitly cite this ground for denying benefits, nor do the brochures of the government nor do those of the boards. Therefore, the victim–offender relationship probably is not a very prominent factor for the German victims' decision to apply or not to apply.

Another similar finding can be shown when the effects of the offenses are studied. Only 4% of the New York/New Jersey victims experienced no injury, one in five indicated minor harm, 58% received medical assistance, and 16% were hospitalized. Elias emphasized that there are no significant differences between the individual samples (1983, p. 86). His tables, however, show tendencies for nonclaimants to have bigger quotas in the groups without injuries or minor harm and a smaller percentage of victims who required medical assistance or hospitalization (see Elias, 1983a, p. 268, Table B.2).

Those differences in physical effects of the offenses between claimants and nonclaimants were also reported by the German victims. Claimants tended to have more serious forms of injury and were more often reported sick. Maybe future studies with bigger samples will find those aspects worthy of being examined again.

Applying for Compensation

Besides the different levels of physical, social, and psychological effects (see Shapland et al., 1985, pp. 97–108), various other causes can influence the decision to apply for compensation. Often lack of information is seen as a main reason. In the British study, a majority of victims had not heard of any means of obtaining compensation, only 39% had heard of the state provisions (Shapland et al., 1985, p. 124). The American victims seem to be better informed; almost one-half of the non-claimants in the New York/New Jersey study said they had information about the programs (Elias, 1983a, p. 111). Striking results, however, have been found in a Dutch national crime survey. Of the general public less than 3% knew that a compensation fund existed, and of the victims of violent crimes only 14% had heard of the scheme's existence (van Dijk, 1985).

Many of the Hamburg victims also lacked adequate information about the compensation system. Four out of ten nonclaimants knew that in certain situations financial help by the state could be claimed. Yet the analysis also showed that the regulations are important for health insurers and administrators. There are cases in which the insurance companies are reimbursed by the state (Article 19 Bundesversorgungsgesetz, see Kirchhoff, 1983/84, pp. 29–30). So not surprisingly the examination of the files in Hamburg suggested that only 11% of the claimants initiated the procedure for compensation on their own. The great majority of the claims were filed by request of agencies of the state medical insurance system, which was the first time many victims were informed about the provisions.

Processing of Applications

The psychological success of the compensation program is influenced, among other things, by the length of the process. British data show a mean period of time of approximately 9 months, varying from 4 months to 2 years (Shapland et al., 1985, p. 157). The vast majority of Elias's claimants were dissatisfied with the length of their cases, as almost one-half of the cases lasted between 12 and 18 months, followed by 37% lasting between 18 and 24 months and 12% lasting more than 2 years (1983a, p. 184). In contrast, lawyers in Quebec made 9 out of 10 decisions within a year of receiving the applications (Baril et al., 1984, p. 85).

The reason for the long delays in some countries (in Hamburg the applications on average took nearly one year) seem to be manifold. In many cases applicants filled in forms insufficiently or incorrectly. Therefore, the boards had to request additional information. Furthermore, most administrators wait for files of enquiries from other institutions, like the police and hospitals, or want to consider the outcome of the trial. Another important factor, for example, in German application cases is the necessity to get additional medical expert evidence when the medical situation is unclear. Those special inquiries in Hamburg (concerning also reduced earning capacities) sometimes took 12 and more months until the final report was submitted (for the different factors, see also Shapland et al., 1985, pp. 157–158).

Baril et al. point to the fact that rejections in general took longer than awards because they probably were considered longer to ensure that the victim was being treated fairly (1984, p. 85). This is not confirmed by the German data. If a statutory requirement was lacking or could not be proved, applications were refused in the majority of cases within approximately six months. Awards and the special group of denials (or "rejections"), being justified with the victim's causing the injury or with the victim's behavior, on average took longer. It can be assumed that the often-necessary medical statements played an important role in the cases, whereas, in refusals the outcome of the trial had been awaited to be sure that the facts in the decision were correct.

The Compensation Decision

The results of the studies show a very different structure: In England and Quebec most of the applications resulted in some award being made (83%/75%), whereas in New York/New Jersey and Hamburg only small groups of the claimants got positive decisions (38%/18%). There are, of course, many influences on these results. The British compensation program, for example, in contrast to the other ones, covers payment for pain and suffering. Therefore, many victims with minor injuries can receive benefits. At the time of Shapland's study, the general minimum limit of loss and harm covered was £150, so the sums of money awarded ranged from £154 to £3,000, with a mean of £611 (Shapland et al., 1985, pp. 150, 163). The German scheme, however, is not constructed to compensate minor victimizations (see Jung, 1979, p. 389; Kirchhoff, 1983/84, p. 29). Therefore, if many applicants with forms of lesser injuries try to get awards, the rate of denials must be high (see also Weintraud, 1980, p. 165). It should be mentioned that, at least in Hamburg between 1980 and 1985, the structure of decisions has changed in favor of the victims. The quota of positive decisions doubled to nearly 40%, although there was no significant change in the structure of serious violent crime. Yet it is unclear whether this development depends on better victim information, a better selection by health-insurance organizations, or a more liberal application of the compensation regulations.

Concerning the high rate of awards in Quebec, the Canadian data indicate that this structure is not unusual. Hastings found a slight decrease in the percentage of applications refused between 1975 and 1976 (16%), 1976 and 1977 (14%), and 1977 and 1978 (12%), even though overall applications were increasing during these periods (1983, p. 48). In contrast to this, the American averge award rate is lower, approximately 60%. There is a wide variance in benefits made by the various programs, so you can find ranges from 24% in Texas to 99% in the Virgin Islands (McGillis & Smith, 1983, p. 103). Although there is only one legal basis for victim compensation in all individual states, in Germany, too, the statistical data show notable differences concerning the number of awards granted (see Table 5.1). For the American situation, McGillis and Smith try to give an explanation: "... the public may be inadequately informed of the program eligibility and benefit policies, resulting in a large number of inappropriate applications. In other cases, a program's strict adherence to reporting and application time period requirements may result in increased denial rates. The program's approach to handling cases with evidence of contributory misconduct may also significantly affect the denial and award rates. In addition, those programs with strict financial-need criteria may deny a larger number of claims than others" (1983, p. 103). Information about those aspects that were covered by the evaluation studies is summarized as follows.

Reasons for Rejecting Applications

Benefits must be denied when statutory requirements are lacking or cannot be proved. In most programs there are restrictions on the behavior of the

TABLE 5.1. Federal Republic of Germany: Structure of compensation decisions

States	Year	Claims processed	Claims granted	Claims denied because of lack of statutory requirements, evidence	Claims denied because of coresponsibility of the victim; unfairness; noncooperation	Other decisions, e.g. withdrawal of application
Baden-Württemberg	1981	316	120 = 38.0%	160 = 50.6%	Included in other group of denials	36 = 11.4%
	1982	461	162 = 35.1%	237 = 51.4%		62 = 13.4%
	1983	609	195 = 32.0%	365 = 59.9%		49 = 8.0%
	1984	529	189 = 35.7%	298 = 56.3%		42 = 7.9%
Bayern	1981	658	148 = 22.5%	433 = 65.8%	Included in other group of denials	77 = 11.7%
	1982	742	167 = 22.5%	492 = 66.3%		83 = 11.2%
	1983	808	165 = 20.4%	560 = 69.3%		83 = 10.3%
	1984	764	188 = 24.6%	493 = 64.5%		83 = 10.9%
Berlin	1981	1,005	112 = 11.1%	839 = 83.5%	17 = 1.7%	37 = 3.7%
	1982	930	101 = 10.9%	775 = 83.3%	30 = 3.2%	24 = 2.6%
	1983	934	92 = 9.9%	776 = 83.1%	18 = 1.9%	48 = 5.1%
	1984	898	83 = 9.2%	733 = 81.6%	39 = 4.3%	43 = 4.8%
Bremen	1981	62	13 = 21.0%	20 = 32.3%	26 = 41.9%	3 = 4.8%
	1982	107	28 = 26.2%	34 = 31.8%	40 = 37.4%	5 = 4.7%
	1983	176	37 = 21.0%	107 = 60.8%	21 = 11.9%	11 = 6.3%
	1984	123	30 = 24.4%	62 = 50.4%	18 = 14.6%	13 = 10.6%
Hessen	1981	294	58 = 19.7%	191 = 65.0%	Included in other group of denials	45 = 15.3%
	1982	389	82 = 21.1%	233 = 59.9%		74 = 19.0%
	1983	390	95 = 24.4%	215 = 55.1%		80 = 20.5%
	1984	438	165 = 37.7%	241 = 55.0%		32 = 7.3%

					Included in other group of denials	
Niedersachsen	1981	529	93 = 17.6%	390 = 73.7%		46 = 8.7%
	1982	640	92 = 14.4%	446 = 69.7%		102 = 15.9%
	1983	632	120 = 19.0%	443 = 70.1%		69 = 10.9%
	1984	653	90 = 13.8%	472 = 72.3%		91 = 13.9%
Nordrhein-Westfalen	1981	2,339	594 = 25.4%	1,417 = 60.6%	—[a]	328 = 14.0%
	1982	2,783	659 = 23.7%	1,329 = 47.8%	382 = 13.7%	413 = 14.8%
	1983	3,007	836 = 27.8%	1,076 = 35.8%	674 = 22.4%	421 = 14.0%
	1984	3,482	991 = 28.5%	1,239 = 35.6%	814 = 23.4%	438 = 12.6%
Rheinland-Pfalz	1981	375	91 = 24.3%	137 = 36.5%	119 = 31.7%	28 = 7.4%
	1982	386	85 = 22.0%	134 = 34.7%	127 = 32.9%	40 = 10.4%
	1983	394	104 = 26.4%	144 = 36.5%	116 = 29.4%	30 = 7.6%
	1984	380	75 = 19.7%	145 = 38.2%	131 = 34.5%	29 = 7.6%
Saarland	1981	258	33 = 12.8%	172 = 66.7%		53 = 20.5%
	1982	284	81 = 28.5%	171 = 60.2%		32 = 11.3%
	1983	332	72 = 21.7%	223 = 67.2%		37 = 11.1%
	1984	282	78 = 27.7%	176 = 62.4%		28 = 9.9%
Schleswig-Holstein	1981	319	47 = 14.7%	216 = 67.7%	26 = 8.2%	30 = 9.4%
	1982	309	44 = 14.2%	210 = 68.0%	31 = 10.0%	24 = 7.8%
	1983	303	48 = 15.8%	168 = 55.4%	52 = 17.2%	35 = 11.6%
	1984	316	50 = 15.8%	176 = 55.7%	55 = 17.4%	35 = 11.1%
Hamburg	1981	499	156 = 31.3%	277 = 55.5%	3 = 0.6%	63 = 12.6%
	1982	574	228 = 39.7%	284 = 49.5%	24 = 4.2%	38 = 6.6%
	1983	513	206 = 40.2%	217 = 42.3%	27 = 5.3%	63 = 12.3%
	1984	429	148 = 34.5%	209 = 48.7%	18 = 4.2%	54 = 12.6%
	1985	388	154 = 39.7%	164 = 42.3%	18 = 4.6%	52 = 13.4%
	1986	368	141 = 38.3%	161 = 43.8%	19 = 5.2%	47 = 12.8%

[a] Included in other group of denials.

victim (for example, responsibility for the injury or when it would be unfair to grant compensation for other reasons or when noncooperation with the authorities is observed). It can be assumed that the stereotypes of the "innocent" and "unworthy" victim are relevant for all groups in the decision-making process.

For the first category—lack of evidence that an offense was committed or an application not meeting statutory requirements—the analysis shows that administration officers fear fraudulent claims. Yet most of the studies did not investigate whether in the staff's opinion special groups of victims were often suspected of false or exaggerated claims. Shapland et al. noted the feeling among those administering the scheme that everything an applicant says should be checked (1985, p. 171). They also described "extra enquiries," but there are no findings on the type of victim who runs into more problems than other applicants when trying to evidence his victimization.

In the German study, too, no clear-cut results could be found. However, there was a tendency to see victims aged 60 years or older as more worthy of belief (see also Geis, 1976, p. 254). These victims were seldom under the influence of drink, the offenders were more often unknown, the victimization places were more likely to be in public and seemed to be less disreputable, and the times of victimization seldom were after midnight. This impression that older victims therefore are given more "credit" was confirmed by the interviews with the board officials. Obviously, those victims belong to the group of "innocent, worthy" victims.

On the other hand, there is a very unclear picture concerning the characteristics of the so called "problematic" victim. It seemed to us that the aspect "having been in drink" reduced the chances of being regarded as worthy of belief. For other factors, like being a member of the "milieu," the study could not show that this really influenced the decision. However, more detailed research is necessary (see also Shapland et al., 1985, p. 162).

For the second group of grounds for denials (contribution to the victim's injury, inequity because of the claimant's conduct, noncooperation), often described as specific eligibility criteria to limit compensation to deserving victims, the studies give some examples concerning the difficult problems (see also Carrow, 1980, p. 44–48). In three cases cited by Shapland et al. (1985, pp. 161–162), the claimants were not seen as "innocent victims." Yet the criteria set out are far from clear, so the decisions are very different. The data showed one victim being denied an award because of previous convictions, whereas five other claimants obtained benefits even though they had convictions (Shapland et al., 1985, p. 161). Similar problems are connected with the issue of provocation or victim responsibility for the offense. In six cases, for example, the researchers came to the conclusion that the victim was the first to use violence, and in seven that he was abusive to the offender. Yet only in two cases were benefits denied or reduced for this reason (Shapland et al., 1985, p. 161). Summarizing their findings, the authors state: "The amount of provocation necessary to produce a reduced award or no award at all seems, like the extent of previous bad character, to be a matter of judgement" (1985, p. 162). They agree that it is important to examine how the board builds up the picture of the "innocent victim" and which information is used to decide whether a certain claimant fits into this category or does not. In this context, it has been assumed that the subjective moral judgments and values of the members of the board influence the compensation policy. Thus, an analysis of the board's decisions on victims of sexual offenses not surprisingly found that the regulations are used to carry through predominant values of the middle class and to interdict deviating behavior (Weintraud, 1980, pp. 147–151).

Not only in Britain, but also in other countries, such attitudes can be recognized. McGillis and Smith cite an American program administrator stating that he did not believe that victims involved in assault situations are innocent. In his opinion they involve themselves in "occasions of crime" and so are responsible for their injuries, at least 10% of the time through poor judgment (McGillis & Smith, 1983, p. 71). In another program they found an administrator who had developed for his own use a set of guidelines of percentages of reduction corresponding to levels of provocation. Yet he refused to hand over a copy because of the highly arbitrary nature of the criteria (McGillis & Smith, 1983, p. 72). The high level of discretion with correspondingly inconsistent decisions is also shown by the results of the study in New York and New Jersey where 62% of the applicants had their claims denied. The summaries of the official reasons, however, seemed to be not very similar when those lists for the two samples were compared (Elias, 1983a, p. 298, Tables D 30, 32). So Elias pointed to the official subjectivity: The amount of cooperation (one of the main reasons for denial) sufficient to pursue one's claim had never been defined (1983a, p. 194).

The German research, too, found a different and sometimes very broad interpretation given to statutory grounds for denying applications. The frequency of denials based on such grounds varies widely by state (see Table 5.1) and, therefore, it seems to be of importance where one is involved in a criminal act and applies for compensation (Villmow & Plemper, 1984, p. 83). The data concerning the decisions in Hamburg show a relatively positive development that also can be found in connection with the discussed reasons of denial. Analysis of the files (1978–1980) indicated that only 8% of applications were denied because the victim was held coresponsible or uncooperative. Until 1985/1986, this percentage was reduced to 5% on average. Of course, this does not mean that those decisions altogether were unproblematic. There were, in fact, cases with moralizing arguments when individual victims were referred to as "undeserving victims." Yet the examination did not show concrete indications for strategies to stigmatize certain marginal groups of society, for example,

members of the "St.-Pauli-scene" (*Reeperbahn*), homosexuals or pro-
stitutes. The results of the interviews with board officials confirmed this
assessment. The board members were considerably aware of those
problems because, when reviewing some board decisions, the local
Sozialgericht (social court) had emphasized that not all victims involved in
the subculture were unworthy victims. Add to this the fact that critical
analyses of the regulations (see Baumann, 1980; Stolleis, 1981) in line with
restrictive decisions of the Federal Supreme Social Court showed the
necessity of reviewing the board's criteria. Obviously, in Hamburg the
staff became more careful about the grounds for denying benefits. Yet the
statistical data show that there is no similar development in all German
states (see Table 5.1).

Concluding Remarks

Analysis of the application of some compensation programs showed very
diverse results. Therefore, one can understand that the judgments are not
corresponding. Concerning the main official goals of compensation
schemes—repaying a substantial proportion of victims of violent crime,
improving attitudes and cooperation among people toward criminal
justice, victim compensation, and government—American and Dutch
evaluation research comes to the conclusion that the programs generally
are a failure (see van Dijk, 1985; Elias, 1984, pp. 111–113). Many
respondents were dissatisfied with delays, inconveniences, poor information, inability to participate, and the restrictive eligibility requirements.
Especially applicants whose claims have been rejected express negative
attitudes and their willingness to cooperate in the future is minimal. Thus
claimants were often more discontented than nonclaimants (Elias, 1984,
p. 111).

Yet British victims, too, expressed reservations although they had a high
rate of applications resulting in an award. Only 50% of those interviewed
were satisfied or very satisfied, whereas 41% felt dissatisfied or very
dissatisfied (Shapland et al., 1985, p. 164). Similar ambivalent reactions
can be found when Canadian applicants comment on their experiences
(Baril et al., 1984, pp. 122–136).

Of course, compensation programs have provided valuable aid to
thousands of victims. German data, for example, show that overall about
140 millions Deutschmarks had been paid out by the end of the year
1986. It is, however, in all countries only a minority who receive benefits
from the existing schemes. Therefore, some contributors criticize victim
compensation in its present form as "only a symbolic policy that served
to justify strengthened police forces, provided political advantages to
supporters, facilitated social control of the population and yet substantially
failed in providing most victims with assistance" (Elias, 1983b, p. 213; see

also Miers, 1983). Even if not every aspect of this negative statement can be totally accepted, it seems obvious that necessary improvements in victim compensation should be made, otherwise characterizations like those of van Dijk (1984) will be found again: "It gives too little, too late to too few of the crime victims" (p. 81).

There are many suggestions for improving the situation, which concentrate upon new information strategies, better administration, and enlarged scope of the schemes. Consideration should not only be given to certain forms of damage or offense, but also to certain groups of victims who are at present excluded (Elias, 1986, pp. 187, 190; Joutsen, 1987, pp. 268, 275) and—not seldom—stigmatized. This however, calls for an overhaul of our preconceived notions of the worthy and unworthy victim—and it is well known that certain forms of prejudice persist a long time.

References

Baril, M., Laflamme-Cusson, S., & Beauchemin, S. (1984). *Crime victims compensation. An assessment of the Quebec JVAC Program* (Crime victims working paper No. 12). Ottawa: Department of Justice of Canada.

Baumann, J. (1980). Zurechnungskriterien beim Opferentschädigungsgesetz. *Die Sozialgerichtsbarkeit, 27*(6), 221–227.

Bundesregierung (1974). Entwurf eines Gesetzes über die Entschädigung für Opfer von Gewalttaten. Deutscher Bundestag, 7. Wahlperiode. *Drucksache 7/2506* vom 27.8, 1974. Bonn: Universitäts-Buchdruckerei.

Burns, P. (1983). A comparative overview of the criminal injuries compensation schemes. *Victimology, 8*(3–4), 102–110.

Canadian Federal Provincial Task Force on Justice for Victims of Crime (1983). *Report.* Ottawa: Department of Justice of Canada.

Carrow, D. (1980). *Crime victim compensation. Program model.* US Department of Justice. Washington, DC: National Institute of Justice.

Council of Europe (1978). Compensation of victims of crime. Strasbourg: Publications Section.

Elias, R. (1983a). *Victims of the system: Crime victims and compensation in American politics and criminal justice.* New Brunswick, NJ: Transaction Books.

Elias, R. (1983b). The symbolic politics of victim compensation. *Victimology, 8*(1–2), 213–224.

Elias, R. (1984). Alienating the victim: Compensation and victim attitudes. *Journal of Social Issues, 40,* 103–116.

Elias, R. (1986). *The politics of victimization. Victims, victimology, and human rights.* New York: Oxford University Press.

Galaway, B. (1981). The use of restitution. In B. Galaway & J. Hudson (Eds.), *Perspectives on crime victims* (pp. 277–289). St. Louis: Mosby.

Geis, G. (1976). Crime victims and victim compensation programs. In W.F. McDonald (Ed.), *Criminal justice and the victims* (pp. 237–256). Beverly Hills, CA: Sage.

Harland, A.T. (1981). *Restitution to the victims of personal and household crimes.*

Washington DC: US Department of Justice.

Hastings, R. (1983). *A theoretical assessment of criminal injuries compensation in Canada. Policy, programmes and evaluation*. (Crime victims working paper No. 6). Ottawa: Department of Justice of Canada.

Hindelang, M.J. (1982). Victimization surveying: Theory and research. In H.J. Schneider (Ed.), *The victim in international perspective* (pp. 151–165). Berlin: de Gruyter.

Hoffmann-Riem, W. (1980). *Bürgernahe Verwaltung? Analysen über das Verhältnis von Bürger und Verwaltung*. Neuwied: Luchterhand.

Joutsen, M. (1987). *The role of the victim of crime in European criminal justice systems. A crossnational study of the role of the victim*. Helsinki: Helsinki Institute for Crime Prevention and Control.

Jung, H. (1979). Entschädigung des Opfers. In G.F. Kirchhoff & K. Sessar (Eds.), *Das Verbrechensopfer* (pp. 379–395). Bochum: Brockmeyer.

Kirchhoff, G.F. (1983/84). The German victim compensation act. *Victimology Newsletter, 3*, 17–36.

Kirchhoff, G.F., & Kirchhoff, C. (1979). Untersuchungen im Dunkelfeld sexueller Viktimisation. In G.F. Kirchhoff & K. Sessar (Eds.), *Das Verbrechensopfer* (pp. 275–299). Bochum: Brockmeyer.

Knudten, R.D. & Knudten, M.S. (1979). Opfer- und Zeugenprogramme in den Vereinigten Staaten. In G.F. Kirchhoff & K. Sessar (Eds.). *Das Verbrechensopfer* (pp. 459–478). Bochum: Brockmeyer.

Mayntz, R. (1985). *Soziologie der öffentlichen Verwaltung*. Heidelberg: C.F. Müller.

McGillis, D. & Smith, P. (1983). *Compensating victims of crime: An analysis of American programs*. Washington, DC: National Institute of Justice.

McKie, C. (1987). *Victim assistance: Criminal injuries compensation in Canada*. Paper presented at the meetings of the American Society of Criminology, Montreal.

Miers, D.R. (1980). Victim compensation as a labelling process. *Victimology, 5*(1), 3–16.

Miers, D.R. (1983). Compensation and conceptions of victims of crime. *Victimology, 8*(1–2), 204–212.

Shapland, J. (1984). Victims, the criminal justice system and compensation. *British Journal of Criminology, 24*(2), 131–149.

Shapland, J., Willmore, J. & Duff, P. (1985). *Victims in the criminal justice system*. Aldershot: Gower.

Stolleis, M. (1981). Entschädigung für Opfer von Gewalttaten—erste Konkretisierungen durch die Rechtsprechung. In W. Gitter, W. Thieme & H. Zacher (Eds.), *Festschrift für G. Wannagat* (pp. 579–598). Köln: Heymanns.

van Dijk, J.J.M. (1984). State assistance to the victim of crime in securing compensation: Alternative models and the expectations of the victim. In Helsinki Institute for Crime Prevention and Control (Eds.), *Towards a victim policy in Europe* (pp. 80–89). Helsinki.

van Dijk, J.J.M. (1983). Compensation by the State or by the offender: the victim's perspective. Research and Documentation Center. Den Haag: The Ministry of Justice.

Vaughn, J., and Hofrichter, R. (1980). Programme visibility in State victim compensation programmes. *Victimology, 5*(1), 30–41.

Villmow, B., & Plemper, B. (1984). Opfer und Opferentschädigung: Einige statistische Daten und Probleme. *Monatsschrift für Kriminologie und Strafrechtsreform, 67*(2), 73–85.

Villmow, B., & Plemper, B. (1987). *Praxis der Opferentschädigung.* Hamburger Entscheidungen und Erfahrungen von Opfern von Gewaltdelikten. Pfaffenweiler: Centautus-Verlagsgesellschaft.

Weigend, T. (1981). *Assisting the victim. A report on efforts to strengthen the position of the victim in the American system of criminal justice.* Freiburg: Max-Planck-Institut.

Weintraud, U. (1980). *Staatliche Entschädigung für Opfer von Gewalttaten in Großbritannien und der Bundesrepublik Deutschland.* Baden-Baden: Nomos Verlagsgesellschaft.

Williams, K. (1983). *Community resources for victims of crime* (Research and Planning Unit Paper 14). London: Home Office.

6
Fear of Crime and Its Relationship to Directly and Indirectly Experienced Victimization: A Binational Comparison of Models

Harald Arnold

Introduction

Since the President's Commission on Law Enforcement and Administration of Justice (1967a) issued its General Report *The Challenge of Crime in a Free Society* two decades ago, fear of, and concern about, crime emerged as a public problem in the context of the discussion of crime as a national issue in the United States. Followed by the task force report, *Crime and its Impact*, (President's Commission, 1967b) and supported by the rich material of the early field surveys (Biderman, Johnson, McIntyre, & Weir, 1967; Ennis, 1967; Reiss 1967), a debate was initiated in political circles and scientific communities alike that focused on the causes and consequences of fear of crime and how to reduce it. Some conclusions have been as far reaching as to name fear of crime as serious a problem as crime itself. The impact of fear on the quality of individual and community life became and still is of direct concern for possible public policy and has important social-policy implications (Research & Forecasts, 1983; Skogan, 1983).

Contemporary fear of crime is one of the topics on the victimological research agenda (Garofalo, 1981; Mayhew, 1985). Collective and individual perceptions of and reactions to victimization, including fear, and related aspects, are central to the understanding of the whole process of victimization (Skogan & Maxfield, 1981). Although fear of crime has interested social scientists for over two decades, and despite the fact that considerable research work has been done in the field of correlates of fear of crime, results have been inconsistent, inconclusive, and far from unequivocal. Notwithstanding some successful approaches toward theoretical conceptualization, a general theory in this area is still unavailable.

Most of the research has been done in the United States where fear of crime is a widespread, significant social problem. Few researchers have looked beyond the borders, thereby ignoring the opportunity to improve concepts at a higher level of generalizability by making use of the advantages of international comparisons (Arzt, 1979; Block, 1984, 1987; Kerner, 1978, 1980; Maxfield, 1984a; Reuband, 1983; for more general discussion, see Ali, 1986; Beirne, 1983; Klein, 1988; Newman & Ferracuti, 1980). This disregard for comparative research contributes to our inability to identify similarities and differences in the situations in Western industrial societies, and by this means learning from each other and gaining new insight into the functioning of general social processes. Relevant variables that are related to fear of crime in one nation may have the same relationship in other countries, and discovered differences may help explain the fear of crime and its divergent causal structure (Block 1987; 1989; Maxfield 1987b; for more general discussion, see Krebs & Schuessler, 1987; Sommers & Kosmitzki, 1988).

After presenting some general background information, this chapter examines the relationship between fear of crime as well as direct and indirect (vicarious) victimization in an international perspective. Based on the data of predesigned sample surveys in the Federal Republic of Germany and the United States, models are developed to explain fear of crime for each country and to examine both differences and similarities.

Fear of Crime: Some General Considerations

An introductory overview on empirical and theoretical research on fear of crime can be found in a number of articles published elsewhere (see e.g. Baumer, 1978; DuBow, McCabe, & Kaplan, 1979; Garofalo, 1979, 1981; Lewis & Salem, 1986; Skogan, 1986b, 1987; Skogan & Maxfield, 1981; Stafford & Galle, 1984; Warr & Stafford, 1983). Here we concentrate on some features that are typical for the state of the art in this field and that characterize the knowledge in the phenomenon discussed (see, e.g., Baker, Nienstedt, & McCleary, 1983; Brantingham, Brantingham, & Butcher, 1986; Greenberg, 1986; Krahn & Kennedy, 1985; Liska, 1985; Maxfield, 1984a, 1984b; Silverman & Kennedy, 1985; Warr, 1987).

Despite the nearly comprehensive, widespread literature on the issue, there is a lack of consensus regarding the basic cognitions. These inconsistencies in research results may explain why a general theory is lacking, and why only short-range models can be found. Even the understanding of the term *fear of crime* and how it should be indicated or measured is not commonly accepted (see, e.g., Gibbs, Coyle, & Hanrahan, 1987). Certainly, that women admit more fear of crime than men in surveys is one of the valid, indisputable results, although this finding seems trivial. In addition to the cognitive aspects, the impact of victimization on fear of crime is important in questioning the causes of fear of crime. Research results on the influence of victimization experiences on fear of crime, however, show all possible outcomes, from negative to positive correlations as well as no significant relationship. Similarly, theoretical explanations have failed to explain adequately the role of experience in the production of fear of crime. Moreover, the problem is even more complicated when it is differentiated according to direct and indirect victimization, reference period of victimization events, type of offense, victim characteristics, demographic subgroups, and so forth.

Even with these difficulties, however, some promising results have been achieved in the development of models of fear of crime in recent years: the victimization model, the social-control model, or the community-concern model (see, e.g., Baumer, 1985; Box, Hale & Andrews, 1988; Lewis & Salem, 1986; Garofalo, 1981; Gomme, 1988; Maxfield, 1987; Skogan & Maxfield, 1981; Taylor & Hale, 1986). In addition, newer studies can show, by using a more appropriate and different methodology such as panel analysis, that some of the problems can be solved, and that formerly discovered anomalies and incongruities are being resolved (Skogan, 1987; see also Liska, Sanchirico, & Reed, 1988).

Salient results from research on fear of crime and review of the literature reveal some problems to be essential for an analysis of fear of crime as a relevant issue.

A number of different suggestions and divergent definitions have emerged under the topic of the fear of crime (see, e.g., DuBow et al., 1979; Gibbs et al., 1987). In addition, in empirical and theoretical studies some terms are used synonymously or interchangeably, while others are used competitively: anxiety for/concern with/worry about crime, feelings of insecurity/safety, fear/perceived risk/subjective probability of victimization, perception of crime. This leads to concurrent concepts and constructs if different operationalisms and indicators are used, and hinders comparison of results between studies. Theoretically, conceptual confusions are possible, making comparison of results more difficult because studies are conducted on different levels of aggregation: international, national, multimetropolitan aggregate, individual metropolitan area, single municipality, neighborhood. Consequently, outcomes are often valid and generalizable over a different range.

Another significant issue concerns the kind and number of independent variables included in a study. For example, when dealing with the topic under this chapter—the impact of criminal victimization on fear of crime—the reference period for victimization events (periods of 6 months, 12 months, 3 years, and up to lifelong have been used) and the nature of the offenses that are included (more serious nonvictim crimes, personal or violent crimes excclusively, or any kind of victimization in general) will affect the model in a very systematic way.

That methodology influences results has already been mentioned. Some recent studies, by looking for interaction effects among relevant independent variables, have shown some interesting new insights into the structure of variable relationships (e.g., the "age as leveler" hypothesis) (Box, Hale,

& Andrews, 1988; Maxfield, 1987b; Ortega & Myles, 1987). In addition, causal effects underlying a relationship may be reciprocal and contingent on another variable so that the use of nonrecursive path models or simultaneous equations is required to allow for feedback loops (Liska, Sanchirico, & Reed, 1988).

Research on Fear of Crime in Germany

A Short Overview on Studies

Three different sources of information have to be considered if to gain an overview on the topic under discussion: (a) public-opinion surveys; (b) social-indicator research and social-welfare research, and (c) criminological and victimological studies.

As in the United States and in many other nations, questions on fear of crime, among other crime issues (e.g., the crime rate, the death penalty, confidence in the criminal-justice system, punishment of criminals) are periodically included in public-opinion polls for many years (Noelle-Neumann & Institut für Demoskopie Allensbach, 1981; Noelle-Neumann & Piel, 1983). Because fear-of-crime items have been used by opinion polls since the mid-1960s, they are the only source from which to get an idea of the development of feelings of insecurity within society over a larger period of time. With a few exceptions (Kerner, 1980; Reuband, 1983), these data have not been used for criminological analysis in a narrow sense, although criminal-justice officials make use of it in crime-policy debates. In order to gauge public perception of crime along with official crime measurement and to get an impression of the impact of crime, crime rates, and crime development, opinion polls on those topics are still requested by criminal-justice institutions. Because public-opinion surveys seldom combine questions of fear of crime with questions about crime victimization, little insight into the relationship of these two indicators can be gained.

A second source of information appears in research in the fields of social indicators and social welfare which include studies of anxieties and fears of different origin. These studies have pointed out the relevance of both security feelings and freedom from crime for the perceived quality of life and subjective well-being (Murck, 1978, 1980). Again, with few exceptions, experiences with crime (i.e., criminal victimization) have not been a subject in these studies and therefore the crime/victimization-fear relationship could not be a focus of analysis. Crime victimization has been measured poorly in this kind of research.

Most of the research on fear of crime, not surprisingly, has been done in the field of criminology and victimology (Kerner, 1986), although the number of studies is small compared to the United States (Kirchhoff & Kirchhoff, 1984). Traditionally, the victim survey has included items of fear of crime and similar issues (e.g., perceived risk of victimization, crime situation in the neighborhood, development of crime rates) (Stephan, 1976, 1982). When the focus has been more on victimological research issues, as opposed to mere alternative crime measurement (i.e., the so-called dark-field or dark-number studies), issues like feelings of insecurity have been of special interest (Gefeller & Trudewind, 1978). In addition, special studies on the state of so-called interior security, a term referring to a rather complex construct meaning a society free of crime, without protests and riots, maintaining democratic order and so forth, have addressed the issues of the general threat and fear of crime as social problems (Kerner, 1980). The surveys in this project were not victim surveys, included no question on victimization experiences, and, consequently, the nature of the research design precluded investigation into the relationship of victimization and fear.

Other more specialized criminological studies covering fear of crime and victimization focused on other issues (e.g., the impact of architectural design on crime) and thus have made use of the data from perspectives that are of only limited interest here (Rolinski, 1980, 1986).

Finally, the so-called KOL (knowledge and opinion about law) studies have to be mentioned because they, in part, have included questions on fear of crime and related subjects, but likewise have not gathered general data on victimization (Smaus, 1985). Thus, no use can be made of those cognitions for the answering of the question under discussion here.

Research on Fear of Crime in Germany

One of the first German victim surveys was carried out in Stuttgart, a large city in the southwest (Stephan, 1976, 1982). Several variables on attitudes toward the importance and extent of crime as well as fear of becoming a victim were included. The crime-oriented perceptual measures cover a wider range, including aspects of concern, worry, fear, or risk estimations. Besides the descriptive and bivariate presentation of fear-related results in the demographic context focusing on sex, age, and socioeconomic status, no bi- or multivariate analysis of the fear of crime that includes the victimization variables was reported in Stephan's research. Instead, a reference point was given in a multidimensional analysis contrasting victims and nonvictims of property and violent crimes. Entering 39 variables related to crime, crime control, and fear, a number of significant differences could be found between victims and nonvictims, showing that victims of property crimes as well as victims of violent crimes are more concerned about crime and personal risks of victimization. None of the fear indicators had a higher value for nonvictims than for victims, as would be expected. Surprisingly, the differentiation between victims of crime and nonvictims by crime-related attitudes was more successful for victims of property crime than for victims of violent crime, one likely reason being that the analysis was based only on a small number of victims of violent crime.

Another victim survey was carried out in the city of Bochum in northwest Germany (Schwind, 1984; Schwind, Ahlborn, & Weiss, 1978). This study focused on nonreported crime and its meaning to geographical-crime research, but also included an investigation on feelings of insecurity. In a differentiated approach, indicators for the emotional, cognitive, and behavioral aspects of feelings of insecurity were used and analyzed (Gefeller & Trudewind, 1978). As independent variables, indirect and vicarious victimization were tested for their relationship to the fear of crime indicators. Additionally, the influence of population density and official crime rates on fear of crime was investigated, as was the relationship of the specific indicators of feelings of insecurity to general anxiety by means of a trait-anxiety inventory. Nearly all indicators of fear of crime, including emotional, cognitive, and behavioral aspects, were found to show a significant positive covariation with direct and indirect victimization experiences (see replication by Schwind et al., 1989).

Further evidence comes from studies outside the field of mere victim surveys. In a study focusing on security needs of citizens, a survey was carried out in each of two small, middle, and large cities with high and low infrastructural resources, respectively (Murck, 1978, 1980). Part of the research instrument included questions on fear of crime and lifelong criminal victimization. One of the results was that victims had a higher degree of fear although the correlation was low (as in most of the studies already mentioned). The relationships remained stable when age, sex, and education were held constant.

Another project investigating the influence of architectural design on the crime rate in two cities (München, Regensburg) included a small victim survey, as well. A later analysis showed that, in general, victims of crime were more afraid than nonvictims (Rolinski, 1980, 1986).

Whereas these studies refer to the 1970s, a newer survey in the 1980s from Hamburg has to be added to the list for completeness. The central purpose of this research project was to study the acceptance of restitution in lieu of punishment (Sessar, Beurskens, & Boers, 1986). The study included a victim survey asking respondents whether during a reference period of three years they had suffered one or more of 18 types of property or violent offenses included in a crime list on the questionnaire. The relationship between fear of crime and the number of victimizations was curvilinear so that the linear correlation coefficient appeared near zero (see Chapter 8 by Boers & Sessar).

This short overview on German findings on the the fear-victimization relationship can be summarized as follows: Despite the fact that the studies have used various methodologies, have measured the fear of crime and criminal victimization differently, with consequent limited comparability in report results, fear of crime was found to be predominantly stronger among victims, although indicators differed. Nevertheless, correlations were generally weak, and some of the coefficients approach non-significance.

The Study: International Comparative Victim Surveys

The data in the following analysis come from a predesigned victimological survey carried out in Texas (United States) and Baden-Württemberg (Federal Republic of Germany) (Arnold, 1986; Teske & Arnold, 1982a). A victim survey utilizing the same methodology (i.e., the same research instrument and procedures) was carried out in the county of Baranya (Hungary), but results of that later study are presented elsewhere (Arnold & Korinek, 1985; Arnold, 1986).

The findings are based on the results of the first predesigned cross-cultural victimization survey undertaken with the specific intent of making a comparative analysis. (The inclusion of a socialist country in the comparison is of specific salience, a view that is supported by results published recently [Arnold, Teske, & Korinek, 1988]). Whereas many researchers stress the relevance of comparative research, the true number of results coming from comparative projects is rather small in criminology and victimology alike. The output is especially meager if one looks for strictly comparative methodology. The methodological and organizational problems of comparative research and the long period of time such studies require probably deter researchers and research organizations from taking up such projects (see Clinard, 1978, and Sveri, 1982, on victim surveys; for a more general discussion, see Newman, 1977; Newman & Ferracuti, 1980). It is nevertheless important periodically to emphasize the necessity of such research (Block, 1984; 1987; 1989).

The research topics covered by the surveys include direct and indirect measures of victimization and fear of crime as well as criminal justice issues of a broad range (e.g., the death penalty, attitudes toward the criminal-justice authorities, ratings of the work of the police, the courts, and the prisons). A few items were different for each survey because they were oriented toward problems of national concern or have been of special interest to only one of the researchers. Single items as well as multiple indicators were used to measure many of the different concepts (e.g., fear of crime).

Of specific interest for the German situation is that this victim survey is the first one that is representative for a larger part of the nation and, as such, of some significance for the country as a whole. Beyond that, the study has the largest sample size of any current German victim survey. (A first nationwide victim survey has been carried out in Germany, most recently as part of the International Comparative 1989 Telephone Survey.)

Research Procedure

Unlike many other previous victim surveys, data collection for this comparative cross-cultural victimization survey was done by mail surveys (Dillman, 1978; Erdos, 1983). Several strong arguments have been made in favor of a mail-survey approach; first, the costs per respondent are lower in the case of a mail survey than for interviews, face-to-face or telephone alike. Because victim surveys need large samples, total costs would have been too high for any approach other than mail survey. Second, regarding the problems of methodological comparability of data gathering, interviews are far more complicated, especially if one is interested in standardizing the situation of data collection. Although interviewer bias is a major disadvantage of interviews, answers by respondents in face-to-face or telephone interview situations are more spontaneous and immediate, an advantage under some conditions. In the case of a victim survey, however, it seems to be no disadvantage that respondents of a mail survey have more time for answering questions and more time to think them over. If the problems of victim-survey respondents are with memory (i.e., recalling incidents of sometimes low personal significance that happened long ago), then the greater availability of time is an advantage because time pressure is low for respondents in mail surveys. In addition, there is no direct and immediate "social pressure" by an interviewer, which may reduce the influence of social desirability on answers. Respondents may feel less compelled to answer, or to give a special answer, in the case of mail surveys. If someone is willing to answer, he or she can easily refuse a single question or the whole questioning, thereby becoming a refusal or at least a reluctant respondent.

Several methodological studies have found no serious differences regarding several central features between face-to-face, telephone, and mail surveys (Niemi, 1985). Whereas low response rates have been a problem to mail surveys and have been used as an objection for a long time, contemporary methods are well developed, so that acceptable response rates can be obtained rather easily (Dillman, 1978; Erdos, 1983). Therefore, it is not surprising that the use of the mail survey method for purposes of gathering data on victimization has been recommended occasionally.

In the project under discussion, the questionnaire and research procedures were predicated on a previously successful statewide victimization survey conducted in Texas during 1980 (Teske & Moore, 1980). Every effort was made to assure that the questionnaires conveyed the same meaning in both languages to guarantee a high degree of functional equivalence and comparability (Krebs & Schuessler, 1987). Sampling procedures and research format were as identical as possible (Teske & Arnold, 1982a). Systematic random probability samples of 3,830 residents age 18 and over in Baden-Württemberg and 2,000 in Texas have been drawn. The surveys were carried out in the fall of 1981 in Baden-

Württemberg and in spring, 1982, in Texas. Using a presurvey card and two or three follow-up cards with reminders for the nonrespondents, a total of 2,252 and 1,442 completed, usable questionnaires were returned in Baden-Württemberg and Texas, respectively. This represented a return rate of 58.8% and 72.1% of the original samples. After adjusting for nonforwardables and deceased individuals, the return rates were 64.2% and 75.5% in Baden-Württemberg and Texas, respectively. From the 1980 Texas victim survey, the data from which are also presented below, a total of 1,331 completed and usable questionnaires was returned, representing a return rate of 66.6% of the original sample (after adjusting, the return rate was 77.4%). Altogether the return rates were quite satisfactory, which is also true for representativeness of the samples and the data quality on the whole (Arnold, 1986; Teske, Hazlett & Parker, 1983).

The Problem: Fear and Its Relationship to Victimization

How far structural relationship between relevant variables is common in the countries investigated is of central interest to the project. Accordingly, one of the main purposes of this research was to address the issue of whether the same factors are operative in both societies as predictors of victimization and fear of crime. In an earlier paper (Arnold & Teske, 1988; Teske & Arnold, 1987) results of a comparative cross-cultural analysis of factors affecting fear of crime have been presented, showing that four independent variables were working fairly well as predictors in both samples in the same order of significance, thereby accounting for similar amount of explained variation in the dependent variable—fear of crime. Besides the inclusion of two commonly strong correlates of fear of crime (i.e., sex and community size), that model emphasized an analysis of the explanatory power of two crime-oriented perceptual measures, namely, perceived community-crime problem and perceived effectiveness of local police. Because age as a predictor made no significant contribution to the model's strength, it was dropped. Likewise, the respondents' own victimization experiences appeared to be significant only in one sample (Texas); therefore this variable has also been dropped, to arrive at a parsimonious model for both countries.

This research is a continuation of the earlier work but with a different emphasis (Arnold, 1984). In this analysis the focus is on the contribution of victimization experience to the explanation or (statistical) prediction of fear of crime even if it is small. Therefore the aim is less to find a parsimonious model that is valid and applicable to both countries; instead, it is to fit a model that will best describe the respective national data regarding the relationship under discussion. To reach that goal some modification has been made to go beyond the early approach. Whereas, earlier, victimization experience was indicated in a rather common way—taking a reference period of 12 months—the approach here is more global, taking also a lifelong span. Vicarious victimization experience is also included because the relevance of indirect victimization has been stated by different authors (e.g., Box et al., 1988; DuBow et al., 1979; Gomme, 1988; Skogan & Maxfield, 1981; Tyler, 1980). Also the statistical method chosen for analysis is different here, allowing for a differentiated testing of interactional effects between the independant variables. Interactional effects and their analysis have been of interest to researchers in recent publications showing some unexpected insights into complicated relationships between variables (Box et al., 1988; Ortega & Myles, 1987). Finally it is important to note that this is another attempt in the "criminologist's struggle with fear of crime" (Kellens, 1986) to disentangle the correlates of fear of crime, especially the contribution of victimization. In so doing, we will also work on a solution to the apparent paradox of the reverse relationship among population groups between risk of victimization and fear of crime.

Methods and Data

Conceptualization and Measurement of Variables

Although fear of crime as a global construct and latent variable was indicated by different measures in this research (Arnold, 1988a, 1988b), we concentrate on one single indicator here for several reasons. First, the results should be comparable to other research using that or a similar indicator (Gibbs et al., 1987; Skogan & Maxfield, 1981) as well as to our own prior research with that dependent variable (Arnold, 1984; Arnold & Teske, 1988; Teske & Arnold, 1982b, 1987). Second, and more important, a more elaborated indicator is not easy to find or to build. The study covered a broad range with its fear indicators including aspects of concern, worry, and risk estimation alike, thereby taking into consideration the complex nature of fear of crime. A previous factor analysis has shown the different dimensions of the fear of crime complex (Arnold, 1988a). Similar to other research results, the main components well known from attitudinal research (i.e., emotional, cognitive, and behavioral factors) have been found (Baumer & Rosenbaum, 1981; Gefeller & Trudewind, 1978; Gibbs, Coyle, & Hanrahan, 1987; Skogan, 1986b). The variable used in the study was the key variable for the emotional factor that represents the fear of crime dimension in a narrow sense. Results based on the factor analysis and a subsequent scalability analysis will, it is hoped, lead to a more reliable measure of fear of crime that is valid and closer to the theoretical construct. Preliminary work in this direction has been done (Arnold, 1988a, 1988b; Teske & Hazlett, 1983).

The indicator used as the dependent variable here is a type of standard fear of crime variable found in several studies (e.g., the General Social

Survey, Gallup Poll). It asks for any area within 1 mile (in the German survey, 1 kilometer) from one's home where one would be afraid to walk alone at night. Although crime is not mentioned in the question, different authors have argued that the item taps crime-related thoughts and feelings rather well. This assumption has been empirically supported with evidence by a co-researcher (Teske & Hazlett, 1983). In addition, the fear-of-crime item followed other crime-related questions; within the context of the whole questionnaire, crime as a general referent was established. Therefore it seems reasonable to assume that respondents who admit being afraid feel so because of fear of victimization.

As independent and control variables, three victimization measures (recent and former direct victimization and recent vicarious [indirect] victimization) and two demographic variables (gender and community size of the place of living) have been included for testing the model described below. Sex has been a consistent and strong, if not the strongest, correlate among the independent variables in previous analysis and needs no further reason for inclusion. That community size has not been cited as relevant as often as gender stems from the fact that many studies on fear of crime did their analysis on levels (for example, neighborhoods) that did not include this variable. The inclusion of community size is relevant because more advanced analyses have shown the existence of some interaction effects, depending on community size level, if a broad range from urban to rural areas is covered by the study. The same is true of interaction effects for gender; therefore some of the attempts to build and to test models of fear of crime differentiate between models for males and for females, as well as between urban and rural models (Ortega & Myles, 1987).

Two measures of direct victimization experiences were employed in this investigation, one referring to the 12-month period prior to administration of the instrument (recent victimization) and one covering the lifelong span previous to the recent reference period (former victimization). It is thus possible to control the influence of victimization events that usually confound the measures in studies that use only a recent reference period. Failure to control for former victimization influences may be a reason for some of the ambiguities found in previous research.

The measures of victimization are based on responses to questions indicating whether the respondents have been victims of one or more of a number of offences listed in the questionnaire. In addition, a global question for other victimizations was asked. Property as well as violent offenses have been included in these measures. Certainly most of prior research pointed to the fact that the impact of violent victimization is stronger and therefore the predictive trends of personal crime, as opposed to property crime, is to be prefered (Skogan, 1987). Nevertheless, there is evidence for the considerable impact of some property crime events too. Consequently, it was decided to begin with a global measure including property as well as violent crime because the starting point here is the difference between self-defined victims of crime versus nonvictims and its impact on fear of crime.

In addition, a methodological reason should be noted. Crime in its more serious form, especially violent crime, is still a rarer event in Germany than in the United States. Therefore a victimization measure based on violent crime exclusively would be rather restrictive. Taking into account our rather small samples compared to the National Crime Survey, the British crime survey, or other larger national surveys, this would leave too few cases of victims for statistical analysis, a number too small for a sound analysis with the method chosen here (see Teske & Arnold, 1982c).

The measure for vicarious or indirect victimization used here is similar to the measure for self-experienced victimization. Following the questions for their own victimization, respondents were asked if they know someone else in the family, in the neighborhood, at work or any friend or acquaintance who has been victim of the listed offenses in the previous 12 months. In addition, a question about having known a victim of murder was asked for and added to the measure. Data on victimization of others prior to the 12 month-reference period also was gathered by the survey, but only for rape and murder. This variable is not included in the present analysis. Two other variables that are part of the vicarious or indirect victimization concept also are not included here, but are measured by the survey: media exposure and witnessing a crime.

Description of the Dependent and Independent Variables

The univariate distribution of the dependent and independent variables in the surveys is reported in Table 6.1. Data from the previous Texas survey (1980) are presented as well to give additional support for the reliability of the results. The situation has not changed very much in Texas during the two years covered. Neither has fear of crime increased significantly ($\chi^2 = .24$, $df = 1$, $p = .63$) nor recent and former direct victimization ($\chi^2 = 1.51$, $df = 1$, $p = .22/\chi^2 = 1.20$, $df = 1$, $p = .27$) or indirect victimization ($\chi^2 = 2.12$, $df = 1$, $p = .15$). In the international perspective, it is highly significant that the German respondents are burdened by crime to a much lesser degree than Texans, which corresponds to the official data on crime (i.e., the police statistics). Thus in the Baden-Württemberg survey respondents reported fewer recent and former direct-victimization experiences (16% and 30%, respectively, difference from Texas 1982). Similarly, they knew fewer others who had been victims of crime in the past 12 months (29% difference from Texas 1982). Accordingly, they admitted less fear of crime (14% difference from Texas 1982).

The bivariate relationships between dependent and the independent variables are displayed in Table 6.2; once again, each survey is presented separately. The figures (N) are the numbers of respondents per (sub-) population who admitted being afraid. Following in parentheses are the

TABLE 6.1. Description of variables.

Variables	Items (abbreviated) and coding	Texas 1980 N	%	Texas 1982 N	%	Baden-Württemberg 1981 N	%
Fear of crime	Any area within 1 mile[a] from one's home where one would be afraid to walk alone at night. No = 0, yes = 1	0 = 562 1 = 758	(42.6) (57.4)	0 = 592 1 = 829	(41.7) (58.3)	0 = 1,237 1 = 987	(55.6) (44.4)
Sex	Female = 0, male = 1	0 = 683 1 = 648	(51.3) (48.7)	0 = 707 1 = 735	(49.0) (51.0)	0 = 1,130 1 = 1,121	(50.2) (49.8)
Community size	<50.000 = 0 >50.000 = 1	0 = 628 1 = 701	(47.3) (52.7)	0 = 679 1 = 762	(47.1) (52.9)	0 = 1,709 1 = 543	(75.9) (24.1)
	(<20.000 = 0)[b] (>20.000 = 1)					0 = 1,339 1 = 913	(59.5) (40.5)
Recent victimization	Victim of either burglary, motor vehicle theft, other theft, robbery, assault with weapon, rape, arson, vandalism, fraud,[c] other crime in the past 12 months. Not a victim = 0, victim = 1	0 = 884 0 = 447	(66.4) (33.6)	0 = 925 1 = 516	(62.2) (35.8)	0 = 1,766 1 = 447	(79.8) (20.2)
Former victimization	Victim of any of the above crimes[d] prior to the last year. Not a victim = 0, victim = 1	0 = 493 1 = 835	(37.1) (62.9)	0 = 504 1 = 931	(35.1) (64.9)	0 = 1,439 1 = 768	(65.2) (34.8)
Indirect victimization	Knowing a victim of any of the above crimes or a murder victim in the past 12 months. Do not know a victim = 0, know a victim = 1	0 = 374 1 = 955	(28.1) (71.9)	0 = 367 1 = 1,062	(25.7) (74.3)	0 = 1,193 1 = 986	(54.7) (45.3)
TOTAL[e]		N = 1,331		N = 1,442		N = 2,252	

[a] In Baden-Württemberg 1 kilometer (= .62 miles).
[b] Dichotomization used in the fit of models of the Baden-Württemberg data below.
[c] Fraud was explicitly included only in the Texas 1982 survey.
[d] Vandalism was explicitly included only in the Baden-Württemberg survey.
[e] Differences to the sums above due to missing data.

TABLE 6.2. Proportions being afraid (fear of crime by sex, community size, direct and indirect victimization).

	Texas 1980		Texas 1982		Baden-Württemberg 1981	
	N	%	N	%	N	%
Sex						
Male	251	(39.2)	293	(40.5)	253	(22.8)
Female	507	(74.7)	536	(76.8)	733	(65.7)
	$p = .000$		$p = .000$		$p = .000$	
	$C_k = .478**$		$C_k = .488**$		$C_k = .561**$	
Community size						
Small	290	(46.7)	317	(47.7)	497	(37.6)[a]
Large	467	(67.0)	511	(67.7)	490	(54.3)
	$p = .000$		$p = .000$		$p = .000$	
	$C_k = .284**$		$C_k = .281**$		$C_k = .231**$	
Indirect victimization						
Know no victim	180	(48.6)	176	(48.8)	460	(39.2)
Know a victim	577	(60.9)	646	(61.7)	491	(50.2)
	$p = .000$		$p = .000$		$p = .000$	
	$C_k = .156**$		$C_k = .161**$		$C_k = .155**$	
Recent victimization						
Not a victim	499	(56.8)	513	(56.3)	763	(43.9)
Victim	259	(58.6)	315	(62.0)	204	(45.8)
	$p = .541$		$p = .035$		$p = .450$	
	$(C_k = .024)$ns		$C_k = .079*$		$(C_k = .023)$ns	
Former victimization						
Not a victim	277	(56.9)	273	(54.7)	601	(42.5)
Victim	479	(57.7)	552	(60.3)	358	(46.8)
	$p = .768$		$p = .041$		$p = .0554$	
	$(C_k = .011)$ns		$C_k = .077*$		$(C_k = .058)$ns	
Total[b]	759	(57.2)	828	(58.3)	987	(44.4)

Note: Strength of association is given by the corrected coefficient of contingency C_k.
[a] Otherwise dichotomized the values are as follows: small 682 (40.5), large 305 (56.6), $p = .000$; $C_k = .197$; cf. Table 6.1.
[b] Differences to the above numbers due to missing data.
ns = not significant; $p > .05$; $*p < .05$; $**p < .001$.

corresponding proportions of the percentages. Based on the differences between the percentages, an intuitive impression of the relationships can be concluded. Added are coefficients for the strength of association (i.e., the corrected contingency coefficient [C_k] and the probability [p] of [type I] error given).

Not surprisingly, a strong relationship between fear and gender is found; as in many previous studies sex has been the strongest predictor among the independent variables included here. The effect of gender is followed by community size and indirect victimization. The order of significance is the same for all three surveys, even the coefficients for the strength of the relationship are relatively similar except for gender. The result is a bit different, however, with regard to the direct victimization measures. That most coefficients are nonsignificant is not surprising when taking into account that a lot of previous research had results in the same direction, especially when combined victimization measures for property as well as violent crimes have been used. But the result is interesting nevertheless. Whereas both values for the earlier Texas survey (1980) are nonsignificant, the recent Texas survey (1982) shows two significant relationships between fear and victimization. For Baden-Württemberg both values are nonsignificant, one showing a tendency toward significance. However, if one looks at the strength of the relationship, it appears evident that there is really no substantial association between fear and direct-victimization experience on that level of order, even for the significant ones.

The zero-order correlations among the independent variables are shown in Table 6.3. The figures appear to indicate an absence of multicollinearity because the coefficients are rather small. On the whole the coefficients are rather similar between the surveys as well as the nations. The strength of these appear to be weak or nonexistent except among the victimization measures. Interestingly, the strength of association is fairly alike between direct and indirect victimization measures, which could be interpreted substantially as well as methodologically (e.g., reference-group effect vs. recall or sensitivity artifact). No correlation was found between sex and indirect victimization, that is, knowing another victim, whereas males are more often victimized than females, which is not unexpected. The same is

TABLE 6.3. Zero-order correlations of independent variables.

	SEX	COMM	IVIC	RVIC	FVIC
Sex	—				
Community size	.042 ns .003 ns .020 ns	—			
Indirect victimization	.014 ns .019 ns .023 ns	.149** .146** .103**	—		
Recent victimization	.114** .032 ns .122**	.084* .173** .127**	.330** .311** .352**	—	
Former victimization	.146** .125** .107**	.136** .180** .168**	.340** .379** .339**	.299** .411** .362**	—

Note: Coefficients are corrected coefficients of contingency and ordered as follows: Texas 1980 (upper figure), Texas 1982 (middle figure), and Baden-Württemberg 1981 (lower figure). ns = not significant; $p > .05$; $*p < .05$; $**p < .001$.

true for community size and its relationship to victimization: respondents from larger cities are more often directly and indirectly victimized.

Multivariate Analysis and Findings

Method of Analysis: Categorial Regression (GSK)

The data were analyzed using the general linear model approach to complex contingency tables developed by Grizzle, Starmer, and Koch (GSK) (1969). The GSK approach because of its close resemblance to ordinary regression with dummy-variables has been named *categorial regression* or *linear probability modeling* (Kritzer, 1981, 1986; Swafford, 1980). This modification to ordinary regression consists of the application of weighted least squares multiple regression to cell probabilities in contingency tables, thereby allowing us to estimate how various independent variables affect the probability that cases will fall into a given category. Unlike conventional regression methods, GSK avoids the assumptions of interval measurement and normal distribution as well as homoscedasticity (constant variance) for the independent and dependent variables, which are dichotomous in this case. These violations would otherwise affect the estimation of regression coefficients as well as the validity of the tests of significance. Beyond that—computed by means of design matrices of contrast—GSK yields estimates of the relative effect (parameter b) of each independent variable that is comparable to a standardized partial regression coefficient. In addition, it gives a measure of the magnitude and significance of complex interaction effects. The GSK approach allows us to examine the extent to which a stated model—combined of main as well as interaction effect—predicts all probabilities of complex contingency tables. By determining the significance of the difference between observed and predicted cell probabilities, according to the tested model, that is, its effect parameters, a decision on the failure of the model is possible based on χ^2-coefficient for the goodness-of-fit. Additionally, the single main and interaction effects can be examined for significance with a similar procedure.

Contrary to other approaches based on the GOODMAN approach, GSK easily allows testing of hierachical as well as nonhierachical models. In addition, building the design matrix one may not only have the usual parallel dummy variables, but also nonparallel dummy variables, which may be specified as conditional or nested effects. With this program, one may not only analyze linear but also log-linear and other more complex functions derived from a multinominal distribution.

The initial step in the analysis was the construction of a six-way cross-classified contingency table encompassing the five independent variables (also called predictors or factors) and the dependent variable (also called

TABLE 6.4. Fear of crime by independent variables.

SP	SEX	COMM	IVIC	RVIC	FVIC	Texas 1980				Texas 1982				Baden-Württemberg 1981			
						Fy	Fn	N	% Fy	Fy	Fn	N	% Fy	Fy	Fn	N	% Fy
1	F	SC	DV	NV	NV	34	23	57	59.7	32	28	60	53.3	130	147	277	46.9
2	F	SC	DV	NV	V	10	19	29	34.5	16	12	28	57.1	33	27	60	55.0
3	F	SC	DV	V	NV	4	3	7	57.1	3	1	4	75.0	11	8	19	57.9
4	F	SC	DV	V	V	2	2	4	50.0	3	4	7	42.9	6	5	11	54.6
5	F	SC	KV	NV	NV	43	21	64	67.2	52	22	74	70.3	95	52	147	64.6
6	F	SC	KV	NV	V	51	22	73	69.9	46	20	66	69.7	52	10	62	83.9
7	F	SC	KV	V	NV	16	5	21	76.2	9	5	14	64.3	19	6	25	76.0
8	F	SC	KV	V	V	37	18	55	67.3	48	20	68	70.6	24	9	33	72.7
9	F	LC	DV	NV	NV	36	8	44	81.8	25	7	32	78.1	107	37	144	74.3
10	F	LC	DV	NV	V	29	2	31	93.6	18	3	21	85.7	43	9	52	82.7
11	F	LC	DV	V	NV	3	2	5	60.0	5	2	7	71.4	8	4	12	66.7
12	F	LC	DV	V	V	8	1	9	88.9	11	2	13	84.6	11	3	14	78.6
13	F	LC	KV	NV	NV	51	17	68	75.0	53	10	63	84.1	62	20	82	75.6
14	F	LC	KV	NV	V	95	13	108	88.0	94	13	107	87.9	47	7	54	87.0
15	F	LC	KV	V	NV	15	3	18	83.3	15	3	18	83.3	21	4	25	84.0
16	F	LC	KV	V	V	70	12	82	85.4	100	8	108	92.6	31	10	41	75.6
17	M	SC	DV	NV	NV	10	38	48	20.8	17	41	58	29.3	28	217	245	16.4
18	M	SC	DV	NV	V	9	31	40	22.5	9	24	33	27.3	19	54	73	11.5
19	M	SC	DV	V	NV	2	4	6	33.3	0	7	7	0.0	3	26	29	10.3
20	M	SC	DV	V	V	1	12	13	7.7	1	3	4	25.0	4	16	20	20.0
21	M	SC	KV	NV	NV	17	27	44	38.6	15	31	46	32.6	19	84	103	18.5
22	M	SC	KV	NV	V	23	53	76	30.3	28	66	94	29.8	15	65	80	18.8
23	M	SC	KV	V	NV	4	9	13	30.8	1	9	10	10.0	6	23	29	20.7
24	M	SC	KV	V	V	26	44	70	37.1	29	52	81	35.8	14	45	59	23.7
25	M	LC	DV	NV	NV	13	20	33	39.4	15	22	37	40.5	30	105	135	22.2
26	M	LC	DV	NV	V	15	16	31	48.4	13	15	28	46.4	16	35	51	31.4
27	M	LC	DV	V	NV	1	5	6	16.7	1	4	5	20.0	3	7	10	30.0
28	M	LC	DV	V	V	2	3	5	40.0	7	8	15	46.7	7	11	18	38.9
29	M	LC	KV	NV	NV	17	16	33	51.5	19	24	43	44.2	25	36	61	41.0
30	M	LC	KV	NV	V	44	51	95	46.3	52	54	106	49.1	20	49	69	29.0
31	M	LC	KV	V	NV	11	9	20	55.0	7	7	14	50.0	10	19	29	34.5
32	M	LC	KV	V	V	56	50	106	52.8	73	57	130	56.2	24	45	69	34.8
TOTAL						755	559	1,314	57.5	817	584	1,401	58.3	940	1,195	2,135	44.0

Note: Subpopulation (SP), female (F), male (M), community size (COMM), smaller (SC) or larger city (LC), indirect victimization (IVIC), do not know a victim (DV), know a victim (KV), recent (RVIC) or former (FVIC) victimization, no victim (NV), victim (V), fear of crime item: yes (Fy) or no (Fn), number of cases per subpopulation (N), percentage agreeing to fear item (% Fy).

criterion or multi-response), which is displayed in Table 6.4. This table contains the distribution of the frequencies of respondents (N) agreeing (Fy) and disagreeing (Fn) to the fear item depending on the systematic variation of the independent variables that define the respective subgroups. The dependent variable is the proportion in each subgroup who agreed to the fear of crime item ($\%Fy$). These proportions can also be described as probabilities, that is, the probability of a respondent agreeing under the specific conditions given by the combination of categories of the independent variables. Contrary to the individual level analysis where the dichotomous, dependent-variable fear of crime could only vary between zero (no) or one (yes) on the aggregate level, the criterion has now a variation like a metric scale.

One of the assumptions of this analysis is that each subgroup constitutes a representative sample of the entire subpopulation of individuals eligible for inclusion in the sample. Further, the observations of the various subpopulations should be independent of one another. Therefore, appropriate probability-sampling procedures are to be used. Another assumption about the necessary number of cases per subgroup is that no more than a quarter of the subgroups ideally should contain fewer than 25 cases. A violation becomes more problematic if fewer than about 10 cases are contained per subgroup because it endangers sound statistical conclusions by means of the significance test applied and introduces a greater degree of uncertainty. On the other side, the analysis may not necessarily be invalid.

Another point that had been stressed is that extreme events require more observations per subgroup to ensure adequate estimation. The rule $pN = 5$ is recommended as a conservative guideline.

Looking at the data in Table 6.4, it can be ascertained that several of the subgroups have few cases, especially in the Texas surveys because of relative small sample size, which not only falls below the limit ideally suggested but also the minimum required normally. For the Baden-Württemberg data, less than a quarter of the subgroups has fewer than 25 cases and only three subgroups do not meet the rule mentioned above so that the data are sufficient on the whole. The uncertainty about the soundness of the statistical conclusions for the Texas data should be minimized by using two samples the results of which can be compared to each other. In addition the use of an alternative function (logit) in modeling should help to test the reliance in the results.

As noted before, besides using the proportions (p) in the additive (response) model a multiplicative or log-linear model can be chosen by using log-odds, that is the logit transformation of the probability p in the following way: $\ln(p/q) = \ln(p/1 - p)$. This will be done below, too, to test the models specified in the response-model version under condition of a log-linear model. Because $q = 1 - p$, the values of p, p/q, or $\ln(p/q)$ are in unequivocal relation to each other. On the other side, whereas p is limited between 0 and 1, p/q can vary from 0 up to infinity and $\ln(p/q)$ is totally unlimited, or, in other words, can take any value from negative to positive infinity. This latter feature advantageous for statistical reasons, especially for estimating parameters. The difference in results between additive models versus logit models is especially substantial if the distributions in the subgroups are skewed. In other words, the choice of the function has implications for the procedure used to estimate model parameters and for the interpretation of model results.

To summarize, the starting point of the analysis is the dependent variable, that is, the frequencies in the subgroups. These frequencies are transformed into conditional probabilities and the corresponding metrics is rewritten as a vector. After creating these dependent-variable functions, a series of dummy variables are specified to represent the effects of the independent variables. The coding of these predictors (main effects) and their interactions by effect coding $(1/-1)$ or dummy coding $(1/0)$ is similar to the coding scheme used in ordinary regression or analysis of variance. The aim is the creation of the so-called design matrices that include the effects specified in hypotheses. If the approach is more explanatory, the starting point is the saturated model, which includes all possible main effects and interactions as predictors. In the saturated model, the number of predictors, that is, the constant, main effects, and interactions, equals the number of observations (i.e., the proportions of the dependent variable in the categories defined by the independent variables). This model yields perfect predictions and recreates the original proportions but is unsatisfactory because it is not parsimonious.

The models can be easily expressed in equation form, like the familiar regression equation. The proportion of the response variable (probability estimates) can be viewed as a linear combination of a set of coefficients (parameters) and dummy (design) variables. But contrary to ordinary regression prediction, it is not for an individual case, but rather the respective probability that a case in a given subgroup will fall into a given category (the cases of which are homogenous) with respect to the dependent variable. So the emphasis of this analysis is more on structural effects.

A variety of models may be used in different strategies chosen to find an acceptable (so-called "best" or "final") model. This best or final model is not the true and real model in a narrow sense but a compromise in reducing complexity by fitting the model to empirical data with the aim of a parsimonious model. The most simple model in conceptualization and interpretation is a main-effect model, that is, a model including only predictor (independent) variables but without its interactions (we do not consider and discuss a mean model, i.e. a model including only the constant [mean] effect as a model in a narrow sense, here, although it may be used for predictions and is indeed the most simple type of model).

Several strategies for settling on an acceptable model are possible. In the exploratory approach, one generally starts with a saturated model, using a backward selection procedure with the aim of discovering which terms (parameters) of the saturated model can be eliminated without introducing statistically significant distortion in predictions, in which case the model provides a poor fit. The procedure is repeated until there is a correspondence between observed proportions and the proportions predicted by the model tested, that is, the chi-square due to error is large enough to be nonsignificant. Contrary to usual testing, the goodness of fit-of-model is acceptable if the value of the chi-square statistic is nonsignificant. A level of significance beyond $p = .25$ is recommended to use for testing a model's goodness of fit. In addition to the model as a whole, the single effects (parameters) are tested for significance as well as the whole equation including these predictors. For the single terms in the equation, usual levels of significance ($p = .05$ or $p = .01$) are to be used.

Developing Models

A series of analysis using the GSK approach (i.e., the program NONMET) has been done based on the survey data for each study separately. Starting with the saturated model, a selection of results of these analyses is reported in Tables 6.5 to 6.7. Models numbered 0 are always the saturated models and include the mean (constant), the main effects, and the interaction effects as terms (parameters). Because of limited space, only those terms that are significant or have a certain tendency toward significance are given. To compare the response models, corresponding logit models have been tested with the same terms. Chi-square values for the tested models indicating the goodness of fit (GOF) of the whole model, as well as the significance of the equations with the parameters are reported. Corresponding are two measures that indicate the variation in the target variable (criterion) and that signify the impact of the independent variables with respect to the predictors of the model. One measure (W) refers to the aggregate level, or subgroups. Because

$$W = \chi^2_{\text{equation}} / \chi^2_{\text{equation}} + \chi^2_{\text{GOF}},$$

the value is relatively high in general. The other measure (V) is a usual coefficient of association that explains variation on the individual level. This coefficient

$$V = \chi^2_{\text{equation}} / N (c - 1)$$

tends to be significantly lower than the former. Both measures are primarily useful to compare the strength of the models built based on the data of a single survey. For example, it can be concluded that the correspondence between observed and predicted values is better for proportions than for logits. In the response models the measure of variation explained is always higher, or, in other words, there is less error variation left. Comparing the saturated models for the surveys, the overall

TABLE 6.5. A selection of tested response and logit models of the Texas 1980 data.

Model no.	Response model	GOF	Equation	Logit Model	GOF	Equation
0	Saturated[a]/ S, C, I; CF, SCI,** CIF,* SIRF**	—	$\chi^2 = 448.33$ $df = 31$ $p = .000$ $V^2 = .341$	Saturated[a]/ S, C, I; CF, IR*, CIF*, SIRF**	—	$\chi^2 = 208.67$ $df = 31$ $p = .000$ $V^2 = .159$
1	S, C, I	$\chi^2 = 38.64$ $df = 28$ $(p = .086)$[b] $W^2 = .914$	$\chi^2 = 409.65$ $df = 3$ $p = .000$ $V^2 = .312$	S, C, I	$\chi^2 = 25.88$ $df = 28$ $p = .580$ $W^2 = .876$	$\chi^2 = 182.79$ $df = 3$ $p = .000$ $V^2 = .139$
2	S, C, I; CF; CIF, SIRF	$\chi^2 = 23.47$ $df = 25$ $p = .550$ $W^2 = .948$	$\chi^2 = 424.87$ $df = 6$ $p = .000$ $V^2 = .323$	S, C, I; CF*, CIF**, SIRF	$\chi^2 = 16.87$ $df = 25$ $p = .886$ $W^2 = .919$	$\chi^2 = 191.80$ $df = 6$ $p = .000$ $V^2 = .146$
3	S, C, I; C < I1 < F2	$\chi^2 = 19.14$ $df = 27$ $p = .865$ $W^2 = .957$	$\chi^2 = 429.19$ $df = 4$ $p = .000$ $V^2 = .327$	S, C, I; C < I1 < F2	$\chi^2 = 18.09$ $df = 27$ $p = .900$ $W^2 = .913$	$\chi^2 = 190.58$ $df = 4$ $p = .000$ $V^2 = .145$
4	S, C, I; C < I1 < F2, S < I2 < R1 < F1	$\chi^2 = 15.56$ $df = 26$ $p = .946$ $W^2 = .969$	$\chi^2 = 434.78$ $df = 5$ $p = .000$ $V^2 = .329$	S, C, I; C < I1 < F2, S < I2 < R1 < F1*	$\chi^2 = 15.10$ $df = 26$ $p = .956$ $W^2 = .929$	$\chi^2 = 193.75$ $df = 5$ $p = .000$ $V^2 = .147$

Note: Abbreviations of factors: sex (S), community size (C), indirect victimization (I), recent victimization (R), former victimization (F). More than one letter, e.g., CF, indicate interaction between these factors; letters with figures, e.g., F2, indicate conditional effects. W^2 is analogous to the amount of explained variation on the aggregate level; V^2 is a similar measure related to the individual level.
[a] For the saturated model only coefficients which are significant or approach significance are presented. All parameters are significant at the $p = .05$ level or below except if indicated: $*p < .10$; $**p < .20$. Mean (constant) omitted.
[b] Model does not fit well to the data; p value below acceptable level ($p = .25$).

TABLE 6.6. A selection of tested response and logit models of the Texas 1982 data.

Model no.	Response model	GOF	Equation	Logit Model	GOF	Equation
0	Saturated[a]/ S, C, I, F**; SRF**	—	$\chi^2 = 506.97$ $df = 31$ $p = .000$ $V^2 = .362$	Saturated[a]/ S, C, I, F*; SRF**	—	$\chi^2 = 222.32$ $df = 31$ $p = .000$ $V^2 = .159$
1	S, C, I	$\chi^2 = 22.28$ $df = 28$ $p = .768$ $W^2 = .956$	$\chi^2 = 484.69$ $df = 3$ $p = .000$ $V^2 = .346$	S, C, I	$\chi^2 = 17.98$ $df = 28$ $p = .927$ $W^2 = .919$	$\chi^2 = 204.34$ $df = 3$ $p = .000$ $V^2 = .146$
2	S, C, I, F	$\chi^2 = 17.35$ $df = 27$ $p = .922$ $W^2 = .966$	$\chi^2 = 489.62$ $df = 4$ $p = .000$ $V^2 = .349$	S, C, I, F**	$\chi^2 = 15.96$ $df = 27$ $p = .954$ $W^2 = .928$	$\chi^2 = 206.36$ $df = 4$ $p = .000$ $V^2 = .147$
3	S, C, I, F; SCRF**	$\chi^2 = 15.92$ $df = 26$ $p = .938$ $W^2 = .969$	$\chi^2 = 491.05$ $df = 5$ $p = .000$ $V^2 = .351$	S, C, I, F**; SCRF***	$\chi^2 = 15.47$ $df = 26$ $p = .948$ $W^2 = .930$	$\chi^2 = 206.85$ $df = 5$ $p = .000$ $V^2 = .148$
4	S, C, I, F; R < S2 < C1 < F1	$\chi^2 = 9.49$ $df = 26$ $p = .999$ $W^2 = .981$	$\chi^2 = 497.49$ $df = 5$ $p = .000$ $V^2 = .355$	S, C, I, F; R < S2 < C1 < F1*	$\chi^2 = 10.76$ $df = 26$ $p = .996$ $W^2 = .952$	$\chi^2 = 211.55$ $df = 5$ $p = .000$ $V^2 = .151$

Note: Abbreviations of factors: sex (S), community size (C), indirect victimization (I), recent victimization (R), former victimization (F). More than one letter, e.g., CF, indicate interaction between these factors; letters with figures, e.g., F2, indicate conditional effects. W^2 is analogous to the amount of explained variation on the aggregate level; V^2 is a similar measure related to the individual level.

[a] Coefficients that are significant or approach significance are presented for the saturated model only. All parameters are significant at the $p = .05$ level or below except if indicated: * $p < .10$; ** $p < .05$; * $p < .20$. Mean (constant) omitted.

TABLE 6.7. A selection of tested response and logit models of the Baden-Württemberg 1981 data.

Model no.	Response model	GOF	Equation	Logit Model	GOF	Equation
0	Saturated[a]/ S, C, I, F**; SI**; CI**; SRF*	—	$\chi^2 = 889.98$ $df = 31$ $p = .000$ $V^2 = .415$	Saturated[a]/ S, C, I, F**; $CI,$**; SRF	—	$\chi^2 = 442.64$ $df = 31$ $p = .000$ $V^2 = .207$
1	S, C, I	$\chi^2 = 45.31$ $df = 28$ $(p = .021)$[b] $W^2 = .949$	$\chi^2 = 841.66$ $df = 3$ $p = .000$ $V^2 = .394$	S, C, I	$\chi^2 = 30.56$ $df = 28$ $p = .337$ $W^2 = .931$	$\chi^2 = 412.08$ $df = 3$ $p = .000$ $V^2 = .193$
2	S, C, I, F	$\chi^2 = 39.95$ $df = 27$ $(p = .052)$[b] $W^2 = .955$	$\chi^2 = 847.02$ $df = 4$ $p = .000$ $V^2 = .397$	S, C, I, F	$\chi^2 = 26.64$ $df = 27$ $p = .483$ $W^2 = .940$	$\chi^2 = 415.99$ $df = 4$ $p = .000$ $V^2 = .195$
3	S, C, I, F; $SCI,$ SRF	$\chi^2 = 17.59$ $df = 25$ $p = .859$ $W^2 = .980$	$\chi^2 = 869.38$ $df = 6$ $p = .000$ $V^2 = .407$	S, C, I, F*; $SCI,$* SRF	$\chi^2 = 16.03$ $df = 25$ $p = .914$ $W^2 = .964$	$\chi^2 = 426.60$ $df = 6$ $p = .000$ $V^2 = .200$
4	S, C, I, F; $S < R1 < F2,$ $C < S1 < I1$	$\chi^2 = 15.72$ $df = 25$ $p = .923$ $W^2 = .982$	$\chi^2 = 871.26$ $df = 6$ $p = .000$ $V^2 = .408$	S, C, I, F; $S < R1 < F2,$ $C < S1 < I1$	$\chi^2 = 14.22$ $df = 25$ $p = .958$ $W^2 = .968$	$\chi^2 = 428.42$ $df = 6$ $p = .000$ $V^2 = .201$
5	S, C, I; $F < S1 < R1,$ $I < S1 < C1$	$\chi^2 = 13.37$ $df = 26$ $p = .982$ $W^2 = .985$	$\chi^2 = 873.71$ $df = 5$ $p = .000$ $V^2 = .409$	S, C, I; $F < S1 < R1,$ $I < S1 < C1$	$\chi^2 = 13.08$ $df = 26$ $p = .983$ $W^2 = .970$	$\chi^2 = 429.54$ $df = 5$ $p = .000$ $V^2 = .201$

Note: Abbreviations of factors: sex (S), community size (C), indirect victimization (I), recent victimization (I), former victimization (F). More than one letter, e.g., CF, indicates interaction between these factors; letters with figures, e.g., $F2$, indicate conditional effects. W^2 is analogous to the amount of explained variation on the aggregate level; V^2 is a similar measure related to the individual level. All parameters are significant at the $p = .05$ level or below except if indicated: *$p < .10$; **$p < .20$. Mean (constant) omitted.

[a] For the saturated model only coefficients that are significant or approach significance are presented.

[b] Model does not fit well to the data; p value below acceptable level ($p = .25$).

impact of the whole set of independent variables measured by the coefficient of association V is rather high for the response models, quite similar in strength for the Texas surveys, and highest for the Baden-Württemberg study. Looking at the independent variables, in all the surveys the main effects of sex, community size, and indirect victimization were significant, as has been expected, whereas the main effects for recent victimization were nonsignificant. This finding also holds true for the logit models. Only one other term, the interaction of community size and former victimization, was significant and that only for the Texas 1980 survey. Some tendency toward significance has been found for other terms, which are reported in Tables 6.5 to 6.7 and will not be discussed further.

In the next step, main models, including the three strongest predictors, have been tested showing an overall GOF for the logit models with a significant equation as well as significant single terms. Conversely, only the response model for the 1982 Texas data fitted well, whereas both other models provided a poor fit, indicating that too much error variation was unexplained. Adding the two measures of direct victimization as main effects to the models yielded a significant single term for former victimization that could be entered to the equation for the 1982 Texas and the Baden-Württemberg data. The explained variation did not increase largely, however, so the GOF for the Baden-Württemberg model remained poor. Testing the single effect of recent victimization as an additional main effect was unsuccessful, indicating that this variable did not contribute to the prediction.

Without describing all of the individual steps that led to the final models, we can summarize: A sequential forward-and-backward selection procedure to include and eliminate different interaction terms was established and preliminary models have been found for each survey including a constant (mean), main effects, and interaction terms. Those models were quite sufficient and parsimonious because they include only a small number of predictors, for example, 6 terms in the Baden-Württemberg model compared to 32 in the saturated model at the beginning, which provided a good fit. Even when comparing the response model to the logit model, the result was quite satisfactory.

Finally, a last step was taken in specifying interaction terms as nested (conditional) effects (i.e., specifying an effect within a level of another term). This is a somewhat difficult procedure, especially if higher-order interaction terms have to be specified. No former solution to this problem has been suggested, theoretical guidelines have to be found (for example, we may have found a significant interaction effect of sex and direct victimization [SR] on fear of crime; further we may state that according to previous research the impact of victimization is predominant for women compared to men; therefore, we look for the effect of victimization within the group of women and specify the nested effect $R S_1$). With higher-order interaction effects given, several possible solutions (i.e., specifications) may be found that require theoretical reasoning (e.g., as will be seen, for the Baden-Württemberg data two alternative and convincing models have been tested that are both quite satisfactory; see model 3 as starting point and model 4 and 5 with alternative specifications in Table 6.7).

The "Best" Models

The result of the analysis is summarized in Table 6.8, which gives the coefficients for the final (best) models. Table 6.8 displays response models as well as corresponding logit models for each survey. Given are the parameters (predictors) included in the models, their effect strength, and the significance of the coefficients. Table 6.9 displays the design matrices for the fitted best models and reveals that a structural difference between the models is attributable to the interaction effects but not to the main effects. This is amplified by the (rather unusual condensed (nested) version of the) matrices given in Table 6.9. In addition, Table 6.10 reports the proportion and logit observed and predicted under the best models described in Table 6.8. Confronting observed and predicted values (in Table 6.10) clarifies the point that larger error is found in those subgroups

TABLE 6.8. Coefficients for the "best models."

Parameter	Response model		Logit model	
	b	p	b	p
Texas 1980				
1 Mean	0.5510	0.0000	0.2066	0.0036
2 S	0.1863	0.0000	0.7683	0.0000
3 C	−0.0797	0.0000	−0.3670	0.0000
4 I	−0.0461	0.0003	−0.2326	0.0011
5 $C < I1 < F2$	−0.1338	0.0000	−0.5676	0.0052
6 $S < I2 < R1 < F1$	−0.0657	0.0483	−0.2864	0.0838
Texas 1982				
1 Mean	0.5440	0.0000	0.2187	0.0027
2 S	0.1923	0.0000	0.8928	0.0000
3 C	−0.1022	0.0000	−0.5104	0.0000
4 I	−0.0396	0.0047	−0.2041	0.0041
5 F	−0.0319	0.0114	−0.1576	0.0290
6 $R < S2 < C1 < F1$	0.1076	0.0050	0.5801	0.0226
Baden-Württemberg 1981				
1 Mean	0.4746	0.0000	−0.1236	0.0274
2 S	0.2389	0.0000	1.0900	0.0000
3 C	−0.0736	0.0000	−0.3261	0.0000
4 I	−0.0275	0.0087	−0.2352	0.0000
5 $F < S1 < R1$	−0.0605	0.0002	−0.2879	0.0012
6 $I < S1 < C1$	−0.0785	0.0002	−0.2615	0.0185

Note: Independent variables: sex (S), community size (C), indirect (vicarious) victimization (I), recent (R) and former (F) (direct) victimization; cf. text for explanation of nested effects.

TABLE 6.9. Design matrices for fitted "best models."

$Xb =$

	1 MEAN	2 S	3 C	4 I	5a C < I1 < F2	6a S < I2 < R1 < F1	5b F	6b R < S2 < C1 < F1	5c F < S1 < R1	6c I < S1 < C1	
	1.00	1.00	1.00	1.00	0.00	0.00	1.00	0.00	1.00	1.00	$b0$
	1.00	1.00	1.00	1.00	1.00	0.00	-1.00	0.00	-1.00	1.00	$b1$
	1.00	1.00	1.00	1.00	0.00	0.00	-1.00	0.00	0.00	1.00	$b2$
	1.00	1.00	1.00	-1.00	1.00	0.00	-1.00	0.00	0.00	1.00	$b3$
	1.00	1.00	1.00	-1.00	0.00	1.00	1.00	0.00	1.00	-1.00	$b4$
	1.00	1.00	1.00	-1.00	0.00	0.00	-1.00	0.00	-1.00	-1.00	$b5$
	1.00	1.00	1.00	-1.00	0.00	0.00	-1.00	0.00	0.00	-1.00	
	1.00	1.00	1.00	1.00	0.00	0.00	1.00	0.00	0.00	-1.00	
	1.00	1.00	-1.00	1.00	-1.00	0.00	-1.00	0.00	1.00	0.00	
	1.00	1.00	-1.00	1.00	0.00	0.00	1.00	0.00	-1.00	0.00	
	1.00	1.00	-1.00	1.00	-1.00	0.00	1.00	0.00	0.00	0.00	
	1.00	1.00	-1.00	1.00	0.00	0.00	-1.00	0.00	0.00	0.00	
	1.00	1.00	-1.00	-1.00	0.00	1.00	1.00	0.00	1.00	0.00	
	1.00	1.00	-1.00	-1.00	0.00	0.00	-1.00	0.00	-1.00	0.00	
	1.00	1.00	-1.00	-1.00	0.00	0.00	-1.00	1.00	0.00	0.00	
	1.00	1.00	-1.00	-1.00	0.00	0.00	1.00	0.00	0.00	0.00	
	1.00	-1.00	1.00	1.00	1.00	0.00	1.00	-1.00	0.00	0.00	
	1.00	-1.00	1.00	1.00	0.00	0.00	-1.00	0.00	0.00	0.00	
	1.00	-1.00	1.00	1.00	1.00	1.00	-1.00	1.00	0.00	0.00	
	1.00	-1.00	1.00	1.00	0.00	0.00	1.00	0.00	0.00	0.00	
	1.00	-1.00	1.00	-1.00	0.00	1.00	-1.00	-1.00	0.00	0.00	
	1.00	-1.00	1.00	-1.00	0.00	0.00	1.00	0.00	0.00	0.00	
	1.00	-1.00	1.00	-1.00	0.00	0.00	1.00	0.00	0.00	0.00	
	1.00	-1.00	1.00	-1.00	0.00	0.00	-1.00	0.00	0.00	0.00	
	1.00	-1.00	-1.00	1.00	-1.00	-1.00	1.00	0.00	0.00	0.00	
	1.00	-1.00	-1.00	1.00	0.00	0.00	-1.00	0.00	0.00	0.00	
	1.00	-1.00	-1.00	1.00	-1.00	0.00	-1.00	0.00	0.00	0.00	
	1.00	-1.00	-1.00	1.00	0.00	0.00	1.00	0.00	0.00	0.00	
	1.00	-1.00	-1.00	-1.00	0.00	0.00	1.00	0.00	0.00	0.00	
	1.00	-1.00	-1.00	-1.00	0.00	0.00	-1.00	0.00	0.00	0.00	
	1.00	-1.00	-1.00	-1.00	0.00	-1.00	-1.00	0.00	0.00	0.00	
	1.00	-1.00	-1.00	-1.00	0.00	0.00	1.00	0.00	0.00	0.00	

Note: Columns 5 and 6 have to be substituted, respectively, to get the adequate matrix; compare Table 6.8 for abbreviations.
[a] Texas 1980 (Model = S, C, I, $C < I1 < F2$, $S < I2 < R1 < F1$). [b] Texas 1982 (Model = S, C, I, F, $R < S2 < C1 < F1$).
[c] Baden-Württemberg 1981 (Model = S, C, I, $F < S1 < R1$, $I < S1 < C1$).

TABLE 6.10. Proportions and logits observed and predicted by "best models."

SP	Texas 1980					Texas 1982					Baden-Württemberg 1981				
	P_o	P_p	L_o	L_p	N	P_o	P_p	L_o	L_p	N	P_o	P_p	L_o	L_p	N
1	.596	.612	0.39	0.42	57	.533	.563	0.13	0.24	60	.469	.474	−0.12	−0.15	277
2	.345	.478	−0.64	−0.15	29	.571	.626	0.29	0.55	28	.555	.595	0.20	0.42	60
3	.571	.612	0.29	0.42	7	.750	.563	1.10	0.24	4	.579	.534	0.32	0.13	19
4	.500	.478	0.00	−0.15	4	.429	.626	−0.29	0.55	7	.545	.534	0.18	0.13	11
5	.672	.638	0.72	0.62	64	.703	.642	0.86	0.65	74	.646	.685	0.60	0.72	147
6	.699	.704	0.84	0.91	73	.697	.706	0.83	0.96	66	.839	.806	1.65	1.29	62
7	.762	.704	1.16	0.91	21	.643	.642	0.59	0.65	14	.760	.746	1.15	1.00	25
8	.673	.704	0.72	0.91	55	.706	.706	0.88	0.96	68	.727	.746	0.98	1.00	33
9	.818	.771	1.50	1.17	44	.781	.767	1.27	1.26	32	.743	.699	1.06	0.91	144
10	.935	.905	2.67	1.75	31	.857	.831	1.79	1.58	21	.827	.802	1.56	1.48	52
11	.600	.771	0.41	1.17	5	.714	.767	0.92	1.26	7	.667	.760	0.69	1.19	12
12	.889	.905	2.08	1.75	9	.846	.831	1.70	1.58	13	.786	.760	1.30	1.19	14
13	.750	.797	1.10	1.37	68	.841	.846	1.67	1.67	63	.756	.754	1.13	1.23	82
14	.880	.863	1.99	1.66	108	.879	.910	1.98	1.98	107	.870	.875	1.90	1.80	54
15	.833	.863	1.61	1.66	18	.833	.846	1.61	1.67	18	.840	.815	1.66	1.52	25
16	.854	.863	1.76	1.66	82	.926	.910	2.52	1.98	108	.756	.815	1.13	1.52	41
17	.208	.239	−1.34	−1.22	48	.293	.285	−0.88	−0.97	58	.146	.135	−1.77	−1.76	254
18	.225	.105	−1.24	−1.79	40	.273	.241	−0.98	−1.23	33	.115	.135	−2.04	−1.76	61
19	.333	.239	−0.69	−1.22	6	.067	.106	−2.64	−2.13	7	.103	.135	−2.16	−1.76	29
20	.077	.105	−2.48	−1.79	13	.250	.241	−1.10	−1.23	4	.200	.135	−1.39	−1.76	20
21	.386	.397	−0.46	−0.45	44	.326	.365	−0.73	−0.56	46	.184	.190	−1.49	−1.44	103
22	.303	.331	−0.83	−0.74	76	.298	.321	−0.86	−0.82	94	.188	.190	−1.47	−1.44	80
23	.307	.331	−0.81	−0.74	13	.100	.150	−2.20	−1.71	10	.207	.190	−1.34	−1.44	29
24	.371	.331	−0.53	−0.74	70	.358	.321	−0.58	−0.82	81	.237	.190	−1.17	−1.44	59
25	.394	.398	−0.43	−0.47	33	.405	.382	−0.38	−0.53	37	.222	.282	−1.25	−0.98	135
26	.484	.532	−0.06	0.10	31	.464	.446	−0.14	−0.21	28	.314	.282	−0.78	−0.98	51
27	.167	.398	−1.61	−0.47	6	.400	.382	−0.39	−0.53	5	.300	.282	−0.85	−0.98	10
28	.400	.532	−0.41	0.10	5	.467	.446	−0.13	−0.21	15	.389	.282	−0.45	−0.98	18
29	.515	.556	0.06	0.30	33	.442	.461	−0.23	−0.12	43	.410	.337	−0.36	−0.65	61
30	.463	.491	−0.15	0.01	95	.491	.526	−0.04	0.19	106	.290	.337	−0.90	−0.65	69
31	.550	.491	0.20	0.01	20	.500	.462	0.00	−0.12	14	.345	.337	−0.64	−0.65	29
32	.528	.491	0.11	0.01	106	.562	.526	0.25	0.19	130	.348	.337	−0.63	−0.65	69

Note: Proportions observed (P_o) and predicted (P_p), logits observed (L_o), and predicted (L_p), number of cases per subpopulation (N).

where few cases are concentrated. This is dependent on the weighting procedure of the program, which weights each observation by the inverse of its binomial-based variance. The smaller the number of cases on which a proportion or logit is calculated, the larger is its variance.

Discussion

How are the results displayed in Table 6.8 to be intepreted? First, the average fear response (i.e., the weighted mean over all subgroups [grand mean]) in Texas is higher compared to Baden-Württemberg. That result is not surprising if one takes into account the higher crime rate, in particular violent offenses, according to official statistics and survey data alike. For both surveys in Texas the mean is quite similar, which is the same result as on the bivariate level of analysis. The means differ from the proportions reported in Table 6.1 because the average is weighted while controlling for other factors in the models. The same is true of the other main effects explained below, which are measures of the direct impact of variables relative to the model under consideration and which are therefore within each model guarded against spurious correlation through control of the other predictors. Comparability regarding significance in all three surveys is the relevance of the single (main) factors in the models. Gender (S) is the most important factor in all tested models. Its effect is similarly strong in the Texas surveys and a little bit stronger in the German study. The importance of gender as the most influential factor explaining fear-to-crime variation in the data is congruent with prior research on that issue. Analogous to the strongest effect are the relations of the strength of the effects of the remaining variables: Again in both countries, community size (C) is the second strong main effect followed by indirect victimization (I). The similarity of the results in both countries goes even further: With the exception of the 1982 Texas Study the data show no importance of direct recent victimization (R) or former direct victimization (F) as single (main) factors of explanation in the final models, for either response models or for the logit models. On the other hand, all models show influence of recent and former victimization on fear of crime in their interaction terms.

Because one is free to choose between two clear and vivid versions of interpretation, the coefficients may be interpreted as follows: One is based on the proportions, the other is a kind of probabilistic view of the results. For reasons of explanation we discuss both methods for interpreting the results. In doing so, we restrict ourselves to the demonstration of only some of the main effects in the 1982 Texas and the Baden-Württemberg data.

In the 1982 Texas sample, the proportion admitting fear of crime within the group of women ($S < 1$) is .19 above the (weighted) average for all subgroups (grand mean = .54). Stated otherwise (i.e., the effect of gender interpreted by contrasting men and women), the effect of gender on the proportion admitting fear among women ($S < 1$) is twice ($2 \times .19 = .38$) that of males ($S < 2$). In total, the proportion of women admitting fear in the Texas sample is .54 (mean) plus .19 (gender effect), which equals .73, whereas the corresponding proportion of men admitting fear is .35, that is, half the size of women being fearful. Similarly, the other main effects also must be interpreted in an additive way. Based on the main effects, the most fearful group results if the effects of gender (S), community size (C), indirect victimization (I), and former direct victimization (F) for the 1982 Texas data are added: For the group of women ($S < 1$) who live in larger cities ($C < 2$) and who know a crime victim in the last year ($I < 2$) and, in addition, who have been a former victim of crime ($F < 2$), the proportion admitting fear is .90 (as can be readily calculated by adding the single main effects to the mean: $.54 + .19 \ [S] + .10 \ [C] + .04 \ [I] + .03 \ [F] = .90$).

Turning to the Baden-Württemberg data, we can see that being a female raises the probability of admitting fear of crime by .24 above the average for all subgroups of .47 (grand mean), which totals a probability of .71. That is a measure close to that of the 1982 Texas data calculated above (.73). Stating the effect of gender otherwise: Being a female rather than a male raises the probability of admitting fear by twice .24, which equals .48. Accordingly, the probability for males admitting fear is .23 (.24 with the nonrounded coefficients), which is somewhat below the corresponding value for Texas males (.35).

Noteworthy, the gender effect on fear of crime over all subgroups seems to be somewhat stronger in Germany compared to the United States. The main effects of community size are about two to three times smaller than the gender effect. The relationships between community size and indirect victimization are similar in size, the community effect being two to three times greater than that of vicarious victimization.

Contrary to the main effects mentioned above, the interaction terms are somewhat more difficult to interpret, especially if one is interested in solving that problem by trying to specify so-called conditional effects. Table 6.8 shows the suggested solutions. The interactions included in the equations have been specified as nested effects, which are all significant at the 5% level or better except for parameter 6 in the logit model of the 1980 Texas data, which shows only a tendency toward significance by narrowly missing the 5% level. Interaction terms are difficult to interpret because often there are several possible and acceptable solutions, especially when higher-order interactions are included. This highlights the point that model fitting makes necessary theoretical assumptions and decisions on the relationships of variables. Only if this has been achieved can a sound and convincing specification of interaction effects be obtained. Now, what is the interpretation of the interactions and what can be concluded from the conditional effects? Because the specifications of interaction effects are different for each of the surveys, we have to look on the results separately.

In the 1980 Texas response model, the parameter 6 ($C < I1 < F2$) may be interpreted as follows: In addition to the general (main) effect of community size (C) on fear of crime, there is a special (conditional) effect of community size for that group, which is characterized by former (direct) victimization experience ($F2$) and not knowing another victim in the past year ($I1$). This conditional effect shows the same direction as the main effect but is even stronger ($-.08$ vs. $-.13$). So for those living in large cities ($C2$), the proportion admitting fear is $-.08$ higher than the average fear for all subgroups ($-.55$) and again another $-.13$ higher if those have former direct victimization experience ($F2$) and do not know another victim of the past year ($I1$). The second and weaker interaction term ($S < I2 < R1 < F1$) shows the effect of gender (S) in that group with no former ($F1$) and no recent ($R1$) direct victimization experiences, but recent indirect ($I2$) victimization (knowing another crime victim in the past year). Interestingly, the specified nested effect of sex shows a direction different from the main effect. On the other side, it is smaller and narrowly significant, which should be interpreted carefully. The result could be interpreted as follows: Whereas the mean fear response ($.55$) is raised for women (S) by $.19$, the score for women with no direct but indirect victimization is diminished at the same time by $.07$ so that the net increase of those later females is $.12$. The opposite is the case for males: Whereas mean fear for men is $.19$ below the general mean ($.55$), it is raised for men with no direct but indirect victimization experience by $.07$. How could this different influence of gender be explained? First, one should remember that the effect is close to the level of significance in the response model and misses in the logit model. If an interpretation is approached anyway, two different hypotheses could be thought of: (1). Women use information and experience of direct and indirect victimization in a distinct way from men, thereby they exert a different control on their emotions (fear). (2) Men have a much higher victimization rate than women; therefore there is a greater chance that if someone knows a victim, this person is a man. In addition, men are more often victims of fear-provoking crimes as violent offenses or victimizations by strangers. Hence, to know another victim of crime might, through identification processes, increase the risk perspective of men contrary to that of women. Additionally, both factors could work together in that special subpopulation.

Now let us change over to the second model on Texas survey data. As mentioned earlier, the mean and the main effects are quite similar to that for the model on the earlier data. On the other side, as a comparison of Tables 6.5 and 6.6 shows, a parsimonious model with the main effects of sex, community size, and indirect victimization was rather well fitting to the 1982 Texas data (cf. model 1 in Table 6.6) contrary to the same model of the 1980 Texas data (cf. model 1 in Table 6.5). In addition to the common three main factors, there is a single main effect of former victimization (F) in the "best model" for the 1982 Texas data (cf. Table 6.8). The effect is rather weak and significant only on the 5% level. Of more interest is the third-order interaction $(R < S2 < C1 < F1)$, which is specified as nested effect. It indicates the effect of recent victimization (R) in the group of men $(S2)$ with no former direct victimization $(F1)$ and no recent indirect victimization $(C1)$. In that group recent victims have a lower probability (.11) of giving a fear response, whereas the nonvictimized have a greater tendency to indicate fear of crime. The group described by this conditional effect should be labeled as a special one because, as males, they have no former victimization mentioned in the survey and in addition they do not know any other recent crime victim.

Finally, in the Baden-Württemberg model, again a model with five factors has emerged showing the well-known triad of main effects of gender, community size, and indirect victimization. The signs of these effects are in the same direction as in the Texas models and even the strength of the effects is quite similar. Perhaps gender differences seem to be a bit stronger in Germany compared to the American situation, but differences are minor in total. How may these highly significant interactions be interpreted? Firstly, there is an effect $(F < S1 < R1)$ of those women $(S1)$ with no recent victimization $(R1)$. These women have a higher fear-level (.06) if they have prior victimization experience, whereas fear is diminished (by .06) if they have never been victimized. Secondly, we found an effect $(I < S1 < C1)$ of indirect victimization (I) also in the female group $(S1)$ coming from smaller communities $(C1)$. For women from smaller cities, knowing another victim increases the possibility of admitting fear not only by .03 (main effect) but to an additional degree that is nearly three times as high (.08), so that the total effect of vicarious victimization in this group is .11.

Let us summarize the main results and the interpretation of the models discussed: In the 1980 Texas data, being a woman rather than a man raised the probability of agreeing to fear of walking at night within 1 mile from her home by .37 (twice the effect of gender) controlling for community size and direct and indirect victimization. In the 1982 Texas study, the corresponding probability was .38 and in Baden-Württemberg, .49. Living in a larger city rather than a smaller one increased the probability of agreeing to the fear question by .16 in the 1980 Texas data and by .20 two years later. For Baden-Württemberg the increment was .15. Knowing a victim augmented the fear level by .09 in the 1980 Texas survey and .08 in the 1982 Texas data. The increase in Baden-Württemberg for that variable was .06.

Besides these main effects, several interaction terms have been modelled that are specified as conditional effects. In addition a single main effect has emerged for the 1982 Texas survey. In the 1980 Texas data, the probability of agreeing to the fear question was raised by a large .26 for respondents with former direct victimization experience and no recent indirect victimization if they live in a large city rather than a smaller one. In this group, the effect added to the general effect of community size, making the urban effect stronger than the gender effect. An extra gender effect (with a different influence) was found for respondents with no prior direct victimization experience but who know other recent victims. For women in this group the probability of agreeing to the fear item was diminished by .13 compared to men—this shows a different direction than the common (main) gender effect.

In addition to three main effects already mentioned for the 1982 Texas study, former victimization proved to be a main factor. Fear increased by .06 for those who have been victims longer ago, as compared to those with no earlier victimization experience. A strong interaction effect of recent victimization was found for men with no former victimization experience and who did not know another victim. Surprisingly, the influence took the opposite direction than expected. Recent victims in this group had a lower probability of admitting fear of .21 compared to the nonvictims.

Finally for the Baden-Württemberg data two interactions have been specified that met our expectations. Among women who have not been victims recently, former victimization experience increased the proportion responding fearfully by .12 compared to nonvictims. Another increase of the probability by .15 to agree to the fear question was found for women living in smaller cities, if they knew another recent crime victim. For this group, the effect of indirect victimization totalled .21 and was the second strongest after the single (main) gender effect.

Conclusions

Several findings are central and noteworthy:

Based on data from predesigned international comparative victim surveys, the variables used as predictors of fear of crime are quite similar in structure and effect within the models examined here. The relative size and order of strength of the relevant independent variables are similar in the three surveys for the two nations. Consequently, because the same factors are operative in predicting fear of crime in both nations, this gives some support to the supposition of a more general process of the societal production of fear of crime, at least in the nations under discussion.

Single main effects of direct recent and former victimization experiences on fear of crime appear to have little or no influence on the fear of victimization. In contrast, indirect (vicarious) victimization contributes significantly to the prediction of fear of crime within all three surveys. This holds true with the operationalization of fear of crime undertaken in this study. The kind of indicator used as a dependent variable is relevant regarding the decomposition of effects of the independent variables and must be kept in mind when interpreting the results. Additionally, because global victimization measures (i.e., no differentiation between property crime and crimes of violence or according to seriousness of offenses experienced) have been used, results may differ to some degree if the indicators of victimization are modified. A preliminary test of this showed only small changes and differences; thus it seems that the main results represent a true tendency.

By analyzing interactions new insights into the complex relationships of variables have been found that are of some interest. Regarding the central issue discussed here (i.e., the relation of victimization to fear of crime), interesting relationships of remarkable strength emerge if interaction terms, including victimization as a component, are specified as nested effects. Accordingly, the relevance of victimization experiences for the origin and rise of fear of crime is less evident on the general level (i.e., over all subgroups averaged), but differ within subgroups defined by specific respondent characteristics.

Regarding the other independent variables, some of the main effects are outweighed in strength by corresponding interaction effects. In some instances, the variable interaction effect exhibited a different direction from that of the main effect.

This knowledge, gained by analyzing variable interaction, should be of some significance for developing a general theory on fear of crime as well as relevant for more practical reasoning with policy implications, especially because the latter makes necessary knowledge of the influences acting on fear of crime as a prerequisite to fighting the fear of crime.

Finally, the models examined should be viewed as rather preliminary efforts that need to be improved and developed by further research in differentiating and specifying other aspects of possible causation of fear of crime. (The restriction and limitation of the models tested have been necessary, given the method of analysis and the design of the study.)

We believe that investigating models on an international comparative level moves toward generalization, and represents a step in the right direction.

Acknowledgments. This is a revised version of a paper presented at the 10th International Congress on Criminology, Hamburg/FRG, September 1988. The author is grateful to Raymond H.C. Teske, Criminal Justice Center, Sam Houston State University, Huntsville, Texas, who provided data from the Texas Crime Polls. His support and assistance has been greatly appreciated during the project.

Allan L. McCutcheon was helpful with 'native speaker" advice to the translation.

References

Ali, B. (1986). Methodological problems in international criminal justice research. *International Journal of Comparative and Applied Criminal Justice, 10*, 163–176.
Arnold, H. (1988a). *Fear of crime: An empirical analysis of a concept and its*

structural components. Unpublished manuscript, Max-Planck-Institut für Ausländisches und internationales Strafrecht, Freiburg.

Arnold, H. (1988b). *Global and violent criminal victimization and their effects on fear of crime*: A test of broad vs. specific indicators in a fear model. Unpublished manuscript, Max-Planck-Institut für Ausländisches und internationales Strafrecht, Freiburg.

Arnold, H. (1986). Kriminelle Viktimisierung und ihre Korrelate. Ergebnisse international vergleichender Opferbefragungen. *Zeitschrift für die gesamte Strafrechtswissenschaft, 98*, 1014–1058.

Arnold, H. (1984). Verbrechensfurcht und/oder Furcht vor Viktimisierung— Folgen von Viktimisierung? In H.J. Albrecht, & U. Sieber (Eds.), *Zwanzig Jahre Südwestdeutsche Kriminologische Kolloquien.* (pp. 185–236). Freiburg: Max-Planck-Institut für Ausländisches und Internationales Strafrecht.

Arnold, H., & Korinek, L. (1985). Kriminalitätsbelastung in der Bundesrepublik Deutschland und Ungarn: Ergebnisse einer international vergleichenden Opferbefragung. In A. Böhm, H. Eckert, W. Feuerhelm, F. Hamburger, & G. Sander (Eds.), *Kriminologie in sozialistischen Ländern* (pp. 65–136). Bochum: Brockmeyer.

Arnold, H., & Teske, R.H.C., Jr. (1988). Factors related to fear of crime. A comparison of the Federal Republic of Germany and the United States. In G. Kaiser, & I. Geissler (Eds.), *Crime and criminal justice* pp. 355–384. Criminological research in the 2nd decade at the Max Planck Institute in Freiburg: Max-Planck-Institut für Ausländisches und Internationales Strafrecht.

Arnold, H., Teske, R.H.C. & Korinek, L. (1988). Viktimisierung, Verbrechensfurcht und Einstellungen zur Sozialkontrolle in West und Ost. Ergebnisse vergleichender Opferbefragungen in der Bundesrepublik Deutschland, den Vereinigten Staaten und Ungarn, pp. 909–942 in G. Kaiser, H. Kury & H.-J. Albrecht (Eds.), *Kriminologische Forschung in den 80er Jahren. Projektberichte aus der Bundesrepublik Deutschland.* Freiburg: Max-Planck-Institut für Ausländisches und Internationales Strafrecht.

Arzt, G. (1979). Responses to the growth of crime in the United States and West Germany. *Cornell International Law Journal, 12*, 43–64.

Arzt, G. (1976). *Der Ruf nach Recht und Ordnung. Ursachen und Folgen der Kriminalitätsfurcht in den USA und in Deutschland.* Tübingen: Mohr.

Baker, M.H., Nienstedt, R.S., & McCleary, E.R. (1983). The impact of crime wave: Perceptions, fear and confidence in the police. *Law and Society Review, 17*, 319–335.

Baumer, T.L. (1985). Testing a general model of fear of crime: Data from a national sample. *Journal of Research in Crime and Delinquency, 22*, 239–255.

Baumer, T.L. (1978). Research on fear of crime in the United States. *Victimology, 3*, 254–264.

Baumer, T.L., & Rosenbaum, T. (1981). *Measuring fear of crime: Perceptual, affective and behavioral dimensions.* Unpublished manuscript, Westinghouse Evaluation Institute, Evanston, IL.

Beirne, P. (1983). Generalization and its discontents: The comparative study of crime. In I.L. Barak-Glantz & E.H. Johnson (Eds.), *Comparative criminology* (pp. 19–38). Beverly Hills, CA.: Sage.

Biderman, A., Johnson, L.A., McIntyre, J., & Weir, A.W. (1967). *Report on a pilot study in the district of Columbia on victimization and attitudes toward law enforcement* (President's Commission on Law Enforcement and Administration of Justice, Field Surveys No. 1). Washington, DC: US Government Printing Office.

Block, R. (Ed.) (1984). *Victimization and fear of crime: World perspectives.* Washington, DC: US Department of Justice, Bureau of Justice Statistics.

Block, R. (1987). A comparison of victimization, crime assessment, and fear of crime in England/Wales, the Netherlands, Scotland, and the United States. Council of Europe, Committee on Environment and Town Planning, Barcelona, Spain, November 18, 1987.

Block, R. (1989). Violence, culture, and demography: A preliminary analysis of the demography of assault prevalence in four national crime surveys. Law & Society Association, Madison, WI, June 11, 1989.

Box, S., Hale, C., & Andrews, G. (1988). Explaining fear of crime. *British Journal of Criminology, 28,* 340–356.

Brantingham, P.J., Brantingham, P.L., & Butcher, D. (1986). Perceived and actual crime risks. In R.M. Figlio, S. Hakim, & G.F. Rengert (Eds.), *Metropolitan crime patterns* (pp. 139–159). Monsey, NY: Criminal Justice Press.

Clinard, M.B. (1978). Comparative crime victimization surveys: Some problems and results. *International Journal of Criminology and Penology, 6,* 221–231.

Dillman, D.A. (1978). *Mail and telephone surveys. The total design method.* New York: Wiley.

DuBow, F., McCabe, E., & Kaplan, G. (1979). *Reactions to crime: A critical review of the literature.* Washington, DC: US Government Printing Office.

Ennis, P.H. (1967). *Criminal victimization in the United States: A report of a national survey* (President's Commission on Law Enforcement and Administration of Justice, Field Surveys II.) Washington, DC: US Government Printing Office.

Erdos, P.L. (1983). *Professional mail surveys.* Malabar, FL: Krieger.

Garofalo, J. (1981). The fear of crime: Causes and consequences. *Journal of Criminal Law and Criminology, 72,* 839–857.

Garofalo, J. (1979). Victimization and the fear of crime. *Journal of Research in Crime and Delinquency, 16,* 80–97.

Gefeller, I. & Trudewind, C. (1978). Bedrohtheitsgefühl: Erfassung, Verteilung und Beziehungen zu ökologischen Variablen und Persön lichkeitsvariablen. In H.-D. Schwind, W. Ahlborn, & R. Weiss (Eds.), *Empirische Kriminalgeographie* (pp. 309–337). Wiesbaden: Bundeskriminalamt.

Gibbs, J.J., Coyle, E., & Hanrahan, K.J. (1987). *Fear of crime: A concept in need of clarification.* Unpublished manuscript, School of Criminal Justice, Rutgers University, New Brunswick, NJ.

Gomme, I.A. (1988). The role of experience in the production of fear of crime: A test of a causal model. *Canadian Journal of Criminology 30,* 67–76.

Greenberg, S.W. (1986). Fear and its relationship to crime, neighborhood deterioration, and informal social control. In J.M. Byrne & R.J. Sampson (Eds.), *The social ecology of crime* (pp. 47–63). New York: Springer.

Grizzle, J.E., Starmer, C.F., & Koch, G.G. (1969). Analysis of categorial data by linear model. *Biometrics, 25,* 489–504.

Kellens, G. (1986). The criminologist in the "fear of crime" struggle. In K. Miyazawa & M. Ohya (Eds.), *Victimology in comparative perspective* (pp. 232.–235). Tokyo: Seibundo.

Kerner, H.-J. (1986). Verbrechensfurcht und Viktimisierung. In W.T. Haesler (Ed.), *Viktimologie* (pp. 131–159). Grüsch: Rüegger.

Kerner, H.-J. (1980). *Kriminalitätseinschätzung und Innere Sicherheit. Eine Untersuchung über die Beurteilung der Sicherheitslage und über das Sicherheitsgefühl in der Bundesrepublik Deutschland, mit vergleichenden Betrachtungen zur Situation im Ausland.* Wiesbaden: Bundeskriminalamt.

Kerner, H.-J. (1978). Fear of crime and attitudes towards crime. Comparative criminological reflections. *Annales internationales de criminologie, 17,* 83–99.

Kirchhoff, G.F., & Kirchhoff, C. (1984). Victimological research in Germany—Victim surveys and research on sexual victimization. In R. Block (Ed.), *Victimization and fear of crime: World perspectives* (pp. 57–74). Washington, DC: US Department of Justice, Bureau of Justice Statistics.

Klein, M.W. (1988). Epiloque: Workshop discussion and future directions, pp. 425–4438 in M.W. Klein (Ed.): *Cross-national research in self-reported crime and delinquency.* Dordrecht: Kluwer.

Krahn, H., & Kennedy, L.W. (1985). Producing personal safety: The effects of crime rates, police force size, and fear of crime. *Criminology, 23,* 697–710.

Krebs, D. & Schuessler, K.F. (1987). *Soziale Empfindungen. Ein interkultureller Skalenvergleich bei Deutschen und Amerikanern.* Frankfurt: Campus.

Kritzer, H.M. (1986). Using categorial regression to analyze multivariate contingency tables. In W.D. Berry & M.S. Lewis-Beck (Eds.), *New tools for social scientists. Advances and applications in research methods* (pp. 157–201). Beverly Hills, CA: Sage.

Kritzer, H.M. (1981). NONMET II. A program for the analysis of contingency tables and other types of nonmetric data by weighted least squares (Version 6.11). Madison: Department of Political Sciences, University of Wiscosin.

Lewis, D.A., & Salem, G. (1986). *Fear of crime. Incivility and the production of a social problem.* New Brunswick, NJ: Transaction Books.

Liska, A.E. (1985). *Victimization and fear of crime.* Paper presented at the 5th International Symposium on Victimology, Zagreb/Yugoslavia.

Liska, A.E., Sanchirico, A., & Reed, M.D. (1988). Fear of crime and constrained behavior: Specifying and estimating a reciprocal effects model. *Social Forces 66,* 827–837.

Maxfield, M.G. (1987a). *Explaining fear of crime: Evidence from the 1984 British Crime Survey.* London: Home Office.

Maxfield, M.G. (1987b). Incivilities and fear of crime in England and Wales, and the United States: A comparative analysis. Paper presented at the 1987 Annual Meeting of the American Society of Criminology, Montréal, Québec, Canada.

Maxfield, M.G. (1984a). *Fear of crime in England and Wales* (Home Office Research Study No. 78). London: HMSO.

Maxfield, M.G. (1984b). The limits of vulnerability in explaining fear of crime: A comparative neighborhood analysis. *Research in Crime and Delinquency, 21,* 233–250.

Mayhew, P. (1985). The effects of crime: Victims, the public and fear. In *Reserch on Victimisation. Collected Studies in Criminological Research* (Vol. 23, pp. 65–103) Strasbourg: Council of Europe.

Murck, M. (1980). *Soziologie der öffentlichen Sicherheit. Eine staatliche Aufgabe aus der Sicht der Bürger.* Frankfurt: Campus.

Murck, M. (1978). Die Angst vor Verbrechen und Einstellungen zur öffentlichen

Sicherheit. *Kriminologisches Journal, 10*, 202–214.

Newman, G.R. (1977). Problems of method in comparative criminology. *International Journal of Comparative and Applied Criminal* Justice, *1*, 17–31.

Newman, G.R., & Ferracuti, F. (1980). Introduction: The limits and possibilities of comparative criminology. In G.R. Newman (Ed.), *Crime and deviance: A comparative perspective.* (pp. 7–16) Beverly Hills, CA: Sage.

Niemi, H. (1985). Uhritutkimuksen käyttökelpoisuss. *The uses of victimization surveys.* (Trans. from Finnish.) Helsinki: National Research Institute of Legal Policy.

Noelle-Neumann, E. & Institut für Demoskopie Allensbach (Eds.). (1981). *The Germans. Public Opinion Polls 1967–1980.* Westport, CT: Greenwood Press.

Noelle-Neumann, E. & Piel, E. (Eds.) (1983): *Allensbacher Jahrbush der Demoskopie 1978–1983* (Bd. 8). München: Saur.

Ortega, S.T. & Myles, J.L. (1987). Race and gender effects on fear of crime: An interactive model with age. *Criminology, 25*, 133–152.

President's Commission on Law Enforcement and Administration of Justice (1967a). *The Challenge of Crime in a Free Society.* Washinton, DC: US Government Printing Office.

President's Commisson on Law Enforcement and Administration of Justice (1967b). Task Force Report: *Crime and its Impact—An Assessment.* Washington, DC: US Government Printing Office.

Reiss, A.J., Jr. (1967). *Studies in Crime and Law Enforcement in Major Metropolitan Areas.* (President's Commission on Law Enforcement and Administration of Justice, Field Surveys III). Washington, DC: Government Printing Office.

Research & Forecasts, Inc. with A. Friedberg (1983). *America Afraid. How fear of crime changes the way we live.* New York: NAL Books.

Reuband, K.-H. (1983). *Fear of crime in West Germany and the United States 1965–1982. A cross national comparison.* Paper presented at the 9th International Congress of Criminology, Vienna, Austria.

Rolinski, K. (1986). Fear of victimization: An empirical investigation of its particular criminal extent in connection with one- and multi-dimensional analysis of its influential sociological and differential-psychological factors. In Miyazawa, K. & M. Ohya (Eds.), *Victimology in comparative perspective* (pp. 294–301). Tokyo: Seibundo.

Rolinski, K. (1980). *Wohnhausarchitektur und Kriminalität.* Wiesbaden: Bundeskriminalamt.

Schwind, H.-D. (1984). Investigations of nonreported offenses. In R. Block (Ed.), *Victimization and fear of crime: World perspectives* (pp. 65–74). Washington, DC: US Department of Justice, Bureau of Justice Statistics.

Schwind, H.-D., Ahlborn, W., & Weiss, R. (1989). *Dunkelfeldforschung in Bochum 1986/1987. Eine Replikationsstudie.* Wiesbaden: Bundeskriminalamt.

Schwind, H.-D., Ahlborn W., & Weiss, R. (1978). *Empirische Kriminalgeographie. Bestandsaufnahme und Weiterführung am Beispiel von Bochum.* ("Kriminalitäsatlas Bochum"). Wiesbaden: Bundeskriminalamt.

Sessar, K. (1989). The forgotten non-victim. *The International Review of Victimology, 1* (forthcoming).

Sessar, K., Beurskens, A. & Boers, K. (1986). Wiedergutmachung als Konfliktregelungsparadigma? *Kriminologisches Journal, 18*, 86–104.

Silverman, R. & Kennedy, L.W. (1985). Loneliness, satisfaction and fear of crime: A test for non-recursive effects. *Canadian Journal of Criminology, 27*, 1–13.

Skogan, W.G. (1987). The impact of victimization on fear. *Crime & Delinquency, 33*, 135–154.

Skogan, W.G. (1986a). Fear of crime and neighborhood change. In A.J. Reiss, Jr. & M. Tonry (Eds.), *Crime and Justice: vol. 8. Communities and crime* (pp. 203–229). Chicago: University of Chicago Press.

Skogan, W.G. (1986b). The fear of crime and its behavioral implications. In B.A. Fattah (Ed.), *From crime policy to victim policy* (pp. 167–188). New York: St. Martin's Press.

Skogan, W.G. (1983). Fear of crime in America. In *America's crime problem*. Testimony presented to oversight hearings before the Subcommittee on Crime of the Committee on the Judiciary, House of Representatives (Serial No. 129). Washington, DC: US Government Printing Office.

Skogan, W.G., & Maxfield, M.G. (1981). *Coping with crime*. Individual and neighborhood reactions. Beverly Hills, CA: Sage.

Smaus, G. (1985). *Das Strafrecht und die Kriminalität in der Alltagssprache der deutschen Bevölkerung*. Opladen: Westdeutscher Verlag.

Sommers, S. & Kosmitzki, G. (1988). Emotion and social context: An American-German comparison. *British Journal of Social Psychology, 27*, 35–49.

Stephan, E. (1982). The Stuttgart victimization survey. In Criminological Research Unit (Ed.), *Research in Criminal Justice* (pp. 34–49). Freiburg: Max-Planck-Institut für Ausländisches und Internationales Strafrecht.

Stephen, E. (1976). *Die Stuttgarter Opferbefragung. Eine kriminologisch-viktimologische Analyze zur Erforschung des Dunkelfeldes unter besonderer Berücksichtigung der Einstellung der Bevölkerung zur Kriminalität*. Wiesbaden: Bundeskriminalamt.

Sveri, K. (1982). Comparative analyses of crime by means of victim surveys—The Scandinavian experience. In H.J. Schneider (Ed.), *The victim in international perspective* (pp. 209–219). Berlin: de Gruyter.

Stafford, M.C., & Galle, O.R. (1984). Victimization rates, exposure to risk, and fear of crime. *Criminology, 22*, 173–185.

Swafford, M. (1980). Three parametric techniques for contingency table analysis: A nontechnical commentary. *American Sociological Review 45*, 664–690.

Taylor, R.B., & Hale, M. (1986). Testing alternative models of fear of crime. *Journal of Criminal Law and Criminology, 77*, 151–189.

Teske, R.H.C., Jr., & Arnold, H. (1987). A comparative analysis of factors related to fear of crime in the United States (Texas) and the Federal Republic of Germany (Baden-Württemberg). *International Journal of Comparative and Applied Criminal Justice, 11*, 33–45.

Teske, R.H.C., Jr. & Arnold, H. (1982a). A comparative investigation of criminal victimization in the United States and the Federal Republic of Germany. In Criminological Research Unit (Ed.), *Research in criminal justice* (pp. 63–83). *Stocktaking of criminological research at the Max-Planck-Institute for Foreign and International Penal Law after a decade*. Freiburg: Max-Planck-Institut für Ausländisches und Internationales Strafrecht.

Teske, R.H.C., Jr., & Arnold, H. (1982b). *The relationship between victimization and the fear of crime: A further evaluation*. Unpublished manuscript, Max-Planck-Institut für Ausländisches und Internationales Strafrecht, Freiburg.

Teske, R.H.C., Jr., & Arnold, H. (1982c). Comparison of the criminal statistics of the United States and the Federal Republic of Germany. *Journal of Criminal Justice 10*, 359–374.

Teske, R.H.C., Jr., & Hazlett, M.H. (1983). *A scale for the measurement of fear of crime*. Paper presented at the annual meeting of the American Society of Criminology, Denver, Colorado.

Teske, R.H.C., Jr., Hazlett, M.H., & Parker, L.M. (1983). *Texas Crime Poll: 1982 Survey*. Huntsville, Texas: Criminal Justice Center, Sam Houston State University.

Teske, R.H.C., Jr. & Moore, J.B. (1980). *Texas Victimization Survey 1979. A special Texas Crime Poll Survey*. Huntsvillie, Texas: Criminal Justice Center, Sam Houston State University.

Tyler, T.R. (1980). Impact of directly and indirectly experienced events: The origin of crime-related judgements and behaviors. *Journal of Personality and Social Psychology, 39*, 13–28.

Warr, M. (1987). Fear of victimization and sensitivity to risk. *Journal of Quantitative Criminology, 3*, 29–46.

Warr, M., & Stafford, M.C. (1983). Fear of victimization: A look at proximate causes. *Social Forces, 61*, 1033–1043.

7

Do People Really Want Punishment? On the Relationship between Acceptance of Restitution, Needs for Punishment, and Fear of Crime

KLAUS BOERS AND KLAUS SESSAR

Introduction

In modern societies the violation of personal values (personal property, health, honor, liberty) is widely regarded as a violation of social values. While personal values are primarily protected by civil law, criminal law with its penalties is supposed to defend the same values inasmuch as they are defined to be of social relevance. This distinction, of course, is not obvious. In early Germanic and Frankish law the concept of negative sanctions covered both restitution and vengeance, restitution predominating over and even superseding vengeance (Schafer, 1968; Schmidt, 1965).

This two-fold application disappeared after the sovereign took the place of the suffering party (the victim), redefining the victim's violation as a violation and insult against himself. "Besides its immediate victim, the crime attacks the sovereign: it attacks him personally, since the law represents the will of the sovereign; it attacks him physically, since the force of the law is the force of the prince" (Foucault, 1979, p. 47).

It is important to note that this distinction between individual and collective reactions to unlawful behavior (i.e., between restitution and punishment), was not initiated from below, by the common members of the society, but from above, by the sovereign or the state.

Initially, therefore, the *Gemeinschaft* took part in settling and regulating social conflicts between its members. The transformation of a violation of prsonal goods into a violation of the legal order led to a situation in which the nature of the offense as an interpersonal conflict was lost sight of (Christie, 1977). At the same time the use of punishment increased, and not only superseded personal restitution but sometimes even came to be considered as a personal restitution. At least in Germany, this led to a strange development. The German civil law provides for so-called damages for pain and suffering as an immaterial restitution in cases of serious physical harm and insult. This sanction derives from the premedieval institution of "penance money" (*Geldbusse*) that an offender had to pay to the victim. Nowadays this sanction is defined as a civil satisfaction, however, with punitive features. Some German courts, with civil jurisdiction, have decided that damages for pain and suffering to the victim can be reduced if the offender has been punished severely enough. The logic of these decisions is that the victim's satisfaction through punishment can replace demages for pain and suffering, just because they are themselves seen as a form of punishment (Sessar, 1986, p. 393). Thus, the victim gets "stones instead of bread"

Our central hypothesis is that the distinction between criminal law and civil law has created a situation that is fundamentally in conflict with the interests of the victim. We assume that every human being who has been harmed physically or materially, or who has been insulted, needs some sort of compensation and that the original idea of an immediate restitution between offender and victim has always retained this significance in the mind of the public. From a sociological point of view, restitution is a negative sanction, which can incorporate elements of punishment. Thus, contrary to the above-cited court decisions, traditional penalties can be reduced or abolished after successful restitution. In cases of incidents involving serious crimes, our initial hypothesis has to be modified in the sense that a relationship between the type of victimization and the acceptance of restitution is assumed.

If the criminal justice system ignores those priorities, victims might react to the neglect of their interests with hostility, requiring the punishment of the offender. This is why we furthermore assume a relationship between the satisfaction of victims' needs for and interests in restitution and in punishment, an assumption that we will not discuss in this chapter.

Because victims are merely members of society who have been affected by crimes more intensely than other members, and because every member is a potential victim, our hypothesis has been extended to society as a whole.

The investigation of our rather global hypothesis was based on the use of attitude measurements. We were less concerned to investigate restitution as an alternative to the criminal law or to punishment than to find out whether cases involving social conflicts require criminal law and punishment in addition to private conflict resolution and restitution. Thus, the question was less whether restitution will be accepted in addition to the criminal law, but rather why and under what conditions it will not be accepted. In other words, our main interest is in the question of the legitimation of punishment (and thereby of criminal law).

Methods

The study was conducted in the city of Hamburg/Germany (1.6 million inhabitants). The central survey referred to a random sample of the

Einwohnerzentralregister (central residents' register). In addition, several further populations were studied:

All civil and criminal judges and prosecutors (Hamburg)
Social workers involved in the criminal justice systems of the state of Hamburg and several other federal states
A random sample of first- and eighth-semester university students at the University of Hamburg, with law students as the experimental group and students of modern languages as the control group
A nonsystematic sample of convicts in prison and on probation
A nonsystematic sample of officially appointed mediators

Our discussion is confined to the survey of citizens supplemented by discussion of the survey of judges and prosecutors.

The main tool of attitude measurement was a pretested questionnaire, divided into two parts: general and special. The general section of the questionnaire was given to every participant in the study. It included the following questions:

Attitudes toward everyday noncriminal deviant behavior
Ways of dealing with such everyday conflicts
Social distance toward deviant persons
Attitudes toward crime and criminals
Feeling of insecurity and risk assessment (fear of crime)

The point of focal interest was participants' attitudes toward the acceptance of restitution. The respondents were asked how they would react to various kinds of crime situations, how they would advise a victim about prosecution of an offender, or what advice they would give a judge for sentencing should consideration of the victim's interests be legally permitted. One of the main questions included 14 descriptions of fictitious crime incidents. Six cases were presented in the same standard form to all participants. Each of the other 8 cases had 4 variants, varied according to crime type, seriousness of incident, relationship between victim and offender, and the way in which the victim contributed to the incident. This added up to a total of 38 cases.

As it is not advisable to present all cases to each respondent (Rossi, Waite, Bose, & Berk, 1974), the item was broken down into 4 subgroups. Every respondent was given 14 cases: the 6 standard cases and one version of the other 8 cases. Each of these subgroups was again broken down into 2 groups, one with a 30-year-old male as an offender, the other with a 17-year-old juvenile, both unmarried and without previous records.

The *special part of the citizen questionnaire* consisted of a comprehensive victim survey. Those respondents who indicated that they had been victims of one of the 19 listed crimes during the 3-year period prior to the interview were asked how they, as a judge, would have sentenced "their" offender. One fourth of the respondents, victims as well as nonvictims, was asked whether they take general precautions or restrict their behavior in order to prevent potential victimization.

The *special part of the questionnaire for the subpopulations* focused on questions referring to social and professional circumstances. For example, criminal judges and prosecutors were asked about their readiness to use restitution as a sanction. They were also asked to describe practical difficulties they might encounter in using restitution in specific cases or with respect to specific offenders (and victims). We anticipated that a comparison of their attitudes with the attitudes of citizens, students, or civil judges would reveal a punitively oriented professional socialization of criminal judges and prosecutors. Any discrepancy between their attitudes and those of the general population would then constitute part of the overall legitimation problem.

The survey was conducted by mail in 1984 and 1985. To those who did not respond, an additional postcard, a letter, and even a second questionnaire were sent. Altogether, 1,799 usable responses were returned. In addition, 317 questionnaires were returned as undeliverable or because the client was deceased. The adjusted return rate now represents 44.1%.

In comparison with many American surveys, the return rate seems low. However, the study was conducted in a large city where people are less willing to participate in research interviews. More important is a nationwide suspicion of any kind of data collection that became apparent in 1983 as a reaction to the government's plan to conduct a macrocensus and to use the data for a number of different purposes, including social control. The German *Bundesverfassungsgericht* (Federal Constitutional Court) thwarted this plan one year prior to the start of our study. Since that time the collection of data, even for scientific purposes, has encountered severe problems.

A comparison of the random sample with the returned sample reveals only slight distortions in the three available variables: sex, age, and marital status. Males are slightly overrepresented compared to females (by 2.6%), as are married compared with nonmarried respondents (by 7.9%), and the age group between 38 and 67 compared with younger and older respondents (by 9.1%)

Attitudes of the citizen group to the hypothetical crime cases will be compared with those of criminal judges and prosecutors, followed by an investigation of a number of variables possibly connected with the attitudes to fear of crime of the citizens along.

Findings on Attitudes

Attitudes in the General Population

Following the practice of numerous other studies on restitution, we asked not only whether restitution would be acceptable in addition to punishment but also whether it would be acceptable instead of punishment (Gandy & Galaway, 1980). However, we differed from other authors in our interest in finding out whether the respondents were willing to replace criminal proceedings by private conflict resolution, both with and without a mediator.

We investigated this question by using the hypothetical cases (see Appendix). A fixed-response menu with five alternatives was presented to the respondents:

1. Victim and offender should privately agree on restitution or reconciliation (with the help of a third person if needed).
2. Victim and offender should agree on restitution or reconciliation mediated by an officially appointed person.
3. The criminal justice system should initiate an agreement on restitution between victim and offender. The agreement should be supervised, for example, by the probation officer.
4. The offender should be punished. If he provided restitution to the victim, the punishment should be dispensed with or reduced.
5. The offender should be punished. Even if he provides restitution to the victim, the punishment should not be dispensed with or reduced.

Rates of response for each of the 38 cases are shown in Figure 7.1 (the cases are marked with their number—see Appendix —and with a cue). Percentages of responses for each of the five proposed forms of reaction are graphed, from left to right. The first and second alternatives are unshaded, the third is lightly shaded, the fourth and fifth alternatives are dark-shaded. The rank order of the cases was determined by the acceptance score (see Table 7.1).

The results are extraordinary. Restitution instead of punishment is accepted for most of the hypothetical criminal incidents, not merely in addition to the criminal process but also instead of it, that is, within the framework of private settlement and reconciliation. Taken over 38 cases, the frequency of the responses to the five proposals is as follows: 23.9% for private agreement; 18.5% for private agreement with the help of a mediator; 17.4% for private agreement initiated and supervised by the criminal justice system; 18.8% for punishment to be mitigated or abolished in the event of successful restitution; 21.4% for punishment without consideration of restitution.

In more than 50% of cases, the respondents were ready to accept private settlement of the conflict with or without a mediator (first and second alternative; 20 cases if the third variation is added). On the other hand, in only 5 cases was the demand for punishment without consideration of restitution higher than 50% (including the 4 rape cases).

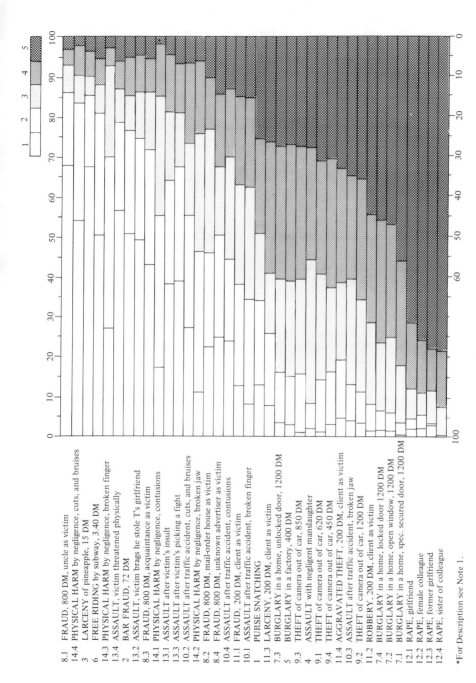

8.1	FRAUD, 800 DM, uncle as victim
14.4	PHYSICAL HARM by negligence, cuts, and bruises
3	LARCENY of pineapple, 15 DM
6	FREE RIDING by subway, 3.40 DM
14.3	PHYSICAL HARM by negligence, broken finger
13.4	ASSAULT, victim threatened physically
2	BAR FRAUD, 72 DM
13.2	ASSAULT, victim brags he stole T's girlfriend
8.3	FRAUD, 800 DM, acquaintance as victim
14.1	PHYSICAL HARM by negligence, contusions
13.1	ASSAULT after victim's insult
13.3	ASSAULT after victim's picking a fight
10.2	ASSAULT after traffic accident, cuts, and bruises
14.2	PHYSICAL HARM by negligence, broken jaw
8.2	FRAUD, 800 DM, mail-order house as victim
8.4	FRAUD, 800 DM, unknown advertiser as victim
10.4	ASSAULT after traffic accident, contusions
11.1	FRAUD, 200 DM, client as victim
10.1	ASSAULT after traffic accident, broken finger
1	PURSE SNATCHING
11.3	LARCENY, 200 DM, client as victim
7.3	BURGLARY in a home, unlocked door, 1200 DM
5	BURGLARY in a factory, 400 DM
9.3	THEFT of camera out of car, 850 DM
4	ASSAULT with negligent manslaughter
9.1	THEFT of camera out of car, 620 DM
9.4	THEFT of camera out of car, 450 DM
11.4	AGGRAVATED THEFT, 200 DM, client as victim
10.3	ASSAULT after traffic accident, broken jaw
9.2	THEFT of camera out of car, 1200 DM
11.2	ROBBERY, 200 DM, client as victim
7.4	BURGLARY in a home, locked door 1200 DM
7.2	BURGLARY in a home, open window, 1200 DM
7.1	BURGLARY in a home, spec. secured door, 1200 DM
12.1	RAPE, girlfriend
12.2	RAPE, female colleague
12.3	RAPE, former girlfriend
12.4	RAPE, sister of colleague

*For Description see Note 1.

FIGURE 7.1 Attitudes toward sanctioning for 38 crime cases (30-year-old offender without previous record). For description see Appendix.

TABLE 7.1. Mean scores and standard deviations and percentage of private agreement for 14 crime incidents in descending order of restitution acceptance, for the Hamburg population in comparison with criminal judges and prosecutors.

Case no.[a]	Citizens			Criminal judges			Prosecutors		
	Mean	S.D.	Private agreement (%)[b]	Mean	S.D.	Private agreement (%)[b]	Mean	S.D.	Private agreement (%)[b]
8.1	1.096	.378	93.2	1.260	.578	80.8	1.371	.683	74.2
3	1.107	.399	92.5	1.342	.650	75.3	1.597	.819	61.3
6	1.123	.438	90.9	1.357	.660	74.2	1.403	.688	71.0
14.1	1.159	.399	85.3	1.167	.475	87.4	1.344	.602	72.1
2	1.179	.485	86.6	1.315	.598	75.4	1.468	.740	67.7
13.1	1.224	.506	81.6	1.493	.709	63.1	1.475	.721	65.6
11.1	1.513	.735	63.2	1.945	.780	32.8	2.226	.777	21.0
10.1	1.517	.738	62.9	1.740	.790	48.0	1.887	.812	38.7
1	1.706	.809	51.7	2.164	.799	24.6	2.516	.671	9.7
4	1.817	.828	45.0	1.983	.805	32.7	2.316	.783	19.3
5	1.894	.791	37.0	2.247	.778	20.5	2.541	.594	4.9
9.1	1.895	.842	41.1	2.219	.731	17.8	2.452	.670	9.7
7.1	2.286	.800	21.7	2.403	.725	13.9	2.629	.520	1.6
12.1	2.589	.700	12.4	2.639	.564	4.2	2.758	.468	1.6

[a] For description see Appendix.
[b] Percentage of the first three response alternatives combined, see text.

Most of the incidents are minor crimes, but they are those the criminal justice system has to deal with most frequently and they are incidents in which restitution almost never plays a role. On the other hand, restitution is accepted for a number of crimes that are usually rated as serious, such as assault with negligent manslaughter (case 4), aggravated assault (cases 10.1 and 10.3), burglary in a factory (case 5), theft under aggravated circumstances (case 11.4), unlawful entry into a private home (case 7.3), and even burglary of a private home (cases 7.2. and 7.4).

Comparison of Public Attitudes with the Attitudes of the Judicial Authorities

Again, when attitudes of the population are compared with those of criminal judges and prosecutors, the data may be distorted as the return rate did not exceed 40%. However, compared to the original total population of these groups, sex and age are equally distributed, thereby excluding distortion in this respect at least. A total of 73 criminal judges and 62 prosecutors from the Hamburg judicial system took part in the survey.

The comparison is limited to the 14 hypothetical cases that were given to the judges and prosecutors, or cases 1 to 6 and the first version of cases 7 to 14 (7.1, 8.1, etc.). For the comparison it was necessary to develop a scale on the basis of the 5 responses. Because the ranking of these alternatives does not reflect a scale of equal intervals, we rated them subjectively. We could not find a theoretically based distinction between purely private and private settlement aided by a mediator or even by the criminal justice system for the distinction between restitution and punishment; therefore, we collapsed the first three categories into one and rated them "1". The Fourth category (abolition or reduction of punishment in the case of successful restitution) was rated "2". The fifth category (pure punishment) was rated "3". In combining the rates given by each respondent, an acceptance score was developed, ranging from 1 to 3 for all 14 cases. (For a discussion of the method, see also Wolfgang, Figlio, Fracy, & Singer, 1985, p. vi). For example, case 3 (larceny of pineapples) was scored 1.107, case 12.1 (raping the girlfriend) was scored 2.589.

In Table 7.1, the mean scores of the citizen survey are compared with the scores of criminal judges and prosecutors. In addition, the percentage of restitution acceptance by way of private agreement between victim and offender, that is without criminal trial and sentencing (combination of the first three response alternatives), for each case is displayed. The rank order of the cases apparently reflects a diminishing acceptance of restitution as expressed by mean scores and percentages. The following two main observations can be made.

First the evaluations of the acceptability of restitution instead of punishment yielded similar rank orderings across all populations. This means that in those cases in which the citizens group did not require punishment, some form of restitution is also accepted by the justice system. In other words, if the attitudes of the overall population were taken as the basis for crime-severity measurements, the rank orderings by citizens and legal professionals would show a fairly close similarity for given classes of crime (see also Sellin & Wolfgang, 1978, p. 268).

Here the significant similarities between the two groups end.

Second, the results reveal remarkable divergences concerning the question of whether the criminal trial and sentencing functions of the criminal-justice system are necessary. Whereas in 9 out of 14 cases more than 50% of the citizens, and in 6 out of 14 cases more than 80% of the citizens favored private settlement in one way or another (see percentage column in Table 7.1), there are 6 cases (50% level) and 2 cases (80% level) in which criminal judges, and 6 cases (50% level) and 0 cases (80% level) in which prosecutors advocated pretrial reactions to the crime in question. For example, twice as many respondents from the general population as judges were sympathetic to resolution via private agreement in the cases involving purse snatching (case 1) and theft of a camera (case 9.1), and three times as many in the case of rape (case 12.1) (although, not unexpectedly, rape was commonly considered to be too serious an act to be included in victim–offender agreements).

The discrepancies between the general public and prosecutors in many cases are even more conspicuous because the citizens' readiness to accept restitution exceeds by far that of the prosecutors (see cases 1, 5, 7.1, 9.1, 12.1). When a cut is made at the mean value "2" (scores higher than this may be taken as indicative of tendencies toward punishment without restitution), 2 out of the 14 cases in the general population lie above the cut (and may hence be classified as punitively oriented) whereas among judges 5 cases, and among prosecutors 7 cases lie above the cut.

The overall pattern seems to be that the public and the legal profession diverge in their assessment of the appropriate sanction: the less severe the incident, the less the public considers it to be necessary to react with punishment or even with a criminal trial. On the other hand, the more severe the incident, the more a trial and sentencing is demanded (although restitution still plays an important role). The legal profession, by contrast, is more rigorous. Thus, from the public point of view, there is little justification for this professional rigorism, except in cases involving the most severe crimes (rape and partly burglary cases) where a consensus among all respondents was revealed.

These results may be regarded as valid, subject to two possible restrictions. First, it was specified that the hypothetical offender had no previous convictions. It migt be that traditional punishment would be favored for the same crimes committed by someone with a criminal record. Second, the results presuppose that private agreement or restitution would be successful or at least seriously attempted. Consequently, the possibility that the public might regard criminal law as a necessary reserve procedure for the event that these efforts fail cannot be excluded.

Findings on Fear of Crime and Attitudes

In the past, research into attitudes concerning appropriate responses to crime has prioritized punishment over restitution. The present results ascertaining public acceptance of restitution in lieu of punishment in many areas of crime provoke new insights into questions of criminal policy and new questions about the relationship between punitiveness and restitutiveness. One important question is whether both types of sanctioning attitudes are merely the opposed extremes of a single scale or whether they have to be treated as independent categories when the impact of exogenous variables on them is studied.

Of the exogeneous variables invoked to explain attitudes toward sanctioning, fear of crime is certainly the most "politically" relevant. In addition, sociodemographic variables (sex, age, income) have to be taken into account, either independently or intercorrelated with the fear variable.

In view of the extent of fear of crime in many Western societies, it seems clear that scared people abreact their fear by demanding harsh punishment. Thus, to many policy-makers and decision-makers, tough law enforcement appears to be one of the most efficient means of combatting fear of crime.

However, this is a common-sense (and hence rather simplistic) approach to the problem because fear of crime has been discovered to be unconnected, or only weakly connected, with crime-related factors such as actual experience of victimization, even if controlled for sex and age. Certainly, the connection proves to be somewhat stronger where serious crimes are concerned; on the other hand, an inverse relationship was discovered in cases involving minor victimizations (see Hindelang, Gottfredson, Garofalo, 1978, p. 189.; Skogan & Maxfield, 1981, p. 59.; Hough, 1985, p. 494.; Skogan, 1987, p. 146.; Teske & Arnold, 1987, p. 40.).

The same is true for the few existing studies of the relationship between fear of crime and attitudes to sanctioning. Because the focus is exclusively on punitiveness (while ignoring the relationship between fear and restitution), these studies fail to reveal any notable link between such attitudes and fear of crime (Stinchcombe, Adams, Heimer, Scheppele, Smith, & Faylor 1980, pp. 67–68), and this in spite of a considerable growth in punitive attitudes[1] in the United States between 1965 and 1977. Also

---

[1] The authors analyzed data from the General Social Survey and Gallup Poll. Punitiveness was measured by the respondents' evaluation of the proposition that "the courts are not harsh enough" and by their attitude to capital punishment.

with respect to other exogenous variables such as race, income, education, direct and indirect victimization, Longworthy and Whitehead (1986) could not find significant correlations with punitiveness.[2] In this study, only younger respondents and males exhibited mildly punitive attitudes. The authors conceded that their model of punitiveness was not very powerful (pp. 582, 585).

Slightly different results were found in Germany. Arzberger, Murck, and Schumacher (1979, p. 124.) conducted a survey in two medium-sized West German cities in 1977. They discovered strong connections between repressive attitudes[3] and age (.31). The correlations with variables like fear of crime (.15) and the respondents' perception of public places as dangerous (.12) were much weakes. There was no correlation with sex (.03) and an inverse, but weak correlation with education (−.18) and income (−.09). The respondents were not asked about victimization experiences.

The weak or even nonexistent correlations might be due to unsophisticated measurements of punitiveness involving stereotyped and dichotomized questions. These measures neglect specific situational factors, which would normally affect respondents' judgments of crime incidents.

Even Hough and Moxon (1985), using much more elaborate measurements in the *British Crime Survey* (BCS) of 1984 (see Hough & Mayhew, 1985)[4], could explain a slight variation in punitiveness only by generation, class differences, and fear, but not by sex and victimization. For example, the proportion of respondents favoring long prison sentences rose markedly with age and, in addition, manual workers were more punitive than nonmanual workers (p. 169). As regards fear, those respondents who were "very worried" about burglary were, even if controlled for age, tougher on burglars than those who were "not very worried." Similar

---

[2] To measure "punitiveness" the authors used a dichotomous variable based on the forced-choice question whether the repondents thought the purpose of prison was to punish criminals or to teach them to be useful, law-abiding citizens (p. 580).

[3] "Repressiveness" was measured by the demand for longer and harsher sentences and for more police forces.

[4] In 1984, the *BCS* 6,600 respondents were confronted with 7 hypothetical crime cases (robbery, burglary, rape, shoplifting, car theft for a joy ride, cannabis smoking, and prostitution) and had to propose a sentence for either a 25- or 17-year-old offender with previous convictions. The menu of sentencing options ranged from "no action" over "court warning," "pay compensation," "community service," probation and several fines to imprisonment from under 1 to over 5 years (Hough & Moxon, 1985, 172–173). This measurement of punitiveness is similar to ours, with the exception that the *BCS* designers wanted to compare the respondents' attitudes with the actual practice of sentencing by the courts, whereas we wanted to investigate the public readiness to accept restitution. Punitiveness was understood as the favoring of long prison sentences (1 year or more).

patterns were discovered in other crime cases (p. 170). Unfortunately, the authors did not report findings concerning restitutive responses.

In view of the difficulty of establishing an association between punitiveness and exogeneous factors, two suggestions have to be made:

First, it seems likely that punitiveness is primarily a social-cognitive pattern sui generis that is based on cultural and political "belief systems" (see Converse, 1964); its dependency on emotional and demographic factors might be less than expected. Second, previous research on attitudes to sanctioning may be misleading because it focuses only on punitiveness and its interrelations. To broaden our perspective, restitutiveness has to be analyzed as well.

The Measurement of Fear of Crime and Attitudes Toward Sanctioning

To investigate and explain *sanctioning attitudes*, an index of attitudes toward punishment and restitution (sanctioning attitude scale) was created by summing for each respondent the modified scores ("1" to "3") in the hypothetical cases and dividing the resulting scale into quartiles of equal magnitude (the first quartile marking the most restitution-oriented and the fourth quartile the most punishment-oriented respondents).

Fear of crime is here conceived as an attitudinal construct that involves both affective and cognitive components and is related to coping behavior. Its measurement therefore has to take into account the following three elements:

1. *Feelings of insecurity* as measured by the standard single-item measure ("How safe do you feel walking alone in your neighborhood at night?"). Although the validity of this item has repeatedly been questioned,[5] it is used for the purpose of intranational and international comparisons. Furthermore, we consider this item to be usable as an index of the affective component of fear of crime, provided that it is incorporated into a questionnaire exclusively on crime topics instead of being used in isolation.[6]

---

[5] For a recent critical discussion, see Gibbs, Coyle, & Hanrahan, 1987.

[6] Feelings of insecurity were found to be strongly correlated with sex and age: females and the elderly exhibited a higher degree of insecurity than males and younger respondents: very safe—5.8% (2.0% f, 10.5% m); reasonably safe—33.6% (23.1% f, 46.2% m); somewhat unsafe—42.9% (49.8% f, 34.8% m); very unsafe—17.6% (25.1% f, 8.5% m); Kendall's Tau b .32, $p < .001$, for sex and .24, $p < .001$, for age. There is a slight positive correlation with vicarious victimization involving robbery and assault (Kendall's Tau b .12, $p < .001$), but almost none with frequency and type of victimization.

2. *Perceived likelihood of victimization* taps exactly what Lazarus (1975) in his cognitive-phenomenological theory of emotion calls "primary appraisal." Although the standard question is strongly correlated with personal risk assessment, both must be distinguished from each other. The latter is more heavily affected by a person's cognitive appraisal of the perceived risk of being victimized than by the emotional consequences of violent crime. Personal risk assessment was measured with respect to physical assault, robbery, homicide, rape, harassment, and theft, presenting four responses: "unlikely," "rather unlikely," "likely," and "very likely."[7]

3. Finally, we presented the respondents with a menu of 32 behavioral reactions that was designed to elicit reports about their protective and avoidance behavior in relationship to violent and property crime.[8]

Relationship of Sanctioning Attitudes to Sociodemographic Variables and Victimization Experiences

The first step involves a bivariate analysis of the influence of sociodemographic variables and victimization experiences on attitudes toward punishment and restitution.

Sanctioning attitudes are directly associated with age.[9] A closer look reveals the need for a distinction between restitutiveness (first quartile) and punitiveness (fourth quartile). With increasing age, respondents are not as likely to exhibit less restitutive attitudes. This is not followed, however, by a corresponding increase in punitive attitudes, these being equally distributed across the age groups; with the exception that respondents aged 18 to 21 years are significantly less punitive than all other respondents.

Females are more restitutive and less punitive than males (by 5% in the first as well as in the fourth quartile); the correlation is statistically significant, but Kendall's Tau b is below 0.1 (0.06, $p < .01$). Respondents with higher education are less punitive than those with lower education (by 12% in the fourth quintile), and they are more restitutive (by 15% in the first quartile). Expressing a smaller social distance[10] leads to a preference

---

[7] Almost negligible is the influence of sex (Tau b .08, $p < .01$) and age (Tau b .04, $p < .05$) on risk assessment. The correlations with direct and vicarious victimization are the same as for feelings of insecurity.

[8] The results for the behavioral element of fear of crime are not presented in this chapter.

[9] Tau b .08, $p < .001$.

[10] Social distance was measured by a scale consisting of 8 items. These questions measured the degree of respondents' willingness to interact with a hypothetical

for restitution (by 9% in the first quartile), whereas respondents who endorse a larger social distance tend to favor punishment (by 14% in the fourth quartile). Again, the correlations are significant but rather weak (Tau b $-.07$, $p < .001$ for education, and Tau b $.11$, $p < .001$ for social distance). There is no significant relationship between direct and indirect victimization and sanctioning attitudes.[11]

To substantiate these findings, we analyzed each of the hypothetical cases again and confirmed that mainly age and education exhibit consistent associations with attitudes to sanctioning.

In some cases there was also a weak relationship with sex: as regards purse snatching (case 1), fraud (case 8.1), physical assault (case 10.2), theft out of a car (case 9.1), and theft out of an unlocked writing table (case 11.3), women were more in favor of restitutive responses than men, whereas there was almost no sex difference for punitiveness.

Impact of Fear of Crime on Sanctioning Attitudes

The next stage involves an investigation of the relationship between fear and attituds to punishment and restitution.

Table 7.2 shows a relatively steady increment in punitiveness with growing *insecurity*; likewise preference for restitution increases with decreasing fear (Tau b $.10$, $p < .001$). As with the age variable, the feeling of insecurity seems to have its primary impact less on punitiveness (a difference of 8% between *very safe* and *very unsafe*) than on attitudes to restitution (18% difference). Regarding *risk assessment* (Table 7.3), an increase of punitiveness and—by an equal amount—a decrease of restitutiveness is connected with the growing perception of the likelihood of falling victim to a robbery (Tau b $.09$, $p < .001$). A similar pattern was found for physical assault, but not for homicide, rape, theft, and harassment.

In spite of what seems to be a self-evident positive correlation between fear and punitiveness, the fact is that about two out of five of those respondents feeling *somewhat unsafe* or *very unsafe* favor mainly restitutive responses (first quartile). Conversely some 45% of punitive respondents (fourth quartile) feel *reasonably safe* or *very safe* (Table 7.2). From this we infer that because women are more fearful, but differ from men in preferring restitutive resolutions at least for some of the hypothetical cases, and because age somehow creates tougher attitudes, old men seem to

---

person (e.g., "Would you ask this person to take care of your apartment while you are not at home?" or "Would you lend this person DM 100 [\$170 in 1988, \$300 in 1984]?")

[11] Data not reproduced in tables.

TABLE 7.2. Sanctioning attitudes and feelings of insecurity.

	Sanctioning attitude scale									
	Very restitutive		Restitutive		Punitive		Very punitive		Row total	
	%	No.	%	No.	%	No.	%	No.	%	No.
Feeling of insecurity										
Very safe	35.1	34	19.6	19	21.6	21	23.7	23	100.0	97
Reasonable safe	25.7	147	26.9	154	26.2	150	21.3	122	100.0	573
Somewhat unsafe	21.4	146	26.2	179	26.5	181	25.8	176	100.0	682
Very unsafe	17.1	43	19.8	50	31.3	79	31.7	80	100.0	252
Column total	23.1	370	25.1	402	26.9	431	25.0	401	100.0	1,604

$x^2 = 28.466$, df $= 9$, $p < .001$

TABLE 7.3. Sanctioning attitudes and risk assessment (robbery).

	Sanctioning attitude scale									
	Very restitutive		Restitutive		Punitive		Very punitive		Row total	
	%	No.	%	No.	%	No.	%	No.	%	No.
Risk assessment (robbery)										
Unlikely	34.0	86	25.3	64	21.7	55	19.0	48	100.0	253
Less likely	20.4	167	25.9	212	29.3	239	24.4	199	100.0	817
Likely	22.6	88	21.9	85	27.2	106	28.3	110	100.0	389
Very likely	21.1	16	26.3	20	17.1	13	35.5	27	100.0	76
Column total	23.3	357	24.8	381	26.9	413	25.0	384	100.0	1,535

$x^2 = 33.201$, df $= 9$, $p < .001$

constitute the most punitive and young women the most restitutive groups of respondents.

These possible explanations are to some extent confirmed by a multivariate analysis of punitive and restitutive attitudes by using log-linear models.

Log-linear models are based on multidimensional contingency tables and provide a suitable procedure for the multivariate analysis of categorial and ordinal data (see Goodmann 1970, 1971).

The goal is to build a most parsimonious model, that is, one requiring the least number of theoretically necessary variables to receive a good fit between the observed (cell) frequencies and those predicted by the model.

With log-linear methods one can estimate the main or interaction effects (known as the so-called λ parameters) of variables on the distribution of the predicted frequencies.

Because we viewed sanctioning attitudes as the dependent variable, we built an asymmetric logit-model (see Langeheine 1980, p. 52).

For the purpose of this analysis the sanctioning attitude scale has been classified into the following three categories: *restitutive*, *neither restitutive nor punitive*, and *punitive*; all of the independent variables were dichotomized.

Table 7.4 displays the λ parameters of our final logit-model, using the odds-ratio for the categories restitutive versus punitive only. The model fits well to the data (LR-χ^2 18.62, df 20, $p. > .500$). It encompasses four main effects (sex, feeling of insecurity, social distance, and education) and one interaction-effect (feeling of insecurity × sex).

The most unexpected result of the multivariate analysis is the insignificance of age. According to our assumptions and the bivariate analysis, a first logit-model included *also* the age variable. However, "age" did not have a significant effect in the multivariate analysis. This subsequently led to a rather weak fit of the original model (LR-χ^2 89.86, df 80, $p < .21$). Thus, the age variable was excluded from further analysis.

For the other independent variables, the parameters of the final model confirm what has been ascertained: Generally, the impact of the exogenous variables on attitudes toward sanctioning is rather weak, with social distance and education being somewhat more significant than gender and the feeling of insecurity.

The direction of the signs of the main-effect parameters confirms that being female, feeling safe, exhibiting a small social distance or being educated has a positive effect on restitutiveness.

TABLE 7.4. Logit-parameters for attitudes toward sanctioning (restitutive vs. punitive).

Effects[a]		
Sex		$p < .01$
Female	.195	
Male	−.195	
Feeling of insecurity		$p < .01$
Safe	.190	
Unsafe	−.190	
Social distance		$p < .001$
Low	.237	
High	−.237	
Education		$p < .001$
Lower	−.297	
Higher	.297	
Sex + feeling of insecurity		$p < .05$
Female + safe	−.120	
Female + unsafe	.120	
Male + safe	.120	
Male + unsafe	−.120	
Intercept (grand mean)	.120	

[a] Goodness of fit: LR-$\chi^2 = 18.62$, $df = 20$, $p < .500$

The interaction terms lead to a somewhat different interpretation. Of main interest are the negative signed first and fourth parameters. The first-interaction term *female + feeling safe* means that the presumably additive effect of both characteristics on the preference for restitution is diminished to a certain degree. That is, the restitutive attitudes of women who feel safe do not differ as much from other populations as one might expect, if considering the main effects only.

On the other hand, the punitive direction of the main-effect categories *male* and *unsafe* is additionally strengthened by the forth interaction term. That is, men who feel fearful differ markedly from other populations in their preference for punitive sanctions.

Both of the other two positive signed interaction terms, which have an additional effect on restitutiveness, are of less interest. It should be noted, however, that each interaction term is dominated by a different variable.

In the second interaction term (*female + unsafe*) gender has the stronger effect, while in the third interaction term (*male + safe*) the feeling of insecurity is the dominant variable.

In light of the insignificance of the age variable and the differential impact of the interaction parameters, our assumption that older males dominate the group of respondents who are in favor of punishment has to be reconsidered.

However, this assumption is to some extent supported if it is modified to state that men who feel unsafe have the strongest impact on the distribution of punitiveness. By transforming the log odds of our model into percentage proportions of punitive and restitutive respondents, this finding becomes more obvious (Table 7.5).

Because the focus is on the relationship between fear of crime and sanctioning attitudes, we controlled for social distance and education by examining the categories of *lower* education and *larger* social distance only.

The results show that fear of crime has a serious effect only on the preference of punishment among males: Males who feel unsafe represent a punitive proportion of 50%, compared to 35% of those who feel safe. On the other hand the feeling of insecurity has almost no impact on the distribution of restitutiveness (3% difference among women and 6% difference among men). Also the proportions of women who feel either safe or unsafe (and also of men who feel safe) do not differ with respect to punitiveness (36% and 37%, respectively).[12]

In sum, a multivariate analysis reveals that women differ from men in their greater preference for restitutive sanctions; but whereas women's attitude seem to be less affected by the degree of anxiety, anxious males exhibit a stronger need for punishment.

---

[12] Similar patterns of distribution were found when controlling for the other categories of social distance and education. These distributions, however, were generally characterized by higher proportions of acceptance of restitution.

TABLE 7.5. Attitudes toward sanctioning by sex, feeling of insecurity, social distance (only "high") and education (only "lower").[a]

Female				Male			
Safe (n = 65)		Unsafe (n = 248)		Safe (n = 85)		Unsafe (n = 112)	
Rest.	Pun.	Rest.	Pun.	Rest.	Pun.	Rest.	Pun.
31	36	28	37	26	35	20	50

[a] Percentages of restitutive and punitive respondents based on logit-analysis.

Concluding Remarks

The Public Attitudes

There are two possible interpretations of the high acceptance of restitution by the general public. We may, on the one hand, see restitution as a new kind of sanction alongside traditional sanctions, substantially extending the range of tools with which criminal policy can react to crime phenomena. Restitution contributes much more to conflict resolution than do fines or imprisonment: It takes into account the victim's needs and interests; and it may even be a more effective form of rehabilitation for the offender.

But this is only one side of the coin, and not the most important one. By extending the study to the question of how conflicts (involving legally defined crimes) can be solved outside the criminal-justice system or at least outside the criminal procedure, we also introduced an abolitionist perspective into the study. The question is to what extent criminal law will remain indispensible even should it some day prove possible to develop a peaceful conflict-resolution system to its full potential; that is, without endangering the social order, by integrating offender and victim into these processes. A further question is whether the criminal law may not need and even sustain social discord and peacelessness in order to secure its own position as the only agency entitled to establish and guarantee social peace and social order. Thus, studies on restitution represent a salient contribution to conflict theory.

Studies on restitution are also necessary to the reevaluation of past research on crime severity. One of the main purposes of such surveys is to develop more appropriate measures for sanctioning practices, to improve the deterrent effect of penalties and to assist in the allocation of scarce criminal-justice resources (Wolfgang et al., 1985; Rossi, et al., 1985, p. 233). The common method is to measure public attitudes to the relative seriousness of various offenses in order to construct an offense-seriousness scale (Sellin & Wolfgang, 1978). This approach has been criticized by some scholars because the severity of the penalties was neglected (Sebba, 1978; Sebba & Nathan, 1984). In fact, this refinement is needed but still insufficient as long as surveys of this kind are restricted to the set of penalties to be found in the penal codes, while ignoring all other imaginable sanctions and reactions to crimes, including restitution and nonintervention (see Hough & Mayhew, 1985, pp. 43–50, who included community service, compensation, and discharge or caution). Neglect of extralegal reactions automatically leads to the affirmation of traditional criminal law; inclusion of those reactions, on the other hand, questions the criminal law.

Fear of Crime and Attitudes

Considering the almost nonexistent, or at least weak, relationship between attitudes to sanctioning and fear of crime, direct or indirect victimization, and sociodemographic variables (although more detailed analysis revealed interesting connections with fear, sex, and age), our findings support interpretations of previous research on attitudes to penalties. Thus, it has generally been concluded that repressiveness does depend more on generalized, traditional patterns of attitude than on people's anxieties (Arzberger et al., 1979, p. 126), or that needs for punishment are unaffected by direct experience of crime because those attitudes are based on historically transmitted "belief systems" of a political, ethical, or religious nature (see Stinchcombe et al., 1980, pp. 81, 122 and Karstedt-Henke, chapter 2 in this volume, following Converse, 1964).

Our observation that punitiveness as well as restitutiveness remain stable in the face of short-term events like victimization experiences, or emotional reactions like feelings of unsafety, or unchangeable personal characteristics like sex, leads to similar conclusions, namely, that punitive attitudes seem primarily to reflect an individual's belief systems, which are acquired over the long-term process of learning social values and deriving their general validity from them. The fact that the better educated are more in favor of restitutive sanctions than the less educated provides a further clue to the cognitive structure of sanctioning attitudes.

In other words, despite the fact that some individuals with high fear scores might seek in punishment a cure-all to reduce their fear, it is also possible that other anxious people may be more sensitive to social problems and therefore maintain some distance toward the use of punishment. At the same time, there may be individuals who, while lacking any anxiety, are committed to traditional political or religious beliefs and thus view tough and consistent punishment as a necessary presupposition for the successful functioning of social life.

In summary, political proposals to tackle the social problem of fear of crime by tougher law enforcement receive no support from empirical research. On the contrary, such proposals seem to mirror ideological persuasion rather than serious reflection on a reasonable social and criminal policy.

Appendix

Standard Cases

1. *T* snatches the bag of a pedestrian; the bag contains a purse with DM 180 (the equivalent in 1989 of $100; in 1984, of $60).
2. T leaves a bar without paying the bill of DM 72 ($40 in 1989, $24 in 1984).
3. At a farmers' market, *T* takes two pineapples valued at DM 15 and runs away ($8 in 1989, $5 in 1984).
4. On a social outing with coworkers *T* gets into a quarrel with a colleague that turns into a physical argument between them. To free himself, *T* heavily punches his colleague in the stomach. The colleague stumbles backward, tumbles, and breaks his neck on the edge of a staircase. He dies immediately.
5. T breaks into a factory by smashing a window. He takes away an electric drill and other tools valued at DM 400 ($222 in 1989, $134 in 1984).
6. T goes by subway without paying the fare of DM 3.40 ($2 in 1989, $1.10 in 1984).

Variant Cases

7.   This case varied by type of crime committed.
7.1. *T* wants to get into a dwelling in order to steal something while the owner is at work. The door is locked and secured by certain additional locks. Using all his strength he forces the door open. He takes money and other things totaling DM 1,200 (worth $670 in 1989, $400 in 1984) in value.
7.2. *T* wants to get into a dwelling in order to steal something while the owner is at work. He discovers an open window on the first floor through which he enters the apartment. He takes money and other things totaling DM 1,200 in value.
7.3. *T* wants to get into a dwelling in order to steal something while the owner is at work. He finds the door unlocked, enters the apartment, and takes money and other things totalling DM 1,200 in value.
7.4. *T* wants to get into a dwelling in order to steal something while the owner is at work. He unlocks the door skilfully, enters the apartment, and takes money and other things totaling DM 1,200 in value.

8.   This case varied by type of victim.
8.1. *T* learns that his uncle wants to sell hi-fi equipment for DM 800 ($444 in 1989, $267 in 1984). They agree on the price. *T* takes the equipment and promises to pay the next day although he knows he does not have the money to pay for it.
8.2. *T* orders hi-fi equipment worth DM 800 from a mail-order house

although he knows he does not have the money to pay for it.

8.3. *T* learns that an aquaintance wants to sell hi-fi equipment for DM 800. They agree on the price. He takes the equipment and promises to pay the next day although he knows he does not have the money to pay for it.

8.4. In the daily paper *T* notices an advertisment offering hi-fi equipment for DM 800. He agrees with the seller on a price, takes the equipment, and promises to pay the next day although he knows he does not have the money to pay for it.

9.   This case varied by amount of property lost.

9.1. At a parking lot *T* opens a car door, is able to unlock the bolt of the trunk and removes a camera worth DM 620 ($344 in 1989, $205 in 1981).

9.2. At a parking lot *T* opens a car door, is able to unlock the bolt of the trunk and removes a camera worth DM 1200 ($670 in 1989, $400 in 1984).

9.3. At a parking lot *T* opens a car door, is able to unlock the bolt of the trunk and removes a camera worth DM 850 ($470 in 1989; $283 in 1984).

9.4. At a parking lot *T* opens a car door, is able to unlock the bolt of the trunk and removes a camera worth DM 450 ($250 in 1988; $1,150 in 1984).

10.   This case varied by kind of injury.

10.1. After an accident with his motorcycle *T* gets furious and hits the person involved, breaking his finger.

10.2. After an accident with his motorcycle, *T* gets furious and hits the person involved in such a way that this person sustains some cuts and bruises on the arm.

10.3. After an accident with his motorcycle, *T* gets furious and hits the person involved in such a way that this person breaks his jaw and has to go to hospital.

10.4. After an accident with his motorcycle, *T* gets furious and hits the person involved in a way that this person sustains painful cuts and bruises on his chest.

11.   This case varied by type of crime.

11.1. While visiting a customer in his home, *T* sells a cheap imitation watch worth DM 20 ($11 in 1989, $7 in 1984) for DM 220 ($122 in 1989, $73 in 1984) pretending that this is a special offer.

11.2. While visiting a customer in his home, *T* forces him under threat of violence to surrender his wallet containing DM 200 ($110 in 1989, $67 in 1984).

11.3. While visiting a customer in his home, *T* takes DM 200 out of an unlocked writing table at a propitious moment.

11.4. While visiting a customer in his home *T* breaks into a dresser drawer at a propitious moment. He steals DM 200 out of it.

12. This case varied by victim–offender relationship.
12.1. Leaving a movie, T happens to meet his girlfriend, with whom he had recently quarreled. Because they have to go in the same direction, they decide to walk together. At a solitary spot he makes advances, the women refuses, but he drags her into the bushes nearby and rapes her.
12.2. Leaving a movie, T happens to meet a female colleague. Because they have to go in the same direction they decide to walk together. At a solitary spot he makes advances, the women refuses, but he drags her into the bushes nearby and rapes her.
12.3. Leaving a movie, T happens to meet his former girlfriend, who broke up with him. Because they have to go in the same direction they decide to walk together. At a solitary spot he makes advances, the women refuses, but he drags her into the bushes nearby and rapes her.
12.4. Leaving a movie, T happens to meet a girl which he knows by sight only. He recognizes her as the sister of one of his colleagues. Because they have to go in the same direction they decide to walk together. At a solitary spot he makes advances, the women refuses, but he drags her into the bushes nearby and rapes her.

13. This case varied according to type of victim's behavior.
13.1. At a party T is insulted by an acquaintance. T urges him to retract his comment. As he refuses to do so T punches him in the face and the acquaintance sustains a nose-bleed and a black eye.
13.2 At a party, an acquaintance of T brags in T's presence of having stolen T's girlfriend. T becomes so angry he punches him in his face and the acquaintance sustains a nosebleed and a black eye.
13.3. At a party an acquaintance picks a fight with T. T tries to calm him. As his efforts are useless, T loses patience and punches his acquaintance in the face in such a way that the acquaintance sustains a nosebleed and a black eye.
13.4. At a party an acquaintance picks a fight with T. T tries to calm him. The acquaintance feels attacked, confronts T, and threatens to beat him up. T loses patience and punches him in his face and the acquaintance sustains a nosebleed and a black eye.

14. This case varied by type of injury.
14.1. While riding a bicycle, T overlooks a traffic sign. This results in an accident in which a pedestrian falls and sustains painful cuts and bruises on his chest.
14.2. While riding a bicycle, T overlooks a traffic sign. This results in an accident in which a pedestrain falls, breaks his jaw, and has to go to hospital.
14.3. While riding a bicycle, T overlooks a traffic sign. This results in an accident in which a pedestrian falls and breaks one of his fingers.
14.4. While riding a bicycle, T overlooks a traffic sign. This results in an

accident in which a pedestrian falls and sustains a couple of cuts and bruises on the arm.

References

Arzberger, K., Murck, M., & Schumacher, J. (1979). *Die Bürger. Bedürfnisse, Einstellungen, Verhalten*. Königstein: Verlag Hain Meisenheim.

Christie, N. (1977). Conflicts as property. *The British Journal of Criminology, 17*, 1–15.

Converse, P.E. (1964). The nature of belief systems in mass publics. In D.E. Apter (Ed.), *Ideology and discontent* pp. 206–261. New York: Free Press.

Foucault, M. (1979). *Discipline and punish*. New York: Vintage Books.

Gandy, J.T., & Galaway, B. (1980). Restitution as a sanction for offenders: A public's view. In J. Hudson & B. Galaway (Eds.), *Victims, offenders, and alternative sanctions* (pp. 89–100). Lexington, MA: Lexington Books.

Gibbs, J.J., Coyle, E.J., & Hanrahan, K.J. (1987). *Fear of crime: A concept in need of clarification*. Paper presented at the annual meeting of the American Society of Criminology, Montreal.

Goodman, L.A. (1970). The multivariate analysis of qualitative data: Interactions among multiple classifications. *Journal of the American Statistical Association, 65*, 226–256.

Goodman, L.A. (1971). The analysis of multidimensional contingency tables: Stepwise procedures and direct estimation methods for building models for multiple classifications. *Technometrics, 13*, 33–61.

Hindelang, M.J., Gottfredson, M.R., & Garofalo, J. (1978). *Victims of personal crime: An empirical foundation for a theory of personal victimization*. Cambridge, MA.: Ballinger.

Hough, M. (1985). The impact of victimisation: Findings from the British Crime Survey. *Victimology: An International Journal, 10*, 488–497.

Hough, M., & Mayhew, P. (1985). *Taking account of crime: Key findings from the second British Crime Survey*. (Home Office Research Study No. 85.) London: Her Majesty's Stationary Office.

Hough, M., & Moxon, D. (1985). Dealing with offenders: Popular opinion and the views of victims. Findings from the British Crime Survey. *The Howard Journal, 24*, 160–175.

Langeheine, R. (1980). *Log-lineare Modelle zur multivariaten Analyse qualitativer Daten*. München: Oldenbourg.

Lazarus, R.S. (1975). The self-regulation of emotion. In L. Levi (Ed.), *Emotions: Their parameters and measurements* (pp. 47–67). New York: Raven Press.

Longworthy, R.H., & Whitehead, J.T. (1986). Liberalism and fear as explanations of punitiveness. *Criminology, 24*, 575–591.

Rossi, P.H., Waite, E., Bose, C., & Berk, R.A. (1974). The seriousness of crimes: Normative structure and individual differences. *American Sociological Review, 39*, 224–237.

Rossi, P.H., Simpson, J.E., & Miller, J.L. (1985). Beyond crime seriousness: Fitting the punishment to the crime. *Journal of Quantitative Criminology, 1*, 59–90.

Schafer, St. (1968). *The victim and his criminal. A study in functional responsibility*. New York: Random House.

Schmidt, E. (1965). *Einführung in die Geschichte der deutschen Strafrechtspflege* (3rd ed). Göttingen: Vandenhoek & Ruprecht.

Sebba, L. & Nathan, G. (1984). Further explorations in the scaling of penalties. *The British Journal of Criminology, 23*, 221–246.

Sebba, L. (1978). Some explorations in the scaling of penalties. *Journal of Research in Crime and Delinquency, 15*, 247–265.

Sellin, Th. & Wolfgang, M.E. (1978). Measurement of delinquency. Montclair, NJ: Patterson Smith. (Reprint of the 1964 edition)

Sessar, K. (1986). Offender restitution as part of a future criminal policy. In K. Miyazawa & M. Ohya (Eds.). *Victimology in comparative perspective* (pp. 392–404). Tokyo: Seibundo.

Sessar, K., Beurskens, A., & Boers, K. (1986). Wiedergutmachung als Konfliktregelungsparadigma? *Kriminologisches Journal, 18*, 86–104.

Skogan, W.G., & Maxfield, M.G. (1981). *Coping with crime.* Beverly Hills, CA: Sage.

Skogan, W.G. (1987). The impact of victimization on fear. *Crime and Delinquency, 33*, 135–154.

Stinchcombe, A.L., Adams, R., Heimer, C.H., Scheppele, K.L., Smith, T.W., & Taylor, D.G. (1980). *Crime and punishment—Changing attitudes in America.* San Francisco: Jossey-Bass.

Teske, R.H.C., & Arnold, H.R. (1987). A comparative analysis of factors related to fear of crime in the United States (Texas) and the Federal Republic of Germany (Baden-Württemberg). *International Journal of Comparative and Applied Criminal Justice, 11*, 33–45.

Wolfgang, M.E.: Figlio, R.M.; Tracy, P.E., & Singer, S.I. (1985). *The National Survey of Crime Severity.* (US Department of Justice) Washington, DC: US Government Printing Office.

8
Fines in the Criminal Justice System

HANS-JÖRG ALBRECHT

Introduction

As part of a general penal code revision in 1969 and 1975 the Federal Republic of Germany increased its reliance on fines through substituting short-term imprisonment (up to 6 months) by fines (1969). Another part of the revision has been the introduction of the *day fine system* instead of the system of summary fines (1975). The consequences of implementing fines as a major alternative to imprisonment in the criminal justice system have been a dramatic decrease in the use of prison sentences and a rather sudden though expected decline in the number of prison inmates. Between 1968 and 1971 the proportion of prison sentences decreased from 23% to 7%. The number of prison inmates per 100,000 inhabitants fell from approximately 100/100,000 in 1969 to 66/100,000 in 1971.

Although fines should be regarded as the most important sanction (in quantitative terms) in virtually all criminal justice systems, knowledge is scarce about the use and potential of fines in responding efficiently to crime. Summary evaluation of studies on recidivism reveals that fines have been neglected in criminological research (Lipton, Martinson, & Wilks, 1975, p. 56). Little is known about fines in sentencing as well as about collection or enforcement of fines (Casale, 1981, p. 1). Nevertheless, fast-growing prison populations throughout the industrialized world and serious overload problems have led to a renewed interest in exploring the potential of fines as alternatives to imprisonment even in those countries where fines until now have not received as attention as in the Federal Republic of Germany or Austria (Casale & Hillsman, 1986, p. 4; Hillsman, Sichel, & Mahoney, 1984).

This chapter addresses problems with the use of fines and its extension in the criminal justice system of the Federal Republic of Germany. It is based on a series of research projects including international comparative legal studies and fine systems, research on sentencing (focusing on the choice between fine, suspended prison sentence, and imprisonment as well as the implementation of the day fine system) and the process of fine enforcement (including the use of substitute imprisonment and community service for fine defaulters) as well as research on recidivism after fines, suspended prison sentences, and imprisonment (Albrecht 1980; Grebing 1982; Albrecht 1982a, 1983; Albrecht, & Schädler 1986; Jescheck, & Grebing 1978).

The data described and analyzed so far were collected by investigating two random samples of offenders found guilty and sentenced in 1972 ($n = 1,823$, before introducing the day fine system) and 1975 ($n = 451$, after introduction of the day fine system). The sample includes essentially traffic offenses, property offenses, assault and fraud; those serious crimes, such as robbery, rape, homicide, for which mandatory prison sentences are provided by criminal law were excluded. Data derived from these files cover investigative, prosecution, and sentencing stages as well as fine enforcement and the general correctional phase of the process. Additional data on recidivism were gathered by following up each offender from the 1972 sample for a minimum period of five years using the Central Court Information System (where every conviction is registered) as a data source. Further data on sentencing, enforcement patterns, and attitudes toward sentencing and criminal penalties were gathered through interviews with random samples of judges, public prosecutors, and court administration staff ($n = 50$ from each group) as well as through a general population survey ($n = 863$) (Albrecht 1982b).

Interviews with judges and public prosecutors included sentencing in four simulated criminal cases, a method that seemed appropriate to overcome some of the problems of "black-box"-research associated with the analysis of files (see Albrecht, 1983; Clancy, Bartolomeo, Richardson, & Weelford, 1981; Hogarth, 1971).

The research was conducted in the state of Baden-Württemberg, a state that can be said to reflect fairly well the state of criminal justice in the Federal Republic of Germany.

The Fine as Criminal Penalty: Problems and Promises

The introduction of fines in the criminal justice system of the Federal Republic of Germany has been accompanied by a lively discussion on advantages and disadvantages of fines vis-à-vis imprisonment and probation and on the potential of different fine systems. In the Federal Republic of Germany the advantages of fines, especially the day fine system, finally have been perceived to outweigh the possibly negative side effects of relying heavily on fines; the arguments raised in the legislative process are relevant for any system making use of fines in criminal justice. However, obviously not all countries followed the FRG's line of reasoning: Scandinavian countries, the Netherlands, Anglo-American countries on the one hand never refrained from using short-term imprisonment on a large scale and on the other hand were quite reluctant to adopt fines as a regular device for a wide range of ordinary offences and offenders (Grebing, 1982; Jescheck & Grebing, 1978).

The arguments put forward to support the use of fines in the criminal-justice system point out that short-term imprisonment is not well suited to reach the overall goals of sentencing in terms of individual prevention. Short-term imprisonment is said to make offenders worse than they are before undergoing imprisonment because the experience of prison serves rather to enhance criminal capabilities and to destroy bonds to relevant others as well as society (Newton, 1976). Besides the effect of avoiding the negative side effects of imprisonment, fines are perceived to be convenient to administer and enforce, as well as being less expensive than probation, suspended prison sentences, or imprisonment. Moreover, individual justice is said to be promoted by individualizing the fine along the lines of the day fine system, which breaks down fining into two parts: (1) fixing a number of day fines reflecting solely the gravity and seriousness of the offense; (2) fixing a day rate based upon the offender's daily net income (after certain deductions (e.g., pension contribution) and taking into account the number of dependents). The number of day fines then is multiplied by the day rate.[1]

Critics of heavy reliance on fines suggest that fines are not suited to most of those offenders coming to the attention of the criminal justice system because these offenders come from marginalized segments of society partially dependent on social welfare and not able to pay considerable amounts of money. Because fines should be big enough to serve as a deterrent (see Davidson, 1965, p. 87), a substantial proportion within this group of offenders would have to serve time in prison in the case of fine default (Stein, 1969). Furthermore, they argue that fines may serve as an incentive to commit new crimes in order to be able to pay the fine. Another argument concerns the problem of fining offenders who are dependent on social welfare or unemployment benefits and herewith are required to pay

---

[1] §40 German Criminal Code reads as follows:
1. The fine has to be fixed as day fines. The minimum number of day fines is 5, the maximum number is, if statutes do not require a higher number, 360 day fines.
2. The amount of 1 day fine is determined by the court which has to consider the personal and economic circumstances of the offender. As a rule the day fine has to be based on the average net-income which the defendent actually has per day or which the defendent could have per day. The minimum amount of one day fine is 2 DM, the maximum amount is 10,000 DM.
3. The income of the defendant, his or her means as well as other sources of income which seem to be relevant for determination of the amount of one day fine may be estimates.
4. In the final decision the number as well as the amount of the day fine have to be mentioned.

the fine with money received from state or other agencies in order to maintain a minimum standard of living. Loss of control over the enforcement process insofar as fines can be paid by third parties is also discussed. Fining offenders could result in unjust and unfair results offenders from marginalized and poor segments of society, substitute fines with imprisonment, while the rich person who is sentenced to a fine will always be able to buy his or her way out of the criminal justice system (Hickey & Rubin, 1971). Finally, there is the fear of loss of deterrence after extension of the use of fines and the more recent question of whether fines would disrupt the process of restitution that disables the offender in order to compensate the victim's losses (see the summary assessment in Grebing, 1982).

Fines in the Sentencing Process

Analysis of court statistics in the Federal Republic of Germany shows that the structure of sentences is dominated by fines. This is not only true for the classical field of the application of fines, (i.e., traffic offenses) but also for ordinary crime (property offenses, fraud, assault, drug offenses). Table 8.1 displays the proportions of different sentences in the adult criminal-justice system. Three out of four offenders are fined in the case of ordinary criminal offences, approximately 95% of all traffic offenders are fined. But the use of fines, although criminal law allows for 5- to 360-day fines (which corresponds to prison sentences up to 1 year), is practically limited to a range of 5- to 90-day fines (except tax offenses where courts are more likely to mete out heavy fines).

The distribution that can be observed in court statistics can be said to be the result of a process commencing at the end of the 19th century and ending with the replacement of prison sentences up to 3 months through fines. In 1882 the proportion of all convictions resulting in fines has been 25.3%. The proportion increased to approximately 60% until the major reform of criminal law in 1969. After 1969 the complete abandonment of sentences of less than 1 month and severe limits on the use of prison sentences up to 6 months lowered the use of imprisonment to today's level. These marked effects of the criminal-law reform can be explained at least partially by the statutory inhibition of judicial discretion in the choice between fines and imprisonment, which specified that only in exceptional cases can prison sentences of less than 6 months be imposed (§47 German Criminal Code). These exceptional circumstances are defined as a need for defense of the legal order (promoting the people's respect for the law) or as special needs for individual prevention arising out of the personality of the offender. Another barrier to prison sentences up to 6 months is the requirement for explicit justification in writing that refers to the need for either general or individual prevention.

The reform in short-term imprisonment policy has occurred within a

TABLE 8.1. Sentences broken down by crime types 1985 (adult criminal law).

	Day fines (%)					Imprisonment (%)			Total	
	5–15	16–30	31–90	91–180	>180	<6 months	6–12 months	>12 months	N	%
Public-order offenses	16.0	32.0	26.0	4.3	0.1	12.5	6.6	2.4	15,920	100
Sexual offenses	3.5	12.4	14.4	2.4	0.1	12.8	21.7	32.7	4,434	100
Crimes against persons (assault, etc.)	17.7	29.2	24.0	1.9	0.04	17.0	6.7	3.4	44,661	100
Property crimes (theft)	35.4	23.5	14.6	1.8	0.05	13.2	8.1	3.4	127,761	100
Robbery	0.3	0.9	2.3	0.8	0.06	6.6	23.4	65.7	3,582	100
Other property crimes (fraud, etc.)	19.9	30.9	24.6	2.8	0.3	11.2	7.0	3.4	87,502	100
Traffic offenses	13.1	37.3	37.9	0.8	0.01	1.7	1.4	0.2	239,484	100

Source: Statistisches Bundesamt (Ed.): Strafverfolgungsstatistik, Wiesbaden 1986.

political context that centered on the themes of effective administration of criminal justice and the legitimacy of the legal system. In the 1960s, the number of convicted offenders in the FRG exceeded by far the capacity of the prison system. Furthermore, the sharp increase in reported crimes and apprehended offenders in the 1960s and 1970s led to considerable pressures on the criminal justice system. Fines were perceived to be sufficient responses to most offenses and a kind of punishment lenient enough to be applied in a system of simplified procedures. In the Federal Republic of Germany, the use of fines is backed up by a procedural option for the public prosecutor to choose between regular court proceedings and a full trial and a simplified procedure called *Strafbefehl* (penal order). The use of simplified procedures requires there are no problems of evidence and proof and that a fine is a sufficient punishment. Neither imprisonment nor suspended prison sentences may be ordered by using the simplified procedures. Combining fines with simplified procedure results in a rational and efficient way to dispose of a substantial number of criminal cases (see Table 8.2). Approximately 40% of all criminal cases that come to the attention of the public prosecutor and are brought to court are handled by way of fining offenders in a summary procedure. Fines combined with simplification of procedures thus are indispensable when aiming at maintaining a certain level of punishment and a certain level of swiftness of punishment. Analysis of file data shows that the average time spent (from detection of the offense until final conviction) in the case of fines is 5 months, whereas 10 months are needed in the case of imprisonment (Albrecht, 1982a, p. 160).

Choice of Fines among Criminal Sanctions

What are the criteria employed in choosing between a fine and imprisonment for those offenses for which the laws permit both and what determines the amount of the fine?

Based on the data resulting from analysis of files and interviews with judges and public prosecutors, we observe that the choice between fine and imprisonment is well patterned. Among the criteria investigated, *prior record* appeared to be the most important single variable in separating fines from prison sentences. Analysis of the content of written statements justifying the use of short-term imprisonment shows also that prior record is exclusively used to demonstrate that the personality of certain offenders indicates the need for a prison sentence. When resorting to prison terms, reasons given to legitimize imprisonment refer to the number and seriousness of prior convictions for the same type of offense. Thus a fine is the typical penalty for the first offender whereas repetition of the same type of offense results in a marked escalation of sentencing, starting with fines and ending up with immediate imprisonment. This holds true for

TABLE 8.2. Decision and sentencing structure[a]

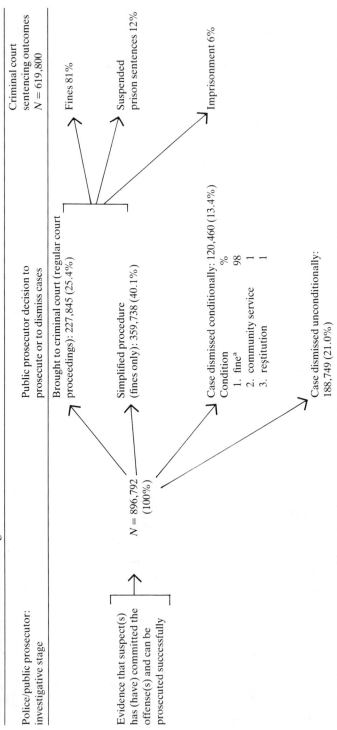

Police/public prosecutor: investigative stage

Evidence that suspect(s) has (have) committed the offense(s) and can be prosecuted successfully

$N = 896{,}792$ (100%)

Public prosecutor decision to prosecute or to dismiss cases

Brought to criminal court (regular court proceedings): 227,845 (25.4%)

Simplified procedure (fines only): 359,738 (40.1%)

Case dismissed conditionally: 120,460 (13.4%)

Condition   %
1. fine[a]   98
2. community service   1
3. restitution   1

Case dismissed unconditionally: 188,749 (21.0%)

Criminal court sentencing outcomes $N = 619{,}800$

Fines 81%

Suspended prison sentences 12%

Imprisonment 6%

Sources: Statistics on public prosecution (based on cases); court statistics (based on adjudicated offenders).
[a] All offenses/offenders, adult criminal law, 1984.
[b] Payment of the fine has to be made to a charitable organization that is to be named by the public prosecutor (e.g., Red Cross, local shelters for battered women).

all categories of offenses, be they traffic, property crime, fraud, or assault. Other variables (such as the victim's injuries or losses, socioeconomic status, marital status, and other offender characteristics) seem to be far less relevant. These findings from the analysis of files and sentencing outcomes are supported by data from interviewing judges and public prosecutors and data from the simulation study on sentencing (Albrecht, 1983). Table 8.3, which displays sentencing outcomes in four simulated cases including drunken driving and theft, demonstrates that there is not much sentencing disparity. Measures of dispersion indicate that strong uniformity exists in sentencing across judges with only few exceptions deviating from the central tendency. When disparity in the choice between criminal penalties shows up, it occurs at two points in the decision-making process: the choice between fine and a prison sentence when the offender has one or two prior convictions for the same type of offense and the choice between suspension of prison sentence and immediate imprisonment.

The overall finding that there are but a few important variables determining the choice between fine and prison sentence can be extended to the decision about the number of day fines imposed. It is obvious and clearly visible in the data (see Table 8.3) that there are certain taxes for certain crime types primarily determined by type of the offense. Strong uniformity and sentencing taxes stem from the requirements of processing considerable numbers of offenders through the system, which results in reduction of information on offense and offender normally provided by police and public prosecutor. The findings show investigations by police and public prosecutor were consistently limited to information that could be drawn from the routine questioning of the suspect or victims as well as from routine reviews of the suspect's record of previous convictions. Consequently, complete information exists as the basis for judicial decision making with respect to (1) the elements of the offense itself, (2) the suspect's identity (name, place, and date of birth), (3) the suspect's prior record, and (4) the material consequences of the offense (financial and other losses). On the other land, considerable deficits in information exist with respect to (1) the offender's personal, social, and economic situation, (2) possible motives for the offense, (3) consequences of the crime for the victim or the defendant's behavior after committing the crime. These findings indicate special problems for implementing the day-fine system because of the central role information on the income and general economic situation of the offender plays in adapting the fine to offense and offender. Although precise information on the offender's income should be seen as a prerequisite of successful implementation of the day-fine system, German criminal law provides an option for estimating the offender's income when adequate information is lacking. Most respondents in the sample of judges interviewed considered the profession of the offender to be the most essential factor in determining the level of income. When asked to assign concrete day rates to particular

TABLE 8.3. Results from a stimulation study on sentencing based on interviews with a random sample of judges/public prosecutors in the state of Baden-Württemberg/FRG.

| | Decisions/sentences | | | | | | | | | | | | | | | | | | | | | | | |
| Case characteristics/offender characteristics | Conditional dismissal (condition: fine)[a] | | | | | Fine (number of day fines) | | | | | | Suspended prison sentence (months) | | | | | | Imprisonment (months) | | | | | | Total N |
	N	%	m(DM)	min.	max.	N	%	m	SD	min.	max.	N	%	m	SD	min.	max.	N	%	m	SD	min.	max.	
Drunken driving: 0.18% BAC; offender: married, no children, blue-collar worker, net income ca. 1,200 DM/month, no prior convictions; 35 years old.																								
Case 1: Minimum statutory punishment: 5 day fines Maximum statutory punishment: 2 years imprisonment						86	100	34	6	20	60													86
Theft of items 50 DM worth in a warehouse; married woman, no children, husband's profession: architect; no information on income available; no prior convictions; 30 years old.																								
Case 2: Minimum statutory punishment: 5 day fines Maximum statutory punishment: 5 years imprisonment	31	37	200	100	500	53	63	10	3, 4	5	20													84
Two aggravated thefts (breaking into cars); items stolen, worth: 1,000 DM, damage caused: 800 DM; 24-year-old blue-collar worker; unemployed; social security benefits/month: 800 DM; 1 prior conviction (driving without a valid license).																								
Case 3: Minimum statutory punishment: 3 months (or a corresponding number of day fines) Maximum statutory punishment: 10 years imprisonment						55	65	83	30	30	180	28	35	4	1, 6	2	7							84
Drunken driving followed by an accident (1 person injured), BAC: 0.2%; 30-year-old employee, not married; net income: 1,500 DM/month; 2 prior convictions (drunken driving 2 and 3 years ago)																								
Case 4: Minimum statutory punishment: 5 day fines Maximum statutory punishment: 5 years imprisonment												55	63	3, 6	1, 1	1	6	32	37	3, 3	1, 0	2	6	87

Source: Albrecht H.-J. (1983). Gleichmässigkeit und Ungleichmässigkeit in der Strafzumessung [Equity and disparity in sentencing]. In Kerner, H.-J., Kury, H., & Sessar, K. (Eds.): Deutsche Forschungen zur Kriminalitätsentstehung und Kriminalitätskontrolle [German research on crime and crime control] (Vol. 2, pp. 1297–1332). Köln: Heymanns.
[a] m = mean; SD = standard deviation; min. = minimum; max. = maximum.

professions, it became obvious that judges have both exact and identical conceptions concerning the incomes of unskilled workers, skilled workers, or employees, which in turn lead to uniform decisions and very limited variation in the fixing of day-rates. Uncertainty in decision making, which resulted in considerable variance in assigning day rates was found for certain independent professions (e.g., physicians, lawyers, etc.) (Albrecht, 1982b). Although offenders holding these professions are of minor quantitative importance for the criminal justice system, problems of equity in determining day rates and fining offenders resulting from lack of information on this small group may only be overcome by concentrating investigative efforts and means inquiries on these types of professions. For the bulk of offenders rough estimations of net income seem to be sufficient.

Collection and Enforcement of Fines

Fine collection and fine enforcement are crucial points in any criminal-justice system that widely uses fines because the credibility of fines as a criminal punishment depends from the degree to which they are actually collected. In the Federal Republic of Germany, the public prosecutor's office takes care of fine collection and fine enforcement. As a great number of fines cannot be paid immediately by offenders because their magnitude surmounts either the monthly income or those parts of the income not needed for maintaining a minimum standard of living, the court, or after passing the sentence, the public prosecutor may grant payment of the fine by installments. If the fine is not paid, there are several instruments to enforce the fine: (1) mere reminder, (2) seizure of property or wages, or (3) if these are not prove successful, substitute imprisonment (corresponding to the number of day fines), which must be ordered (except when serving a subsitute prison sentence had to be considered to be grossly unfair and unjust; see §459f Criminal Procedure Code).

The survey of fine collection and fine enforcement shows (see Figure 8.1) that about half of all fines falling into our sample were paid immediately after sentence. In the remaining group, 63% (or 31.5% of all fined offenders) were allowed to pay their fines by installments: 70% of these offenders either paid punctually, or paid after receiving at least one payment reminder. Fifty percent of those fined, who neither paid immediately nor were permitted to pay by installments nor were granted postponement of payment paid their fines after one reminder of overdue payment. In every tenth case, seizure proceedings were initiated but were proved successful only in a small number of cases (2.1%). A substantial proportion of the sample ended up with an order of substitute imprisonment (15.3%) (Figure 8.1). Most of these offenders had enough means to pay the fine because in two-third of these cases payment was received after ordering substitute

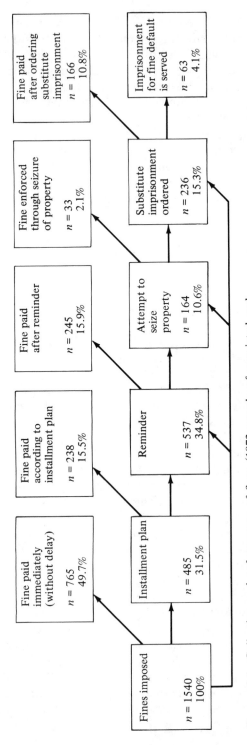

FIGURE 8.1. Collection and enforcement of fines (1972 sample of convicted and sentenced offenders).

imprisonment, whereas one-third actually had to serve a prison sentence (4.1%).

When looking at those variables predicting fine default, low professional status, unemployment, and prior record turned out to be the most important characteristics of fine defaulters (see also Softley, 1973). On the other hand, groups of individuals having below average economic means, such as students, apprentices, or pensioners are not overrepresented in the group of fine defaulters. Moreover, the size of the fine imposed had no effect on fine default. Fine default was independent from the size of the fine. When analyzing the profile of fine defaulters it became evident that fine defaulters were most similar to those offenders having received a suspended or immediate prison sentence.

Although the small number of fine defaulters may be interpreted as underlining the practicability of fines and the day-fine system as a whole, large, fine defaulters still bring a considerable burden upon the prison system (see Table 8.4). As unemployment increased rapidly fast at the end of the 1970s and with it the number of problematic enforcement of fined offenders, all states of the Federal Republic of Germany set up community-service schemes in order to divert fine defaulters from the prison system (Albrecht & Schädler, 1986; Kerner & Kästner, 1986). An offender is eligible for community service if substitute imprisonment for fine default is ordered. The court aide (staffed with social workers) then contacts the offender and offers community-service opportunities. One day fine corresponds to six hours of community service. Although the experiences of community service as alternative for fine defaulters have not yet been thoroughly scrutinized, we may conclude on the basis of small pieces of research that community service is a practicable device. Failure rates observed in the Federal Republic of Germany correspond to those reported from other countries that introduced community service as a sole sanction (Albrecht & Schädler, 1986), ranging from 10% to 20%. However, community service as an alternative to substitute imprisonment in the case of fine defaulters must not be justified by better preventive outcomes or cost-benefit ratios, but by the attempt alone to provide the same chances to every rich and poor offenders alike. With implementation of community service as a measure for avoiding substitute imprisonment, sources of injustice can be reduced that result from the wide use of fines in the criminal justice system on the one hand and the differences in income level and social background of offenders on the other hand.

Other important questions concern the problem who actually pays the fine (the offender or relatives, friends, etc.) and whether the need to pay the fine represents an incentive to commit further crimes (especially property crimes). (Behavior such as prostitution that is especially vulnerable to fines in terms of stipulating repetition has been decriminalized in the Federal Republic of German.) But the questions are not easily answered. Although our findings based on analysis of court files that allow

TABLE 8.4. Fine default – substitute imprisonment.

	1970	1974	1978	1982	1983	1984	1985
Fines	464,818	494,266	507,627	505,917	516,892	502,727	488,414
Prison admissions[a] (total)	—[d]	—	—	—	—	—	51,479
Prison admissions[b] (fine default)	—	14,000	19,000	23,500	23,000	22,000	19,000
Prison population[c] (total)	30,450	30,743	34,868	38,620	40,819	42,140	41,852
Prison population[c] (fine default)	—	1,152	1,623	1,984	1,972	1,876	1,600
Fine/fine default prison admission (%)	—	3	4	5	4	4	4
Prison admissions/fine default Admission (%)	—	—	—	—	—	—	37
Prison population/fine defaulters (%)	—	4	5	5	5	4	4

[a] Sentenced offenders (adult prison sentences only).
[b] Based on estimations derived from surveys stating that the average term of substitute imprisonment is approximately 1 month.
[c] March 31st.
[d] Data not available.

identification under certain circumstances of the person who paid the fine shows that approximately 1% of all fines were paid by other persons than the offender, data cover only those document points in the payment process. But analysis of recidivism causes us to conclude that fines constitute at least a no more powerful incentive to relapse than suspended or immediate prison sentences (at least when assuming that fined offenders are no more capable of escaping detection and conviction for subsequent offenses than are imprisoned offenders). Reconviction data show that reconviction rates for property crimes and fraud are lowest in the group of fined offenders. As for the possible effects of diverting the burden of the fine to the family or relatives (or even social welfare authorities), we have to acknowledge that every sanction implies some kind of suffering for the surrounding group of persons.

Is Fining Offenders a Superior Device?

The deficiencies of data on reconviction or subsequent arrests as measures of success or failure are well known. Moreover, problems arise out of the design as a post facto study. There is no way in the present study to control changes in the period between conviction and the end of the follow-up in variables like marital, socioeconomic, or employment status and it seems impossible to obtain data on offenders other than those from the files covering periods before the final sentence (see Lipton et al., 1975).

In order to keep and evaluate every piece of information available from data on reconvictions, the binary information on recidivism was combined with the actual number of reconvictions, the type of offense, seriousness of the new offense, and time between sentence and reconvictions. Nonserious reconvictions were not excluded as they are sometimes in studies on recidivism (see Stone-Meierhoefer & Hoffmann, 1980).

Findings from the study on recidivism for the sample convicted in 1972 can be summarized as follows: Recidivism occurred in 31% of all cases. Controlling the type of offense, significant differences between single offender groups could be observed. In the case of traffic offenses (causing negligent injuries or the death of another person in an accident), the rate of recidivism was as low as 18%, whereas for traffic offenses such as drunken driving a rate of 31% could be observed. Shoplifting shows up with 33% of the offenders being reconvicted, whereas high-risk groups turned out to be offenders sentenced on the basis of assault, fraud, and aggravated theft (43% to 70%). But only a small fraction of multiple recidivists is resentenced for the same type of crime. Crime switching can be assumed to be responsible for the sentencing patterns observable in the group of recidivists. About half of them were fined again; approximately 25% were punished by immediate imprisonment. It is obvious that a major fraction of offenses occurring in the 5-year follow-up was not considered to be of a serious nature (assessed primarily through reviewing the offenders' records for previous convictions for the same type of offense). Thus, fining offenders is not only an important judicial way of handling first offenders, but also multiple offenders switching between different types of crimes. A detailed analysis of sentencing patterns in the case of recidivists reveals that prior record contributes to an escalation of punishment if (1) previous conviction was for the same offense and (2) the period between earlier conviction and actual conviction did not exceed approximately 3 years.

When assessing the predictive power of variables derived from criminal history, employment status, and family through different multivariate statistical procedures, prior record was found to be the best predictor among a set of several independent variables (including socioeconomic status, marital status, age, and type of offense as well as employment status). Although risk probabilities in groups with and without prior record are modified if other variables like age and marital status are introduced, the overall predictive power is not considerably increased. The fraction of those offenders falling in an unclear range of probability of reconviction (between 40% and 60%) is very low (12%). The group with the lowest risk of reconviction consists of offenders who are (1) aged 40 years or older, (2) married, (3) found guilty of a traffic offense, and (4) have no prior conviction (10% from this group was reconvicted at least once within 5 years). The group with the highest risk is much smaller (about 4% of the sample): Members of this group were found guilty of aggravated theft or fraud and had serious and numerous prior convictions (80% were reconvicted within 5 years). But the overall predictive power of the independent variables introduced in stepwise multiple regression is not satisfying: Explained proportions of variance range between 15% (traffic offenses) and 26% (aggravated theft). Although there are some restraints in applying multiple regression in recidivism studies, multivariate procedures like dummy regression, multivariate nominal scale analysis (MNA), and multiple classification analysis (MCA) did not produce substantial differences in coefficients nor in the amount of explained variance (Albrecht, 1982a; see also Andrews & Messenger, 1973; Cain, 1977).

Comparing rates of reconviction after different sentences (fines, suspended prison sentences, and immediate imprisonment), we have to face first the problem of coping with the effects of "natural experiments." Because there is no way to assign offenders randomly to different kinds of criminal sanctions, "treatment" and control groups appropriate for thorough evaluation of "treatments" cannot be established by making use of a controlled experiment. Therefore, in this study, evaluation efforts concentrated on statistical controls and the relevance of selection criteria. Comparing the groups of offenders with fines, suspended prison sentences, and immediate imprisonment, we observe that there are substantial differences in prior record, marital status, age, socioeconomic status, and employment status, with prior record representing a key variable in sentencing-decisions. These differences let us hypothesize that fined offenders represent the group with the lowest risk of reconviction while offenders with immediate imprisonment represent a high-risk group. Therefore, two alternative and competing explanations of differences in reconviction rates are plausible:

1. Differences in rates of reconviction between the groups are due to differences in the punishment response.
2. Differences in the rates of reconviction are due to differences in those other variables that distinguish the groups.

Obviously, evaluation designs relying on the outcomes of natural experiments do not allow testing of these assumptions. Therefore, I investigated the question of whether and to what degree correlations between rates of recidivism and the punishment variable are overestimated and introduced selection criteria as controls.

Reconviction occurred in the fined group at a rate of 26% whereas the corresponding rates in the case of suspended prison sentences and imprisonment were 55% and 75%. Substantial differences between the groups were found in the number of reconvictions, the seriousness of reconviction, and conviction-free intervals (mean number of reconvictions: fine [.5], suspended prison sentences [1.0], imprisonment [2.0]; two thirds of offenders with recidivism after fines are resentenced to fines, while only 13% are imprisoned; in the case of suspended sentences the rates are 43% and 23%, respectively, and after imprisonment, 26% and 51%). Examination of the subpopulation of fined offenders shows that fine defaulters (about 4% of the group receiving fines) are responsible for a considerable proportion of all reconvictions in this group. Approximately 80% of all prison sentences in the case of reconviction after receiving a fine occurred in the group of fine defaulters. Furthermore, it seems noteworthy that the amount of the fine had no observable effect on the rates of reconviction.

Analysis of covariance was used to assess the stability of coefficients for the relationship between differences in punishment and rates of recidivism.[2] Prior record, marital status, socioeconomic status, employment status, and age were introduced as covariates assuming that these variables represent a valid model of the choice between fines, suspended prison sentences, and imprisonment in the sentencing decision. Controlling for these covariates, differences among the rates of reconvictions of fined offenders, offenders sentenced to suspended imprisonment, and offenders sentenced to immediate imprisonment were reduced dramatically. Differences in the rates of

---

[2] Analysis of covariance was carried out by the ANOVA-procedure as it is available in the Statistical Package for the Social Sciences (SPSS).

reconvictions for traffic offenders could be reduced to practically zero. Although there remained substantial differences after controlling selection criteria in the case of theft and fraud, the overall tendency of considerable reductions in the differences between punishment and recidivism could be observed, too. These findings should be interpreted as supporting for my second assumptions: Differences in the rates of reconviction between groups receiving different kinds of punishment reflect differences in the group structure and the effects of selection. My conclusion is that variation in the punishment response within the relatively narrow boundaries of sentencing options for certain offenses is not followed by substantial differences in rates of reconviction.

The difficulties and problems embodied in evaluating natural experiments that affect criminal justice systems should not be a justification for refraining from the evaluation of large-scale changes in the criminal justice system. However several lines and dimensions of change should form the basis of evaluation. Going beyond the topic of individual prevention and recidivism, respectively, reconviction, analysis of police-based crime statistics and court based offense and offender statistics demonstrates that the overall trends in crime and conviction rates were not affected by replacing short-term imprisonment with fines (Kiwull, 1979; Albrecht, 1980). Furthermore, a comparison of base expectancies of recidivism in the 1960s and 1970s does not reveal any differences that could be attributed to changes in sentencing (Kiwull, 1979).

Evaluating and assessing the potential of fines vis-à-vis imprisonment have to be based as well on the attitudes and perceptions of the population at large as well as the professional groups responsible for the implementation of criminal law: judges and public prosecutors.

The results obtained from interviews with judges and prosecutors showed that they accepted the day-fine system and the range of its application. Approximately 80% of the judges interviewed stated that they proceeded according to the principles of the day-fine system. Approximately half of them said that the day-fine system led to more equity in fixing fines and adopting them to offense and offender (Albrecht, 1982b).

A survey of the general population revealed that a majority (78%) of the population at large accepts fines as reasonable and effective punishment. Individuals who stated that they had been the victim of a criminal offense did not differ from nonvictims in this respect. Although the fine is generally accepted as an appropriate criminal penalty, almost two-thirds of the interviewees expressed mistrust about application with respect of the fine system. This mistrust was expressed as the suspicion that "rich people are more likely to be fined than poor people." Nevertheless, approximately two-fifths (39%) were of the opinion "that judges should impose fines more often as a substitute for short-term imprisonment than is already done." Controlling the attitudes on perceptions toward fines by introducing the dimension "fear of crime" (as measured through perceptions of the probability of becoming a victim of crime and of crime as increasing), these variables were not found to be related to the assessment of fines in general. Moreover, these variables do not differentiate groups that advocate or do not advocate further extension of the fine in the criminal justice system. Finally, attitudes and perceptions of criminal penalties were based on rather exact knowledge about the structure of sentencing outcomes in the Federal Republic of Germany. Approximately 70% assumed correctly that fines were imposed on an overwhelming majority of all sentenced offenders.

Conclusion

Summarizing the findings from research on fines in the criminal justice system, we may conclude:

1. It has been possible to replace imprisonment by fines on a large scale.
2. Changes in sentencing have been encouraged by (1) narrowing the court's discretion on the choice between fines and imprisonment as well as by (2) the administrative convenience of a procedural device combining summary procedure with fines.
3. Possibly the shift from widespread use of prison sentences to the use of monetary penalties indicates a significant move toward a justice system that incorporates administrative and civil (perhaps more civilized) features.
4. Reliance on fines coincides with findings from criminological research indicating that most offenders are but one-time offenders and do not require severe punishment or intervention.
5. Collection and enforcement of fines can be organized efficiently, although the credibility of fines still depends on the threat of substitute imprisonment.
6. The legitimacy of any fine system can be supported by offering alternatives to substitute imprisonment in terms of community service, thus avoiding or reducing the stigma of partial justice.
7. Evaluation of changes in the criminal justice system such as the large-scale trend toward fines has to be multidimensional. The many difficulties evaluation research faces in studying recidivism and deterrence should not confine research to these topics. Questions of acceptance (in the population at large and in professional staff) and implementation (administrative feasibility and the economics of punishment) must be addressed as well.
8. If different lines of evaluation are followed up, the fine experiment in the criminal justice system of the Federal Republic of Germany seems to show that societies can rely on alternatives to prison without affecting the system's performance.

References

Albrecht, H.-J. (1980). *Strafzumessung und Vollstrecking bei Geldstrafen.* Berlin: Duncker & Humblot.

Albrecht, H.-J. (1982a). *Legalbewährung bei zu Geldstrafe und Freiheitsstrafe Verurteilten.* Freiburg: Max-Planck-Institut.

Albrecht, H.-J. (1982b). The fine in the German penal sanctional system. In Criminological Research Unit (Ed.), *Research in Criminal Justice* (pp. 225–245). Freiburg: Max-Planck-Institut.

Albrecht, H.-J. (1983). Gleichmässigkeit und Ungleichmässigkeit in der Strafzumessung. In H.-J. Kerner, H. Kury, & K. Sessar (Eds.), German research on crime and crime control. (Vol. 2, pp. 1297–1332) Köln: Heymanns.

Albrecht, H.-J., & Schädler, W. [Eds.]. (1986). Community service, Gemeinnützige Arbeit, dienstverlening, travail d'interêt général: A new option in punishing offenders in Europe. Freiburg: Max-Planck-Institut.

Andrews, F.M., & Messenger, R.C. (1973). Thaid: A sequential analysis program for the analysis of nominal scale dependent variables. Ann Arbor, MI: Survey Research Center, University of Michigan.

Cain, G.G. (1977). Regression and selection models to improve nonexperimental comparison. In: M. Guttentag (Ed.), *Evaluation studies. Review annual Vol. 2,* pp. 93–113. Beverly Hill, CA, London: Sage.

Casale, S.S.G. (1981). *Fines in Europe: A study of the use of fines in selected European countries with empirical research on the problems of fine enforcement.* London: VERA Institute of Justice.

Casale, S.S.G., & Hillsman, S.T. (1986). *The enforcement of fines as criminal sanctions: The English experience and its relevance to American practice.* New York: VERA Institute of Justice.

Clancy, K., Bartolomeo, J., Richardson, D., & Wellford, Ch. (1981). Sentence decision-making: The logic of sentence-decisions and the extent and causes of sentence disparity. *Journal of Criminal Law and Criminology, 72,* 524–545.

Davidson, R. (1965). The promiscuous fine. *Criminal Law Wuarterly, 8,* 74–93.

Grebing, G. (1982). *The fine in comparative law: A survey of 21 countries.* Cambridge England: Institute of Criminology.

Hickey, W.L., & Rubir, S. (1971). Suspended sentences and fines. *Crime and Delinquency Literature, 3,* 413–429.

Hillsman, S.T., Sichel, J.L., & Mahoney, B. (1984). *Fines in sentencing: a study of the use of the fine as a criminal sanction.* Washington, DC: National Institute of Justice.

Hogarth, J. (1971). *Sentencing as a human process.* Toronto: University of Toronto Press.

Jescheck, H.-H., & Grebing, G. [Eds.]. (1978). *Die Geldstrafe im deutschen und ausländischen Recht.* Baden-Baden: Nomos.

Kerner, H.-J., & Kästner, O. [Eds.]. (1986). *Gemeinnützige Arbeit in der Strafrechtsphflege.* Bonn: Deutsche Bewährungshilfe.

Kiwull, H., (1979). *Kurzfistige Freiheitsstrafen und Geldstrafen vor und nach der Strafrechtsreform, einschliesslich der Entziehung der Fahrerlaubnis und des Strafverbots als Mittel der Specialprävention.* Jur. Diss., University of Freiburg.

Lipton, D., Martinson, R., Wilks, J. (1975). *The effectiveness of correctional treatment: A survey of evaluation studies.* New York: Praeger.

Newton, A. (1976). Alternatives to imprisonment: day fines, community service orders, and restitution. *Crime and Delinquency Literature, 8*, 109–125.

Softly, P. (1973). *A survey of fine enforcement.* (Home Office Research Study No. 16.) London: Her Majesty's Stationery Office.

Stein, P.M. (1969). Imprisonment for non-payment of fines and costs: A new look at the law and the constitution. *Vanderbilt Law Reform, 22*, 611–644.

Stone-Meierhoefer, B., Hoffmann, P.B. (1980). Reporting recidivism rates: the criterion and follow-up issues. *Journal of Criminology, 8*, 53–60.

9
Multiple Offending in Germany
Lessons on the Influence of Police Recording Rules upon Official Crime Rates of Different Age Groups

HANS-JUERGEN KERNER

Introduction: The Legacy of Traditional Offender Classifications

Classic west European criminology has always stressed the importance of studying repeated offense behavior. Partly based on experience gained by practitioners in the different fields of law enforcement, criminal justice, court-related clinics, and corrections, and partly referring to the results of early prison studies scholars concluded nearly unanimously that "criminality" was unevenly distributed among the general population. Criminality was, according to the leading scholars of that time, mainly a domain of young men, particularly among early beginners and, later in life, of adult chronic offenders generally called "multi-recidivists" (see e.g., Exner 1949, 181 et seq.; Mezger 1951, 152 et seq.).

Scholars in those times, discussing theories of crime causation, often used the terms of "criminals" versus "non-criminals." Thus they implied the possibility of drawing a clear-cut line between the completely "innocent people" who never committed any kind of offense and the "bad ones" getting in conflict with criminal law more or less often. That approach seemed to be the guiding research philosophy in a few comparative studies, in Germany as well as in the United States (see e.g., Glueck & Glueck, 1950). But it did not dominate the entire field of research. It was not predominant in criminology textbooks as we can easily detect by skipping the introductory chapters of those textbooks and by looking directly at the detailed discussion of research results.

One central weakness, however, should be mentioned: German authors in those times tended to disregard the influence of hidden criminality. They mentioned the problem in a general way by pointing to the existence of what was then called the "dark field." But not being acquainted with modern methods or techniques of self-report studies, they discussed only singular events or practitioners' experience. This kind of evidence seemed to show a certain regularity between the offenses known to the authorities and those remaining officially undetected. Instead of studying the problem in detail they quickly asserted the existence of a so-called law of constant relationships, meaning that the relationship between officially recorded crime and the dark figure is always constant. That law allowed the scholars to neglect hidden offenses for all practical research purposes when they dealt with the questions of the extent and structure of criminality. Assuming that officially known offenses represented an offender's "true criminality" the scholars developed a rather clearly defined concept. Following this concept they did not distinguish between dichotomous classes of criminals versus non-criminals but thought in terms of a quasi-natural continuum of offending behavior. Offenders were eventually divided into subgroups such as conflict criminals, occasional criminals, recidivists, habitual run-of-the-mill criminals, serious habitual criminals, and, finally, experienced professional criminals. Conflict and occasional criminals were seen as an epiphenomenon of the current state of public customs and moral rules, i.e., representing the general population. Given the wide diversity in modern living conditions and the multiplicity of laws prohibiting or proscribing certain acts it was considered more or less normal that every year many people would be "seduced" to commit an offense. According to the old scholars there also existed varying per-sonality types in the general population and therefore one could find "good characters" as well as "bad characters" among those persons arrested and convicted of a crime. As long as these character variations did not exceed a certain limit (e.g., cross the borderline to psychopathy) they were not considered as the "real causes" of criminality. Their extent would only explain whether or not a given individual might be able to fully resist environmental constraints or temptations. Persons with a strong moral self-concept certainly would resist more temptations. But as far as they shared mankind's universal natural "heritage" they might not have the strength to manage extreme situations of interpersonal conflicts, as, for example, a spouse's infidelity. The concrete solution of the inner conflict may depend on many accidental conditions. Solutions to conflicts could be found, inter alia, through either suicide, illnesses, or alcoholism. But if they were carried out through a crime the classification of the actor as a "conflict criminal" would be basically the same irrespective of the crime being committed, be it a department store theft or a murder caused by jealousy.

Following this classic approach further, we would classify those persons as "occasional criminals" that of course may also not be able to avoid such conflicts but may show a more or less developed general "proneness" to crime in terms of weak inhibitors against environmental influences con-ducive to the breach of norms. Whether they eventually become one-time offenders or moderate repeat offenders may depend upon the number and seriousness of occasions they had been confronted with. In any case they belonged to the normal population. Therefore, as older scholars argued, in order to look for the "real causes of criminality" one would not find much difference between non-offenders and the large number of occasional offenders. Consequently there might be no need for special treatment efforts. Meaningful differences, however, might arise when one would try to compare all these people with those in the remaining offender categories, i.e., the habitual and professional criminals. By taking this classic state of affairs into consideration one could be inclined to assume that at least some parts of the more recent American criminal career and habitual offender research (e.g., Petersilia, 1977) belong to the same theoretical tradition without awareness of that fact. As far as these habitual offender projects focus on long-term prison inmates they are subjected to the same methodological critique that was expressed formerly against the old projects by the labeling approach. The leading argument is that this approach fundamentally confounds the results of selective ascription of responsibility and the effects of discriminatory law enforcement procedures with antecedent "causes of criminal conduct" that probably do not exist at all. This topic shall not be discussed here in detail, nor will I take up the relevant theoretical debate. It may suffice, given the limited space, just to point out the methodological counter-argument, known by all criminologists: The objections raised by labeling theorists and other critical scholars will lose much of their power if research projects are turning down the levels of the social construction of reality. Instead of dealing with confirmed habitual felons in a retrospective design one should choose young first offenders and follow them through a certain period of time in a quasi-prospective design (for Germany see, e.g., Pongratz et al., 1975; Traulsen, 1976). In a further step one might choose a birth cohort of people and evaluate and analyze their lives over a certain period of time, either retrospectively or prospectively. To date birth cohorts offer the best chance to avoid pitfalls in causal attributions. In addition they can also follow a quasi-prospective design, as did the famous Philadelphia Birth Cohort Study I in the first stages (Wolfgang et al., 1972). All other conditions being equal the explanatory power improves, however, if a true prospective design is chosen that combines self-reported and officially registered delinquency, as is the case with the Cambridge Delinquency Development Study (West & Farrington, 1977).

All those studies show that crime is not evenly distributed among the population and give credence to the assumption that "differences" among subgroups of the general population actually do exist and are not just artifacts of societal or state-determined selection procedures. But can we really be sure that the data we are using are always reliable? With regard to official figures on crime and criminality the answer will heavily depend on the counting rules administered in everyday crime recording procedures. Because of a recent revision of police procedures in Germany we can approach the problems on the aggregate level in a more direct way than usually possible. On the individual level recent research results in Germany show quite convincingly that scholars might overcome these difficulties by getting access to unrestricted police files or data bases containing the full range of criminal acts persons are charged with. The German studies so far seem basically to confirm in substance the picture already shown by international studies.

General Counting Problems: Suspects versus Individuals Suspected of Crime

On the aggregate level we may begin by pointing out a rather simple fact with quite serious methodological and substantial consequences: Events constituting a "crime" or an "offense" (felony, misdemeanor, etc.) according to the laws of a given country have to be recognized by the official authorities. Otherwise a criminal act did not occur at all regardless of what the victim, bystanders, or other people think about it. So the same "event" containing one or more socially defined "acts" committed by a single actor or by multiple actors may be counted in the police records in extremely different legal categories. The description and degree assigned to the event officially depend upon the legal tradition of the country where it happened. International crime surveys are plagued by this problem, and although remarkable progress has been achieved in the last decade (see, e.g., the United Nations World Crime Surveys: HEUNI, 1985), the problem is far from being truly solved. I shall not deal here with the details of those questions and will concentrate on the procedures of the Federal Republic of Germany.

German police forces use a large handbook containing a unified coding system for criminal events on a nationwide scale. This handbook is filled with general rules, exceptions, and counter-exceptions. One would be inclined to doubt if a responsible street police officer, a trained backline officer, or a clerk in an overburdened city police department would ever be able to handle all those details in an orderly way. Therefore the police sometimes use rather crude, idiosyncratic, re-simplification rules based on their own experience. The one and with regard to methodological aspects somehow relieving fact is based upon the results of specific studies dealing with this problem. The results show that the large majority of events reported to the police or otherwise coming to their attention have a simple structure, i.e., a single act of hitting or otherwise harming a single victim and, seen in legal terms, meeting the criteria of a single offense type as defined by the penal code or a particular criminal law act.

The German Police Crime Statistic (PCS) recorded 4,356,726 offenses (felonies and misdemeanors) in 1988, excluding traffic offenses and offenses against the state. Because all police departments in Germany participate in the federal data collecting procedure and use the same type of recording rules we could take the results as reliable. However, we cannot avoid the next problematic stage. The main question is under what circumstances a registered crime might be classified as "cleared." Different countries follow very different policies and therefore obstruct cross-national comparisons. However, there is one basic distinction, leading to two general concepts. Those countries using "arrest" as the decisive point in the procedure (such as the U.S.A.) will always get a lower clearance rate than those countries (such as the F.R.G.) using a rather "soft" concept of a more or less concrete "suspicion," all other conditions being equal. The German PCS are prepared and published by the Bundeskriminalamt (Federal Criminal Police Bureau at Wiesbaden). The PCS considers a crime as cleared if there is at least one subject apprehended while committing the act (or shortly after it in near spatial context). If there is no immediate apprehension a clearance will be recorded as soon as the police have identified at least one suspect who might have committed the offense. Of no relevance is whether this suspect is considered to have committed the act alone or together with others. It is also unimportant whether he or she was the real perpetrator or only an accessory before the crime took place or an assistant to the perpetrator or even otherwise engaged.

The resulting German clearance rate is then defined as the annual number of "cleared offenses" compared with the number of "known offenses" registered in the same year. Although regularly published in percent values it is obviously not a real percentage because it does not refer to the same body of events. Thus Clearance rates of more than 100% are possible and actually shown in the PCS yearbooks, e.g., with regard to fencing climbing sometimes up to 106%. The total clearance rate, however, is by far not that convincing: it went down steadily for many years and is now more or less oscillating around 45%.

In 1988 the 2,000,213 offenses cleared by the police (representing a clearance rate of 45.9%) led to 1,314,080 offenders. The official term "Tatverdaechtige" means "suspects" or "persons suspected of a crime" and is used with respect to Article 6 para 2 of the European Convention of Human Rights. This article states that everyone officially charged with a crime is to be considered innocent unless a formal verdict of his or her guilt has been passed. The verdict must be handed down by a competent judicial authority who follows all the prerequisites of due process in criminal matters.

The German PCS recording system was thoroughly changed after 1982 with regard to those "suspects." This main revision of the basic counting procedures produced rather dramatic results. We may consider it as a quasi-natural experiment in order to look more closely at the question of how the "definition of the situation" (of a crime) is determined by conditions that practitioners, policy makers, and scholars alike are not used to considering carefully when evaluating aggregate data.

The immediate effect cannot be shown for the whole Federal Republic, however, because a few of the 11 "Laender" (States) were not able to implement the revision on time. Overall figures for suspects are thus lacking for the year 1983. Figures are available since 1984 but may still be influenced by the relevant difficulties. The state of Baden–Wuerttemberg was among the states experiencing particular problems. Police authorities implemented the new rules with 1 year's delay. This resulted in the "loss" of 35.4% of the suspects between 1983 and 1984 (231,252 vs. 149,332). The loss was higher for male (-39.1%) compared to female (-20.3%) suspects.

How is this effect possible? The classic counting rules applied until 1982/83 were highly similar to those existing in many other countries, among them probably the United States (Uniform Crime Reports). Those rules imply that every individual charged with crime has to be recorded separately whenever a new law enforcement procedure is to be initiated by a competent authority. Within one procedure German rules provide for one "count" for every separate criminal act the person is charged with. If a single act pertains to several official crime categories only the most severe charge will be recorded. Since the PCS forms that have to be filled out at police departments are related to the investigations (with separate sheets both for the acts and the persons implied) multiple charges can rather easily be reduced to either one event or one person as long as only one investigation dealt with the situation. The sheets bear simply the same identification number so a computer can bring the acts and the person involved in the acts together without remarkable delay. Because different investigations will get different identification numbers at different sheets even a computer is not able to make the connection between them unless additional signs are added to the sheets. Eventually this leads to multiple counting of the same individual as if he or she were different "persons." Therefore the number of separate police investigations determines to a large extent the gross number of officially recorded offenders in the whole country. The more active all or some individuals are during any given year the more distorted is the official picture of the "real extent of crime."

With the new system German police were able to reduce this bias. At least as far as the States are concerned a special computer program will be administered to the data stored at the States' Criminal Police Bureau in the yearly PCS tape. This program is able to combine all the data of the multiple investigative procedures within the same police authority or among different police agencies throughout the country. This enables the police to identify offenders who were involved in multiple investigations as the same individual. The Wiesbaden Federal Criminal Police Bureau up to now does not get the individualized files so the former bias continues to exist if someone for example happens to commit a crime both in Bavaria and in Hamburg. Following the data available so far, estimates of the distortion rate reach 5 to 8% of the gross offender count at the entire federal level.

So the Federal Republic of Germany faced a "loss" of 21.9% of offenders between 1982 (the last year with old counting rules) and 1984 (the first year where data on the new system could be provided). Even this new crime statistic might not represent the true picture if we consider the fact that standardized rates used here (persons per 100,000 of the normal population) may vary less than the raw data used in the case of Baden–Wuerttemberg. However, we are able to compare this difference with special data collected in a project with authorities of the State of Northrine–Westfalia. This State is the largest of the Federation, with about 17 million inhabitants. The Duesseldorf Criminal Police Bureau paralleled experimentally the old and the new counting systems for a few years. In 1981 then the difference in offender rates was 17.5%, i.e., less than the difference for the Federal Republic between 1982 and 1984. So at least the general trend in the Federal Republic of Germany seems to be realistic.

Particular Research Studies: Data and Methods

The real test of the new counting procedures lies in the way they reduced the biases of the registered crime distribution among different age groups in the population. In order to evaluate this process in more detail we rearranged at first the already officially available figures for the F.R.G. as a whole and than the similar data sets of two States (Baden–Wuerttemberg and Northrine–Westfalia) and one City–State (Hamburg) in terms of sex and age groups of known offenders. The remarkable losses mentioned above indicated that a large part of the differences might be attributed to the continuous activity of a comparatively small number of repeat or even chronic offenders. Moreover, early local studies had shown a highly skewed distribution of the distorting effect indicating a discrimination against the younger population groups. Therefore we tried to get access to an original State data set containing raw data on all offenders detected during one given year. We started the data analysis with a cross-sectional approach and then created a special system file as the basis for a longitudinal study of offender cohorts. We were lucky insofar as the Northrine–Westfalia Criminal Police Bureau was willing to participate in a joint effort, the partners being that Bureau and the Heidelberg Institute of Criminology. However, after a few first computer runs the Bureau's director retired earlier than expected. At the same time the Crime Prediction Task Force at the Federal Criminal Police Bureau at Wiesbaden, where he and we had previously cooperated for a couple of months and developed our common project, was dissolved. Therefore the project lost its legitimizing foundation and for a couple of other reasons could not be revitalized.

The system file for the cross-sectional calculations was created by using the 1981 Northrine–Westfalia PCS offense tape and the separate PCS offender tape, both containing individualized data sets on all criminal events investigated during the whole year by all police departments all over that state. After screening available computer programs we decided to install a SPSS-6 Mainframe Equipment specially adapted for the Siemens computer already in use at the Criminal Police Bureau's computer center. By administering a particular algorithm successfully tested on several earlier occasions at the Bureau's center all events were repeatedly searched through in order to really personalize the "suspects": By comparing the suspects' data in two given events they were considered to belong to the same individual person if they met several criteria simultaneously. These were (1) same gender, (2) same birth date, (3) same place of residence as defined by the four-digit postal code, (4) same family name up to the first eight letters, and (5) same first name up to the first five letters. Additional control precedures such as, e.g., phonetic alphabetical screening were used in doubtful cases.

The PCS tapes contained more than 1 million cases. Data protection rules required that sensitive data of this kind had to remain within the responsible authorities' files or equipment. So we were not able to use our own resources (mainly the university computer center) but had to adapt to the conditions in Duesseldorf at the Criminal Police Bureau. This meant that because of limited cpu time there, we accepted a restriction in the number of cases to be included in the separate system file.

We received several Northrine–Westfalia PCS Yearbooks and, in addition, scholarly works about the distribution of criminality among the population in general as well as among the youth population in particular. The review led to the following selection which might structurally represent the core criminal behavior of young German persons below the age of 21 years:

All homicide offenses, including negligent manslaughter
All sexual offenses
Robbery offenses, including extortion with violence and feloniously attacking motorcar drivers with the intent to rob them
All simple and aggravated assaults
All offenses directed against personal liberty
Simple theft and aggravated theft (e.g., burglary) with the following categories: bicycle theft, motorcycle theft, motocar theft, theft of sales automats, department store theft, theft at kiosks, theft out of motorcars, theft in/out of inhabited homes, flats etc., theft in/out of basements, open kitchen rooms or other service equipment rooms etc., theft in/out of buildings still in construction or in/out of construction workers' lodgings etc.
Malicious damaging offenses (including vandalism)
All drug offenses

Offenses of open (e.g., violent) opposition against police officers or similar law enforcement personnel while on duty.

We excluded fraud and similar offenses and therefore our data contain a systematic bias with regard to older age groups, groups we were not much interested in. In Germany these crimes' rates start to rise steadily beginning at the age of 25 and gain importance (up to the age of 45) with regard to the PCS. So the figures presented below refer only to the registered crimes typically committed by juveniles and adolescents. The real scale of adult criminal behavior is a more expanded one. General fraud and similar offenses usually sum up to 20% of all offenses recorded for the adult group (21 years and older) in official Police Crime Statistics.

Because our final system file contained a statewide "selected total number" of offenses and offenders but not a probability sample the administering of probability statistics procedures would not have made sense even if we would have got the chance to do so before the file was deleted. Given the large number of cases involved differences between subgroups always were significant: The PCS file contained 307,053 persons; the selection of crime types reduced the total number available for our system file to 280,345 persons. Several special calculations were then made with smaller subfiles. Multiple offending could be checked only for a short period of time, maximally for 1 full year. However, colleagues in Freiburg (at the Max-Planck-Institute for Foreign and International Penal Law, Criminology Division) were luckier in their efforts to begin and continue a birth cohort study. In that still ongoing project all subjects of those born in 1970, 1973, 1975, and 1978 and registered by the Baden–Wuerttemberg Police Department (up to January 1, 1988, N = 20,492 persons) will be followed prospectively with respect to their further criminal career. We were able to use the first results of that study for cross-checking the validity of our own results. In the following we will present a selection of the data. Whenever appropriate other studies are considered comparatively.

Multiple Offending Among Different Age Groups

As already mentioned the general loss of offenders in the PCS due to the revised counting and recording rules was higher than most experts expected. Therefore the officials of the Central Police Authorities, accustomed to explaining rising crime figures and connecting them with demands for more resources, obviously were disturbed by the drastic change. They needed considerable time to find an appropriate official line for public statements. The most important fact, however, was the uneven distribution of the losses in detail. Younger age groups of offenders diminished considerably more than those above 25 or 30 years of age did.

Following the categories officially used in the PCS we can demonstrate the effect for the City–State of Hamburg between 1982 and 1983:

Children (8 to 13) = −28%; juveniles (14 to 17) = −41%; adolescents (18 to 20) = −41%; adults (21 and older) = −28%.

For the State of Baden–Wuerttemberg, changing its system 1 year later; we got the results for male and female offenders separated and present here only figures for males:

Children = −30.5%; juveniles = −51.5%; adolescents = −50.8%; adults = −34.1%.

Even when considering standardized offender rates (offenders per 100,000 of the same age and sex subgroup of the normal population) neutralizing possible population changes, final results will not differ substantially. In the State of Northrine–Westfalia we could calculate the standardized rates for exactly the same year (1981 was the base year of our project) by administering both the old and the new counting rules. As we can see from the following results (only referring to the male offender group) changes were still remarkable but a bit less dramatic than above:

Age group (males)	Offender rate (old rules)	Offender rate (new rules)	Change rate (in per cent)
Children	2,769	2,375	−14.9
Juveniles	8,731	6,532	−25.2
Adolescents	10,612	7,802	−26.5
Young Adults	7,613	5,844	−23.2
Older Adults	2,648	2,283	−15.5

The age group of young adults refers to those persons between 21 and 25 years of age. By distinguishing further adult age subgroups we detected that the differences tended to fade away with increasing age.

What do those data imply in terms of "age and crime"? Obviously the old German PCS counting system was grossly overestimating the "real amount" of juvenile delinquency and crime in terms of the youth population engaging every year in officially registered delinquent and criminal behavior. If we compare the Federal PCS offender rates for male adolescents in 1982 (last year with old rules) we find a rate of 11,782 per 100,000, which exceeds the average male offender rate (4,766) by 147%. In 1984 (first year with results based upon the new rules) their rate dropped to 7,347 offenses per 100,000, which exceeds the male offender rate (3,554) by 107%. The new PCS Counting system thus made the commonly known age–crime curve more even and is less skewed toward the age groups of 14 to 17 and 18 to 21 years which are internationally considered to be the most criminally active groups. However, it did not alter the basic distributional structure. We should bear in mind the revision's limited range: it only cleared the distortion caused by counting a person again and separately at the beginning of every new investigation procedure. So we can assume that the differences in numbers and rates are due to a more or less small part of the population being criminally active over long periods of time. But so far we are not in the position to test this assumption fully in terms of repeated offending with the kind of data available so far. Someone committing only two offenses during a year and being caught twice by police forces would have been counted twice in the PCS. A person committing 160 offenses but getting caught the first time after the fiftieth offense and then not again before having committed 110 additional acts would also be counted twice in the PCS. The two offenders obviously do not belong to exactly the same category. We can get further clarification by looking at other indicators referring to "criminal events" instead of investigation procedures. The German PCS traditionally recorded for every cleared criminal offense whether or not the offender(s) involved was (were) already known to the police. Since 1983/84 this information can be truly individualized but, unfortunately, separate information for different age groups is not yet officially published and scholars were not yet allowed to make their own computer runs with the original raw data tapes. So for the moment we are bound to general figures. According to our national PCS for 1988 about 42% of the apprehended offenders were already known to the police. They were responsible for 54.8% of all crimes cleared during 1988 in Germany. In 61.8% of the aggravated theft cases the offenders were already known to the police and they allegedly committed 82.3% of all aggravated thefts that could be cleared in that year.

Another way of finding out how many repeat offenders will commit different kinds of offenses during one year is to at least evaluate police counting procedures with regard to separate crime events. By now German recording rules require police officials to register every act having a distinct and separable legal quality as a separate crime. It does not matter if the crime is investigated together with other acts in the same procedure or handled apart or in a large time distance from the other acts the same individual is considered to have performed in the same year. In legal terms: really concurring offenses are to be treated distinctively; ideally concurring offenses (i.e., the same act belongs to different legal offense categories) shall be reduced in recording to the offense bearing the highest seriousness in terms of the general penalty provided for by the penal law. Thus every offender gets a separate count for every offense he or she was engaged in. The total number of offenders will than be broken down in the PCS Year-book for each category of crime. So in 1988 out of the 1,007,250 male offenders 263,733 were said to have committed aggravated theft, 103,349 simple theft, 220,096 fraudulent offenses, 209,000 offenses against the person (mainly assaults and robbery offenses), 16,110 sexual offenses, 2,910 homicide offenses (including attempts), 261,857 all other offenses, and, finally, 144,628 offenses violating particular penal law acts, e.g., the drug offense act. Summing up these figures one will get 1,222,111 offenders or 21.33% more than the grand total. If one takes into account the more detailed subcategories the "surplus value" will reach nearly 27% on the next specification level. On the most detailed level fully evaluating the whole four-digit classification system about 30% more offenders can be counted.

Those figures imply that many offenders are quite versatile repeaters in one and the same year. But because only the crime categories are recorded and not additionally the number of counts within each separate category the exact range of multiple offending cannot be calculated precisely. By looking at the different age groups we can detect that those between 16 and 18, 18 and 21, and 21 and 25 again claim the top positions.

The Northrine–Westfalia Criminal Police Bureau was the first law enforcement authority to invent a new approach in the mid-70s that marked a practical "breakthrough" irrespective of theoretical objections one might raise. As part of a statewide juvenile crime prevention campaign the persons responsible for the Bureau's Juvenile Delinquency Division decided to search the already computerized state PCS files for so-called "intensive juvenile offenders." Intensive offenders were considered, following general police experience and an ad-hoc thumb rule, to be all those youngsters between 14 and 18 years of age who were at least caught twice during one year and were at the same time charged with at least six separate offenses. The Juvenile Delinquency Division could easily identify the intensive offenders who turned out to be very active and therefore the procedure was expanded to children and adolescents as well.

We shall not go into detail. In the following we sum up all the data provided by the Criminal Police Bureau for the years 1976 to 1983.

The child intensive offenders represented 2.5% of all offenders in the same age group at any given year but they committed up to 24.4% of all offenses of this age group. The 5.1% juvenile intensive offenders were responsible on the average for 30.2% of all juvenile crimes. Adolescent intensive offenders showed very similar results: 5.0% were held responsible for 31.6% of all crimes for this age group.

When standardizing the figures by calculating the average values for "each 1%" of intensive offenders we got the following results for the last year in consideration: The standardized 1% of child intensive offenders would commit 8.9% of all offenses of the same age group, whereas juvenile intensive offenders would commit 6.4% and adolescent intensive offenders 6.7% of all offenses equally defined.

The impression that child intensive offenders were claiming the top position among minors was confirmed so far when we took all offense counts into account. During the same year the 561 child intensive offenders had committed 11,148 separate offenses; the figures for juveniles are 2,649 persons with 45,398 offenses; the 2,231 adolescents committed 41,089 offenses. The averages per person are 19.1 for the children, 17.1 for the juveniles, and 18.4 for the adolescents.

In addition we allowed the PCS counting program to look at the so-called "serial offenders" who committed 100 or more separate offenses during one year. Children again dominated the scene: the average serial child offender committed 197 compared to 184 for juveniles and to "only" 161 offenses for adolescents. By creating our own system file we started a computer run using the unrestricted data set and, by doing so, avoiding the limits created by the internal police requirement of at least two separate investigation procedures. The results differed in certain respects from those just shown, but did not alter the picture structurally. On the other hand, 73.5% of the delinquent children committed only one offense over the year compared with 66.6% of the juvenile offenders and 64.5% of the adolescent offenders. The average number of offenses for the whole age group was 2.4 among the children, 2.8 among the juveniles, and 2.6 among the adolescents. We then defined as "real intensive offenders" those having committed at least 10 offenses during the year. To get a more detailed picture we also included two other age groups, i.e., the young adults between 21 and 24 years of age and the full adults being 25 or older. Here juveniles ranked the highest with 4.3%; followed by child intensive offenders with 3.3%, adolescents to 2.6%, young adults to 2.1%, and full adults to 1.6% only. So it seemed at first glance that the intensity of "intensive offendership" would slow down with rising age. This impression changed quickly, however, when we again calculated the standardized 1% share with regard to the offense total for each age group. The results were as follows: every 1% of child intensive offenders (with 10 and more offenses) committed 11.8% of all offenses registered for the whole age group; the other values were: for juveniles 10.0%, for adolescents 10.3%, for young adults 11.3%, and for full adults 15.9% respectively.

The last figure led us to assume that perhaps the basic structure of multiple offending would be similar among all age groups. However, we were not able to test this assumption with the unrestricted data set because we had no further access to the data. Therefore we were forced to turn to our selected system file. That file, as we shall recall, did not contain fraud offenses. The consequence of exclusion is that the real extent of crime is higher than shown below and increases with the age groups (at least to the age of 45). Given this systematic distortion it was even more astonishing to detect that in fact differences came out to be smaller than normally expected. We present only three rows of figures here. With regard to the intensive offenders, those with more than 10 offenses in a given year, we can see their percentages are continuously diminishing with increasing age groups. To put it in more simple terms: older people normally are less active than younger ones. But those who remain active do not reduce their offending behavior at all or at least not drastically.

However, we should keep in mind that those figures do not tell us anything about the seriousness of the criminal acts committed by the offenders, making it difficult to draw solid conclusions with regard to criminal career development.

Age group	Intensive offenders (in % of all offenders)	Offense number (average)	Standardized 1% (offense share)
8–13	1.8%	27.8	16%
14–17	1.7%	25.9	14%
18–20	1.2%	23.9	16%
21–24	0.5%	23.0	20%
25–29	0.3%	20.0	18%
30–39	0.3%	26.3	22%
40–49	0.2%	25.9	27%

In addition to our own research Kolbe (1989) could rely upon several samples (each containing 400 persons) taken out of the same PCS Tape and representing the age groups of 10–12, 14–16, 18–20, and 22, respectively. She showed convincingly that among those age groups the intensive offenders normally did just "more of the same," i.e., they committed mostly the same offenses with regard to the legal offense categories compared to the less active offenders. Besides this dominant fact she found an additional trend: with rising age the percentage of more serious offense subcategories, according to the PCS system, was also rising and, all in all, the whole "spectrum" of criminality expanded; violent crimes, however, did not develop disproportionally.

The Path from Multiple Offending to Criminal Careers

Because we were prevented from analyzing in a quasi-prospective design the further development of the young offenders (included in our 1981 system file) between the years 1982 and 1988 we had to rely on other sources.

The Northrine–Westfalia Criminal Police Bureau thus provided us with data out of a study they had performed on their own before joining the common project. For the year 1983 all of the intensive juvenile offenders who were permanent residents on that State were traced. These 2,474 persons were than checked on whether or not they might already have been registered in the 1982 PCS Tape. Actually 363 persons or 14.7% were eventually found. This means that 85.3% of the 1983 intensive offenders between 14 and 17 years of age would have started anew or, after a calm period of one or more years, would have reactivated their career.

Lamnek (1982) was able to deal with that question in more detail by getting access to Munich PCS Tapes for the 10-year period from 1971 to 1980. He limited his analysis to offenders between 8 and 21 years of age and concluded that nearly half of them had been charged with multiple offenses. But the majority did not start a criminal career. About 73% of all repeat offenders were active only during one year; the average length of being registered for committing offenses was 10.5 months.

Krueger (1983) at the Schleswig–Holstein Criminal Police Bureau selected several samples of first offenders between 10 and 22 years of age who were registered at the State's police statistics in 1977. He followed them up until 1982, implying a whole control period of 6 years and a follow-up period of 5 years on the average. Of the entire group of 2,992 first offenders 30.5% were caught again and charged with new offenses. But only eight persons were found to have been active during the whole control period. Allowing for different styles in development we recalculated the data by coding the years an offender had been active at all regardless of the given year in the scale. That means an offender who was active in the first and in the last year of the total control period would get the same mark as another offender who was active during the first 2 years and then quit the career. By doing so we got the following results for the repeat offenders: 1 year activity = 51.5%, 2 years = 23.7%, 3 years = 12.6%, 4 years = 8.4%, 5 years = 3.4%, and, finally, 6 years = 0.9% only.

Walliser (1984) at the Baden–Wuerttemberg Criminal Police Bureau checked a particular police data file created in the 70s with the main aim to relieve the police of their paperwork. He could identify 752,705 individuals charged with offenses at one or more occasions during an 11-year period. Out of that rather large number 63% were charged with a crime only once, 16% twice, 7% three times, 4% four times, and just 2% five or more times. Those identified by the category of intensive offenders used in the Northrine–Westfalia Criminal Police Bureau (i.e., six and more offenses) made up 8% of the total and were responsible for 41% of all offenses registered for the whole offender group during the entire control period of 11 years.

Steffen & Czogalla (1982) at the Bavarian Criminal Police Bureau followed two offender samples also for a period of 11 years, one between the ages of 10 and 21 years and the other between the ages of 18 and 29; the results were very similar to those already mentioned. In both samples one-time offenders dominated (59% vs. 57%), and intensive offenders summed up to about 10%.

In the Berlin birth cohort study Weschke & Krause (1982) found that of all those youngsters having had police contact up to their 21st year of age about 14% committed six and more offenses.

Karger & Sutterer (1988), working on the most recent and rather elaborated German birth cohort study at Freiburg, found the following preliminary results for their four cohorts: The average number of offenses per person and per year at risk was 0.19 for the 1970 birth cohort, 0.19 for the 1973 birth cohort, 0.20 for the 1975 birth cohort, and, finally, 0.18 for the 1978 birth cohort. This obviously is not much of a difference. When looking at the so-called chronics with five or more registered offenses they found 4.7% among the youngest cohort and 15.1% among the oldest one. We recalculated these figures in terms of the standardized 1% share as explained above. Then the picture reversed and showed remarkable similarities to our largely cross-sectional data: each 1% of the chronic younger child offenders (1978 birth cohort) was responsible for 6% of all offenses registered for the whole age group. The values for the other chronics were 4.8% for the older children (1975 birth cohort), 4.3% for the juveniles, and 4.2% for the near-adolescents. Karger and Sutterer calculated "lambda" values for their cohorts. Regarding this offense/offender ratio they could not find uniform patterns in the sense of a rising or falling trend across the age groups. The ratio sharply increased, however, when the cohorts reached the age of 10. The maximum of first police contacts was reached later on at the age of 16.

Discussion and Concluding Remarks

As we saw in the first parts of this chapter aggregate crime figures on Police Crime Statistics levels have to be interpreted with caution if one wants to reach conclusions about the extent of criminality among different age groups. From the victim's perspective, however, it does not make much difference whether he or she was attacked by a young person who had already attacked many persons before, or by a one-time offender. Concerning the old counting rules working in disfavor of the younger generation in Germany it would be interesting to see whether in other countries similar calculations could be made. Up to now we did not find comparable figures in the literature. For the United States nationwide data also seem to lack these statistical procedures but we could find at least a regional study allowing first superficial comparisons. The New York State Criminal Services Division (1976) started a project on juvenile violence in New York City and analyzed the data about all police arrests of children and juveniles between July 1, 1973 and June 30, 1974. Because they concentrated only on 11 specified crimes against the person, from murder to attempted rape (assault and robbery summing up to 85%), the variance is smaller as if they would have included property offenses. Altogether they detected 5,666 arrests of 4,847 youngsters. This result implies that if the NYC police forces would have counted these arrests for the UCR in a way similar to the traditional German way, the NYC media could tell the public that 5,666 young violent criminals had been arrested in that given year but the actual number would be 819 or 14.5% fewer!

With regard to the multiple offending in general and to the criminal career paradigm in particular our German data show quite clearly that repeat offenders can easily be found among all age groups and already by analyzing only a 1-year period. Intensive offenders or "chronics" commit a large part of all offenses registered officially for most age groups. On the other hand belonging to this offender group does not necessarily imply serious offending in terms of the severity of the multiple criminal events nor will it inevitably end in an extended criminal career. One question was not dealt with in our analysis: whether the escalation and specialization of offenders laid the ground for a criminal career. German data available so far cast doubt on the assumption that escalation and specialization do occur at all to a considerable extent. Even if this occurs under certain circumstances, the most recent findings (Albrecht & Moitra, 1988) supported the skeptical assumption that a prior record might not help in predicting how many crimes an individual will commit in the future and in what types of crime he or she will engage in. Needless to say that many questions still remain and need to be answered and will stir up further debates among scholars and policymakers (see also Kerner 1989 with further comments).

References

Albrecht, H.-J., & Moitra, S. (1988). Escalation and specialization. In G. Kaiser & I. Geisler (Eds.), *Crime and Criminal Justice*. Freiburg: Max-Planck Institute Publications Dept.

Exner, F. (1949). *Kriminologie*. 3. Aufl. Berlin: Springer Verlag.

Glueck, S., & Glueck, E. (1950, 3rd ed. 1957). *Unraveling Juvenile Delinquency*. Cambridge, Massachusetts: Ballinger.

HEUNI, Helsinki Institute for Crime Prevention and Control Affiliated With the United Nations, Ed. (1985). *Criminal Justice Systems in Europe*. Helsinki: Valtion Painatuskeskus.

Karger, Th., & Sutterer, P. (1988). On longitudinal research in criminology and first results from the Freiburg Cohort Study. In G. Kaiser & I. Geisler (Eds.), *Crime and Criminal Justice*. Freiburg: Max-Planck Institute Publications Dept.

Kerner, H.-J. (1989). Jugendkriminalitaet, Mehrfachtaeterschaft und Verlauf. *Bewährungshilfe* 36, 202–220.

Kolbe, C. (1989). *Kindliche und Jugendliche Intensivaeter*. Heidelberg: Law Dept. Thesis, Heidelberg University.

Krueger, H. (1983). Rueckfallquote rund 30%. *Kriminalistik*, *37*, 326–329.

Lamnek, S. (1982). Sozialisation und kriminelle Karriere. In H. Schueler-Springorum (Ed.), *Mehrfach auffaellig*. Muenchen: Juventa.

Mezger, E. (1951). *Kriminologie*. Muenchen: C. H. Beck.

New York State, Criminal Services Division (1976). *Juvenile Violence*. New York: CJS Dept.

Petersilia, J. et al. (1977). *Criminal Careers of Habitual Felons*. Santa Monica: Rand.

Pongratz, L., Schaefer, M., & Weise, D. T. (1975). *Kinderdelinquenz. D-aten, Hintergruende und Entwicklungen*. Muenchen: Juventa.

Steffen, W., & Czogalla, P. P. (1982). *Intensitaet und Perseveranz krimineller Verhaltensweisen*. Teil II. Muenchen: Bayerisches Landeskriminalamt.

Traulsen, M. (1976). *Delinquente Kinder und ihre Legalbewaehrung*. Frankfurt a.M.: Lang.

Walliser, F. (1984). Personenauskunftsdatei (PAD), Falldatei (MOD) und Perseveranztheorie. *Kriminalistik*, *38*, 322–328.

Weschke, E., & Krause, W. (1982). Auswertung polizeilicher Unterlagen in Berlin ueber Kinder, Jugendliche und Heranwachsende des Jahrgangs 1953. In *Handlungsorientierte Analyse von Kinder- und Jugenddelinquenz*. Berlin: Fachhochschule fuer oeffentliche Verwaltung und Rechtspflege.

West, D. J., & Farrington, D. P. (1977). *The Delinquent Way of Life*. London: Heinemann.

Wolfgang, M. E., Figlio, R. M., & Sellin, Th. (1972). *Delinquency in a Birth Cohort*. Chicago and London: University Press.

Subject Index

(Note: "f." = including the next following page; "ff." = including several following pages)

Research in Criminology

continued

Multiple Problem Youth:
Delinquency, Substance Use, and Mental Health Problems
D.S. Elliott, D. Huizinga and S. Menard

Selective Incapacitation and the Serious Offender:
A Longitudinal Study of Criminal Career Patterns
Rudy A. Haapanen

Deterrence and Juvenile Crime: Results from a National Policy Experiment
Anne L. Schneider

Understanding Crime Incidence Statistics:
Why the UCR Diverges from the NCS
Albert D. Biderman and James P. Lynch

Developments in Crime and Crime Control Research: German Studies on
Victims, Offenders, and the Public
Klaus Sessar and Hans-Jürgen Kerner (Eds.)